PUBLISHED

Jane Austen: *Emma* DAVID LODGE

Jane Austen: *'Northanger Abbey' & 'Persuasion* B.C.

Jane Austen: *'Sense and Sensibility', 'Pride and Prejudice' & 'Mansfield Park'* B.C. SOUTHAM

William Blake: *Songs of Innocence and Experience* MARGARET BOTTRALL

Charlotte Brontë: *'Jane Eyre' & 'Villette'* MIRIAM ALLOTT

Emily Brontë: *Wuthering Heights* MIRIAM ALLOTT

Browning: *'Men and Women' & Other Poems* J.R. WATSON

Bunyan: *The Pilgrim's Progress* ROGER SHARROCK

Byron: *'Childe Harold's Pilgrimage' & 'Don Juan'* JOHN JUMP

Chaucer: *Canterbury Tales* J.J. ANDERSON

Coleridge: *'The Ancient Mariner' & Other Poems* ALUN R. JONES & WILLIAM TYDEMAN

Congreve: *Comedies* PATRICK LYONS

Conrad: *'Heart of Darkness', 'Nostromo' & 'Under Western Eyes'* C.B. COX

Conrad: *The Secret Agent* IAN WATT

Dickens: *Bleak House* A.E. DYSON

Dickens: *'Hard Times', 'Great Expectations' & 'Our Mutual Friend'* NORMAN PAGE

Donne: *Songs and Sonets* JULIAN LOVELOCK

George Eliot: *Middlemarch* PATRICK SWINDEN

George Eliot: *'The Mill on the Floss' & 'Silas Marner'* R.P. DRAPER

T.S. Eliot: *Four Quartets* BERNARD BERGONZI

T.S. Eliot: *'Prufrock', 'Gerontion', 'Ash Wednesday' & Other Shorter Poems* B.C. SOUTHAM

T.S. Eliot: *The Waste Land* C.B. COX & ARNOLD P. HINCHLIFFE

Farquhar: *'The Recruiting Officer' & 'The Beaux' Stratagem'* RAYMOND A. ANSELMENT

Henry Fielding: *Tom Jones* NEIL COMPTON

E.M. Forster: *A Passage to India* MALCOLM BRADBURY

Hardy: *The Tragic Novels* R.P. DRAPER

Hardy: *Poems* JAMES GIBSON & TREVOR JOHNSON

Gerard Manley Hopkins: *Poems* MARGARET BOTTRALL

Henry James: *'Washington Square' & 'The Portrait of a Lady'* ALAN SHELSTON

Jonson: *Volpone* JONAS A. BARISH

Jonson: *'Every Man in his Humour' & 'The Alchemist'* R.V. HOLDSWORTH

James Joyce: *'Dubliners' & 'A Portrait of the Artist as a Young Man'* MORRIS BEJA

Keats: *Odes* G.S. FRASER

Keats: *Narrative Poems* JOHN SPENCER HILL

D.H. Lawrence: *Sons and Lovers* GAMINI SALGADO

D.H. Lawrence: *'The Rainbow' & 'Women in Love'* COLIN CLARKE

Marlowe: *Doctor Faustus* JOHN JUMP

Marlowe: *'Tamburlaine the Great', 'Edward the Second' & 'The Jew of Malta'* JOHN RUSSELL BROWN

Marvell: *Poems* ARTHUR POLLARD

The Metaphysical Poets GERALD HAMMOND

Milton: *'Comus' & 'Samson Agonistes'* JULIAN LOVELOCK

Milton: *Paradise Lost* A.E. DYSON & JULIAN LOVELOCK

John Osborne: *Look Back in Anger* JOHN RUSSELL TAYLOR

Peacock: *The Satirical Novels* LORNA SAGE

Pope: *The Rape of the Lock* JOHN DIXON HUNT

Shakespeare: *A Midsummer Night's Dream* ANTONY PRICE

Shakespeare: *Antony and Cleopatra* JOHN RUSSELL BROWN

Shakespeare: *Coriolanus* B.A. BROCKMAN

Shakespeare: *Hamlet* JOHN JUMP

Shakespeare: *Henry IV Parts I and II* G.K. HUNTER

Shakespeare: *Henry V* MICHAEL QUINN

James Joyce

Dubliners

and

A Portrait of the Artist as a Young Man

A CASEBOOK

EDITED BY

MORRIS BEJA

M

MACMILLAN

First edition 1973
5th reprint 1984

Published by
Higher and Further Education Division
MACMILLAN PUBLISHERS LTD
*Companies and representatives
throughout the world*

ISBN 0 333 14033 8

Printed in Hong Kong

To my young Dubliners,
Drew and Eleni

CONTENTS

Part Two: Critical Studies

ACKNOWLEDGEMENTS

Maurice Beebe, 'Joyce and Aquinas: The Theory of Aesthetics' from *Philological Quarterly*, vol. 36, 1957 by permission of *Philological Quarterly*; Morris Beja, 'The Wooden Sword: Threatener and Threatened in the Fiction of James Joyce' from *James Joyce Quarterly*, vol. 2 (Fall 1964) by permission of the *James Joyce Quarterly*; Wayne C. Booth, 'The Problem of Distance in *A Portrait of the Artist*' from *The Rhetoric of Fiction* by permission of The University of Chicago Press; Anthony Burgess, 'A Paralysed City' from *Here Comes Everybody* by permission of Faber & Faber Ltd and W. W. Norton & Co. Inc., Copyright © 1965 by Anthony Burgess; Richard Ellmann, *Letters of James Joyce*, vol. II and vol. III by permission of Faber & Faber Ltd and The Viking Press Inc., Copyright © 1966 by F. Lionel Munro, administrator of the Estate of James Joyce: all rights reserved; Richard Ellmann, *James Joyce* by permission of Oxford University Press Inc., Copyright © 1959 by Oxford University Press Inc.; Stuart Gilbert, *Letters of James Joyce*, vol. I by permission of Faber & Faber Ltd and The Viking Press Inc., Copyright © 1957, 1966 by The Viking Press Inc.: all rights reserved; Brewster Ghiselin, 'The Unity of *Dubliners*' reprinted by permission of the author, Copyright © 1956 by Brewster Ghiselin, this selection is Part I of a two-part essay which originally appeared in *Accent*, Spring and Summer 1956; Gerald Gould, review of 'Dubliners' from *New Statesman*, 27 June 1914, reprinted by permission of *New Statesman*; John Gross, 'The Voyage Out' from *James Joyce* (Modern Masters

Series) by permission of Fontana Paperbacks and The Viking Press Inc., Copyright © 1970 by John Gross; George H. Healey, *The Complete Dublin Diary of Stanislaus Joyce*, Copyright © 1962 by Cornell University and George Harris Healey, Copyright © 1971 by Cornell University, used by permission of Cornell University Press; James Joyce, 'The Dead' from *Dubliners* by James Joyce, Copyright © 1967 by the Estate of James Joyce: all rights reserved, reprinted by permission of Jonathan Cape Ltd and The Viking Press Inc.; James Joyce, *Stephen Hero* reprinted by permission of Jonathan Cape, the Executors of the James Joyce Estate and The Society of Authors as the literary representative of the Estate of James Joyce; Hugh Kenner, 'The Portrait in Perspective' from *Dublin's Joyce* by permission of Chatto & Windus and Indiana University Press; Harry Levin, 'The Artist' from *James Joyce, A Critical Introduction*, Copyright 1941 by New Directions Publishing Corporation, New York, reprinted by permission of Laurence Pollinger Ltd and New Directions Publishing Corporation; Ellsworth Mason and Richard Ellmann, 'The Pola Notebook' from *The Critical Writings of James Joyce* by permission of Faber & Faber Ltd and The Viking Press Inc.; Frank O'Connor, 'Joyce and Dissociated Metaphor' from *The Mirror in the Roadway*, Copyright © 1956 by Frank O'Connor, reprinted by permission of A. D. Peters & Co. and Alfred A. Knopf Inc.; Robert Scholes and Richard M. Kain, 'James Joyce, A Portrait of the Artist' and 'Twelve Epiphanies' from *The Workshop of Daedalus: James Joyce and the Raw Materials for 'A Portrait of the Artist as A Young Man'* by permission of The Society of Authors as literary representative of the Estate of the late James Joyce, Jonathan Cape Ltd as publishers, and The Viking Press Inc.; J. I. M. Stewart, *Eight Modern Writers* reprinted by permission of The Clarendon Press, Oxford; unsigned review 'A Study in Garbage' from *Everyman Journal*, 23 February 1917, by permission of J. M. Dent & Sons Ltd; unsigned review of *A Portrait of the Artist* from *Irish Book Lover*, April–May 1917, by permission of The Three Candles Ltd; unsigned review of *Dubliners* from *The Times Literary Supplement*, 18 June 1914, by permission of *The Times*.

GENERAL EDITOR'S PREFACE

Each of this series of Casebooks concerns either one well-known and influential work of literature or two or three closely linked works. The main section consists of critical readings, mostly modern, brought together from journals and books. A selection of reviews and comments by the author's contemporaries is also included, and sometimes comments from the author himself. The Editor's Introduction charts the reputation of the work from its first appearance until the present time.

The critical forum is a place of vigorous conflict and disagreement, but there is nothing in this to cause dismay. What is attested is the complexity of human experience and the richness of literature, not any chaos or relativity of taste. A critic is better seen, no doubt, as an explorer than as an 'authority', but explorers ought to be, and usually are, well equipped. The effect of good criticism is to convince us of what C. S. Lewis called 'the enormous extension of our being which we owe to authors'. This Casebook will be justified only if it helps to promote the same end.

A single volume can represent no more than a small selection of critical opinions. Some critics have been excluded for reasons of space, and it is hoped that readers will follow up the further suggestions in the Select Bibliography. Other contributions have been severed from their original context, to which some readers may wish to return. Indeed, if they take a hint from the critics represented here, they certainly will.

A. E. Dyson

INTRODUCTION

Who killed James Joyce?
I, said the commentator,
I killed James Joyce
For my graduation.[1]

It may seem a gracelessly obvious ploy to quote those lines at the start of a volume such as this one, but hopefully they will indicate that the editor has tried to keep in mind the possible dangers as well as the benefits of literary criticism. Both the risks and the gains become all the more notable when the bulk of criticism devoted to an author becomes as formidable as it has in the case of James Joyce. The body of work on Joyce includes elaborate scholarly editions of letters and manuscripts, biographical memoirs and studies, many critical volumes, untold numbers of essays, and even entire periodicals – indeed one of those periodicals is devoted not to Joyce but, even more exclusively, to a single one of his works.[2]

Joyce, obviously, wrote the sort of literature that generates such studies, so one could argue that, for good or ill, he has received what he deserved. For good, I would urge – on balance, anyway. By and large Joyce has not been unlucky in the quality of the 'commentators' and criticism his work has attracted. Of course there have been excesses and perversities – no one familiar with many of the books and essays on James Joyce could doubt that – but they finally loom no larger among all the relevant studies than do similar embarrassments in the world of Shakespeare criticism, say, or, in Joyce's own century, Lawrence studies. Indeed, few writers of his time have led such tirelessly dedicated scholars and such impressively perceptive critics to record their findings and impressions for the rest of us.

Unfortunately, intelligent and creative criticism can also be misused – indeed, the dangers of excessive dependence upon it may be all the greater because of its quality, while poor or wrong-headed secondary studies are more easily guarded against. So it was probably of respectable secondary experiences as well as of abominable ones that Nikos Kazantzakis – another writer who attempted an epic 'modernisation' of Homer's *Odyssey* – was thinking when he gave the Greek people some notable counsel : 'Don't suffer that which they tell to mock the learned, precise Germans : if they see two doors, on the one written "Paradise" and on the other "Lecture about Paradise", they'll all rush for the second door.'[3] Ideally, the essays in the present volume provide us with keys to the door we want to go through, rather than a by-pass into some other realm.

The world we wish to enter is that of *Dubliners* and *A Portrait of the Artist as a Young Man* – two works which, together comprising the achievements of Joyce's young maturity as an artist, can usefully be associated in a collection such as this one. Appropriately, when the first of the *Dubliners* stories appeared in the *Irish Homestead,* they were published under the pseudonym of 'Stephen Daedalus'.

In 1904 George Russell ('A.E.') had asked Joyce to write a 'simple' story for the *Irish Homestead.* 'It is easy earned money,' he told Joyce, 'if you can write fluently and don't mind playing to the common understanding and liking once in a way.'[4] The result was not only 'The Sisters' (published in August 1904) but, eventually, *Dubliners.* In a letter of that same year to Constantine P. Curran (signed, incidentally, 'S. D.'), Joyce described his attempt at 'a series of epicleti' – invocations, as it were : 'I call the series *Dubliners* to betray the soul of that hemiplegia or paralysis which many consider a city' (see below, p. 35). This and other letters reprinted here indicate in part Joyce's purpose, while the

excerpts from his correspondence with Grant Richards only suggest the prolonged and harrowing dealings that Joyce almost
always had to go through in order to see his books published as
he had written them. Joyce was twenty-two when he began to
write *Dubliners*. Remarkably, he was only twenty-five when
in 1907 – after some delays in publication had already agonised
him – he completed the last of the stories, 'The Dead'. He was
thirty-two by the time the collection finally appeared in print.
The years between saw many frustrations. In 1905 he submitted
his stories to Grant Richards, a London publisher, who accepted
them in February 1906. In April, however, Richards informed
Joyce that a new story, 'Two Gallants', had produced problems
with the printer, who objected to certain passages. Joyce replied
that he had written his book 'in accordance with what I understand to be the classical tradition of my art. You must therefore
allow me to say that your printer's opinion of it does not interest
me in the least.'[5] A tortuous correspondence then ensued : it was
shameful for its own time, and seems ludicrous in ours (one of the
major obstacles to publication was Joyce's use of the word
'bloody'). When Joyce exasperatedly but carelessly asked why
no one had yet objected to 'An Encounter', Richards became
alerted to the dangers of that story as well, and finally he decided
not to publish the book after all.

Looked at charitably, in terms of the laws and publishing practices of his time, Richards' behaviour will seem perhaps more
timid than unconscionable. It is hard to be so generous toward
George Roberts, of the Dublin firm of Maunsel & Co. The book
had been rejected by several publishers after Richards dropped
it when in 1909 Roberts, an old Dublin acquaintance, accepted
it, and a contract was signed in August. But soon Roberts
began to have misgivings about the risks of libel actions because
of various references to actual names in the stories. It has been
said that given the Dublin of 1910, Roberts' fears may have been
justified.[6] Be that as it may, it is impossible to condone his sub-

sequent professional behaviour as a publisher. He delayed without being open about what he was doing and without firmly committing himself to publication or abandonment, and then climaxed three years of his handling of the episode by writing to Joyce, in August of 1912, that his 'legal advisers' had recommended that he proceed against Joyce 'in order to recover all costs, charges and expenses for time, labour and materials expended on the book'. 'I should be extremely sorry to have to take proceedings against you,' Roberts assured Joyce, 'but . . . I must ask you to make a substantial offer towards covering our loss.'[7] Joyce sent no money; as payment he made Roberts the narrator of his satirical broadside, 'Gas from a Burner'. That may have enabled Joyce to give vent to some of his bitter feelings, but *Dubliners* remained unpublished – until Grant Richards made the surprising move of asking to consider the volume again. Apparently feeling that society had caught up with *Dubliners,* Richards published it in June 1914. Times had changed for Joyce : the same year had already seen the start of the serial publication of *A Portrait of the Artist as a Young Man.*

Like *Dubliners,* the *Portrait* had been begun in 1904. Joyce wrote 'A Portrait of the Artist', reprinted here, in one day, 7 January, and then submitted it to John Eglinton for publication in the magazine *Dana.* Eglinton has recorded that 'I handed it back to him with the timid observation that I did not care to publish what was to myself incomprehensible.'[8] Few readers will feel that, aside from the chance to publish the future Great Writer, *Dana* lost very much of intrinsic value in the rejection of the 'Portrait', although the value of the sketch to scholars and students of Joyce is very real indeed. In any case, Joyce now set about in earnest to create his autobiographical novel and in the process to become, as he once wrote to his wife Nora, 'one of the writers of this generation who are perhaps creating at last a conscience in the soul of this wretched race'.[9] The original version, which was much longer than the one he eventually completed and published, was entitled *Stephen Hero*; the surviving portions, concentrating upon Stephen's university days, have been published, and they are extremely important and fascinating.[10] For one thing, although the section of *Stephen Hero* that we can now read deals with only a part of the life of Stephen treated in the *Portrait,* the two volumes are of comparable length, for *Stephen Hero* is more detailed, expansive and explicit. Among the most important of the passages which do not appear in the *Portrait* is the discussion of 'epiphany', which in *Stephen Hero* precedes the discussion of aesthetic theory. Epiphany can be defined as 'a sudden spiritual manifestation, whether from some object, scene, event, or memorable phase of the mind – the manifestation being out of proportion to the significance or strictly logical relevance of whatever produces it',[11] and refers to a concept that had been important to Joyce as well as to Stephen. Both for a time planned on 'collecting many such moments together in a book of epiphanies'. Joyce never did actually publish such a collection, but in one way or another he used a large number of the original epiphanies in his subsequent novels. Out of the forty manuscripts of epiphanies that have survived and have been published[12] the twelve that found their way into the *Portrait* are reprinted here.

In 1907 Joyce began still another revision of his autobiographical novel. By April of 1908 he had finished three of the five chapters of *A Portrait of the Artist as a Young Man* as we now have it; the last two chapters seem not to have been completed until the earlier chapters were being serialised in *The Egoist*. The editor of *The Egoist,* Dora Marsden, had been put on to Joyce's novel through the intervention of Ezra Pound, and the *Portrait* ran in twenty-five instalments between 2 February 1914 (Joyce's thirty-second birthday) and 1 September 1915.

It is perhaps impossible to overestimate the importance of Ezra Pound at this stage of Joyce's career – or the careers of a number of notable literary figures of the time, for that matter. If to some the later career of Ezra Pound must seem one of tragicomic villainy in the 1930s and 1940s, and one of pathos in the last decades of his life, in the first few decades of the century it was one of unquestioned heroism. Pound did not stop his efforts on Joyce's behalf with the serialisation of the *Portrait*, but also helped in the search for a publisher who would be willing to bring the novel out in book form. His championship of Joyce was perceptive but impassioned : he reacted to Edward Garnett's 'reader's report' for the firm of Duckworth & Co. by observing that 'altering Joyce to suit Duckworth's reader' would be 'like trying to fit the Venus de Milo into a piss-pot – a few changes required.'[13] Garnett's report, sent to Joyce's literary agent in 1916 and reprinted here, takes on all the more interest when we realise that it is the product of a reader of genuine intelligence and sensibility – a man who, if he could turn down Joyce's manuscript, could also enthusiastically greet the manuscripts of D. H. Lawrence's *Sons and Lovers* and Virginia Woolf's *The Voyage Out*.[14] He could, then, be receptive to the new – but not sufficiently so for him to welcome *A Portrait of the Artist*.

Dubliners, as we have seen, had already appeared in 1914, and it had received some attention. The stories in the volume, with their spareness and scrupulous meanness, marked a technical revolution in the history of the short story in English, but most of the original reviewers were especially put off by Joyce's revolutionary new content and attitude, or apparent lack of attitude. The common thread running through the reviews of *Dubliners* was the 'morbidity', 'sordidness', and 'unpleasantness' of the stories, though Joyce's talent was usually recognised as well; the review in the London *Times Literary Supplement*, reprinted here, may serve as an intelligent example. Even Gerald Gould, the one reviewer (aside from Pound) to recognise Joyce's 'genius' – and indeed to have had the courage to use that word in all seriousness – could not refrain from thinking it 'a pity' that 'Mr Joyce insists upon aspects of life which are ordinarily not mentioned' (see below, p. 63. A reader coming across Gould's review in this volume

will perhaps be less surprised by his 'narrow puritanism' (his own
term) than heartened by his ability to see beyond it in a way that
other reviewers with similar reservations could not.

A Portrait of the Artist was first published as a book in the
United States in December 1916 by B. W. Huebsch, and in
England early in 1917 by *The Egoist,* and it was widely hailed;
indeed the attention and praise it received are especially striking
when one remembers that it was, after all, only a first novel. Yet
by now references to Joyce's genius were no longer rare, and it
would be a gross distortion to characterise the early reviewers of the
Portrait as clods or philistines. There were still hold-outs, to be
sure : the *Portrait* after all *was* enormously new and bold and different. It is in order to convey a sense of how new and bold and
different it seemed to many readers that, at the risk of providing
a misleading balance, the reviews reprinted here have been chosen.
Still further excerpts are provided by 'James Joyce and His
Critics : Some Classified Comments', an advertisement run in
The Egoist in 1917 which Ezra Pound seems to have had at least
a hand in devising.[15] Not unexpectedly, perhaps, Irish reviewers
tended to be annoyed by the *Portrait.* The anonymous reviewer
in the Dublin *Freeman's Journal,* for example, expressed his
despair that 'English critics . . . are already hailing the author as
a typical Irishman, and his book as a faithful picture of Irish
life.' [16] The review in the *Irish Book Lover* – 'no clean-minded
person could possibly allow it to remain within reach of his wife,
his sons or daughters' – was too irresistible in its brevity to be
omitted from this collection. Even now, to be sure, profound
admiration for the *Portrait* is not universal – as some of the selec-
tions in Part Two of the present volume attest. But only occasionally do the attacks still take the form of an accusation – like
one from the 1960s – that the book represents 'a joyless projection
of adolescent agonies and morbidities'.[17]

This Introduction is not the place for a detailed account of the
history of Joyce's reputation, especially since excellent surveys are

available elsewhere.[18] Nevertheless, a brief attempt at an overview
is probably appropriate, although in fact not much need be said
about the reputations of the two relevant volumes through their
first twenty years or more. For while at first *Dubliners* tended to
be forgotten in comparison to the *Portrait,* that novel was in turn
soon overshadowed by the unprecedented excitement aroused by
the publication of *Ulysses,* first as a serial starting in 1918, then
in book form in Paris in 1922. Despite the widespread attention the
Portrait had received, it sold very few copies at first – then none
at all. In 1924 Joyce reported that 'in one year not a single copy
of *A Portrait of the Artist* has been sold in the United States'; as
late as 1940 he wrote to a friend summarising his American publisher's 'account of sales of my books for the previous half year.
Exiles, 0, *A Portrait of the Artist as a Young Man,* 0, *Dubliners,*
6'.[19] Yet the excitement Joyce's work aroused among many of
those who knew it, especially younger writers, is incalculable.
Interestingly, poets seemed even more receptive than novelists :
the major poets of the time, older and younger, were appreciably
more enthusiastic than the novelists of Joyce's own generation
tended to be. There was of course Pound; T. S. Eliot was an early
champion of Joyce's work; Hart Crane – not yet twenty years
old – found the *Portrait* to be, 'aside from Dante, . . . spiritually
the most inspiring book I have ever read'.[20] In Ireland William
Butler Yeats thought the *Portrait* 'a very great book' and, on the
basis of his reading of the early chapters in *The Egoist,* had
described Joyce as 'the most remarkable new talent in Ireland
today'.[21] For a while, however, Ireland more or less seemed to
be ignoring Joyce's work; the years following the Easter Rising
of 1916 provided, after all, a sufficiency of other controversies.
Yet even during those years a number of Irishmen began to share
Yeats's estimate; in his 1922 revision of a book originally published in 1916, *Ireland's Literary Renaissance,* Ernest Boyd wrote
that 'the simple truth is that *A Portrait of the Artist as a Young
Man* is to the Irish novel what *The Wanderings of Oisin* was to

Irish poetry and *The Playboy of the Western World* to Irish drama, the unique and significant work which lifts the *genre* out of the commonplace into the national literature' (p. 405). But praise was not general all over Ireland. On the last page of his 1926 survey, *Anglo-Irish Literature,* Hugh Alexander Law viewed the possibility that Joyce's work was the harbinger of 'the novels of the future' as 'a dreadful prospect' (p. 301). And Benedict Kiely, the contemporary novelist, remembers what it was like to be young and Irish when Joyce died in 1941 : 'a Dublin daily newspaper, renowned for success through dullness, did the young men of that time a favour by failing to carry even a news report of the death of Joyce, and thus helping to identify and delineate the enemy'.[22]

A number of books were published about Joyce in the 1930s, but inevitably they tended to concentrate on the problems of *Ulysses.* But 1941 saw a landmark in Joyce studies with the publication of Harry Levin's *James Joyce : A Critical Introduction* – arguably still the best introduction to Joyce's work as a whole; the chapter on the *Portrait* is the first piece in Part Two of this book.

During the 1940s and 1950s a good deal of attention was paid by many critics to various aspects of Stephen's aesthetic theories. I have chosen to include Maurice Beebe's 'Joyce and Aquinas : The Theory of Aesthetics' as among the most sensible and useful, though it should also be mentioned that the same year, 1957, saw the publication of Father William T. Noon's *Joyce and Aquinas,* a learned and judicious study, not easily excerpted, which reaches conclusions not unlike Beebe's : as Father Noon puts it, 'the more one comes to learn about Joyce's actual exposure to the thought of Aquinas, the less one is inclined to believe that it was, from a scholarly point of view, systematic or thorough' (p. 3). The interest of critics in Joyce's possible debts to Aquinas was allied to another motif that ran through the criticism of the 1950s – the general relationship between Joyce and Catholicism, an interest reflected

in such books as Kevin Sullivan's *Joyce Among the Jesuits* (1958)
and J. Mitchell Morse's *The Sympathetic Alien* : *James Joyce
and Catholicism* (1959).

Such emphases tended to stress the *Portrait* more than
Dubliners, and indeed during this time Joyce's stories remained
relatively ignored by the critics. In part, that seems to have been
the result of an uncertainty of approach which is still evident in
many studies of *Dubliners.* For critics are frequently unsure how
to react to these tight, spare, yet richly complex and ambiguous
tales by the author of *Ulysses* and *Finnegans Wake,* and they
sometimes in consequence decide to bring in the vast arsenal they
have come (rightly or wrongly) to feel necessary for attacking those
later books. An outstanding early example is Richard Levin's and
Charles Shattuck's 'First Flight to Ithaca : A New Reading of
Joyce's *Dubliners*',[23] a painstaking but finally unconvincing and,
in any case, not very helpful attempt to show that *Dubliners* has
the same sort of Homeric patterning as *Ulysses.* It was presumably
of this sort of essay that Myles na Gopaleen (Flann O'Brien) was
thinking when he could say – as early as 1949 – that Joyce had
'reduced the entire literary world to a state of chronic and helpless exegesis'.[24]

A different sort of exasperation with Joyce is expressed in the
attack by Frank O'Connor reprinted here : 'In reading Joyce' he
feels, 'one is reading Literature – Literature with a capital L' (see
below, p. 123). It is possible to have a two-fold reaction to
O'Connor's complaint, for we may assent to the accuracy of his
remark but not to the attitude behind it – or, as Harry Levin has
expressed it in a chapter he added to his *James Joyce* in 1960,
'we need not disagree; we need merely recognise the sharp decline
in literary standards that could make such an assertion an accusation' (p. 242). Other reactions against Joyce also continued to be
voiced; in the widely read *A Literary History of England,* published in 1948, Samuel C. Chew observed that 'already it is
apparent that startling innovations in technique are not in them-

selves evidence of artistic success' and that 'Joyce's contemporary renown was in part due to factors extraneous to literary excellence'[25] (once again we may agree and disagree – go along with the statements as such, but not with the evaluation of Joyce's work behind them).

But the Joyce Juggernaut rolled on. In time *Dubliners* too received more and more attention, and Brewster Ghiselin's 'The Unity of *Dubliners*' (1956) was a seminal essay in the new consideration being given to the stories – not so much because of its talk about symbols (in itself arguably formulaic), but above all in its stress on the 'symbolic pattern' of the entire collection, which Ghiselin saw as 'a sequence of events in a moral drama'.[26]

By 1948 Seon Givens had been able to compile an impressive collection entitled *James Joyce : Two Decades of Criticism,* which contained a number of important and subsequently influential essays. One of them was Hugh Kenner's 'The *Portrait* in Perspective'; the version printed in our volume is the quite different essay of that title in Kenner's *Dublin's Joyce* (1955). Taken together, these essays have comprised the most influential and controversial argument yet published on the *Portrait,* and Kenner's view of the 'priggish, humourless' and 'indigestibly Byronic' Stephen helped to found what has come to be called the 'Stephen-hating' school, which flourished in the 1950s.

One of the things that eventually balanced things back in Stephen's favour a bit was the appearance of an extremely important contribution to Joyce studies, Richard Ellmann's authoritative biography, *James Joyce* (1959). I have chosen as an excerpt here the chapter on 'The Backgrounds of "The Dead" ', a fine example of how biographical information can be used by a sensitive critic to enhance rather than inhibit one's understanding of a work of fiction, in this case the most famous of the stories in *Dubliners.* In regard to the *Portrait,* throughout his book Ellmann (like others elsewhere to be sure) shows how – although Stephen Dedalus is not James Joyce, a truism which must never be forgotten – Stephen and Joyce share enough attitudes and experiences to put the irony with which Stephen is sometimes portrayed in a much more subdued or oblique perspective than 'Stephen-hating' allows. Indeed, the question of the tone of the *Portrait* in regard to Stephen has remained a recurring one in studies of the novel, as can be seen in several of the essays in this volume, notably Wayne C. Booth's.

Booth's essay is from one of the most influential and widely read critical books of the 1960s, *The Rhetoric of Fiction,* in which he presents important arguments in regard to such elements of fiction as point of view, tone, and the explicit or implicit authorial 'voice'. Of the *Portrait,* Booth states that 'the truth seems to be that Joyce was always a bit uncertain about his attitude toward Stephen. Anyone who reads Ellmann's masterful biography with this problem in mind cannot help being struck by the many shifts and turns Joyce took as he worked through the various versions. There is nothing especially strange in that, of course'. (See below, pp. 194–5). Of course; but in Booth's handling there turns out to be something unmistakably reprehensible in it. Booth's discomfort with the *Portrait* involves his desire for greater clarity and certainty, at least about a number of key issues, such as Joyce's attitude toward Stephen's aesthetics. Such a preference is understandable, but in the end it is not one that all serious readers of literature will feel compelled to share; some will feel that a writer who has powerfully conveyed a sense of ambiguity and uncertainty has not necessarily failed to communicate.

The last two decades have seen the flood of books and essays on Joyce rise higher and higher. Many of these studies have been on individual works, and during this time Joyce's early works of fiction have finally come into their own as objects of investigation. But these years have also been strong on general books covering the whole of Joyce's career. Excerpts from a few such works are in this volume. John Gross's 'The Voyage Out' is a brief, cogent presentation of the case *for* Stephen Dedalus, although it also recognises his real and major limitations. J. I. M. Stewart's contribution is from *Eight Modern Writers*, the twelfth volume in the *Oxford History of English Literature*. Anthony Burgess, who has clearly been influenced by Joyce in his own novels, regards him as one of the truly great artists: 'Shakespeare and Joyce,' he has written, 'in all world literature, come closest in aim, technique and achievement.'[27] Burgess's essay on *Dubliners*, 'A Paralysed City', is from his book on Joyce published in England as *Here Comes Everybody : An Introduction to James Joyce for the Ordinary Reader* and in America more briefly and memorably as *Re Joyce*. Perhaps out of defensiveness arising from his fear that Joyce may be lost among all the scholarship about him, Burgess describes his book as 'commentary rather than criticism' (Faber, 1965, p. 12). There is, actually, a certain irony in Burgess finding himself in the present volume, for he once described his reaction to a collection of critical essays on the *Portrait* as one in which 'my mouth goes dry, as in the witness- or confession-box, and a nightmare illusion of never having read the book (even though I've known it for thirty-odd years) comes upon me'.[28]

Some of the many other works on Joyce published in the 1960s and 1970s – a number of them extremely valuable – are listed with brief descriptions in the Select Bibliography at the end of this book; there are certainly too many to do justice to in this Introduction. But some developments ought to be singled out. For example, 1963 saw the start of the *James Joyce Quarterly*, edited by Thomas F. Staley and published at the University of Tulsa; in addition to articles, notes, and reviews, it prints reports on Joyce symposia, queries, supplemental checklists of Joyce items omitted from the annual *MLA International Bibliography*, and so on.

The most significant publications of the last decade or two have been texts by Joyce himself. In 1957 Stuart Gilbert edited the *Letters of James Joyce*; in 1966 Richard Ellmann brought out two additional volumes, containing some of the most important letters, and all the volumes are now available in a three volume edition. Ellmann and Ellsworth Mason edited Joyce's *Critical Writings* in 1959 (London: Faber; New York: Viking); a number of pieces in that collection are of special interest to readers of the *Portrait*. So is *The Workshop of Daedalus: James Joyce and the Raw Materials for A Portrait of the Artist as a Young Man*, edited by Robert Scholes and Richard M. Kain (1965). This is a volume of great interest and value, which publishes a number of Joyce's manuscripts for the first time: included are all the surviving epiphanies, 'A Portrait of the Artist', several fascinating notebooks, and other materials by and about Joyce.

At last, too, we now have more reliable editions of *Dubliners* and *A Portrait of the Artist*. James S. Atherton edited the *Portrait* for the Heinemann Modern Novel Series in 1964. It is a fine edition: the Introduction is excellent, and at the end Atherton provides notes which are illuminating, concise, and unobtrusive. In the same year in America, Chester G. Anderson (in consultation with Richard Ellmann) produced a welcome edition for the Viking Press. Both editions were aided by the existence of Joyce's 'holograph' of the *Portrait*, now in the National Library of Ireland, in Dublin. Anderson's edition (published in England in 1968 by Jonathan Cape) contains no Introduction or notes, which – despite the high quality of those by Atherton – may lead some readers to prefer it. In any case in 1968 Anderson edited the Viking Critical Library volume of the *Portrait*, which does contain notes (some of them more adventurous than Atherton's perhaps, but extremely useful), as well as numerous other materials, by and about Joyce, relevant to *A Portrait of the Artist as a Young Man* and thoughtfully chosen. In 1967, Robert Scholes, also in consultation with Richard Ellmann, prepared an edition of *Dubliners* for Viking (in England, Jonathan Cape). Two years later Scholes and A. Walton Litz edited the Viking Critical Library volume of the stories, and it too contains useful notes, materials on the background of the stories and their composition, and critical studies. In a single American paperback, *Notes for Joyce : Dubliners and A Portrait of the Artist as a Young Man* (Dutton, 1967), Don Gifford has compiled notes on both books.

Joyce's reputation is greater than ever, but in some ways it remains as controversial. In a conjecture about what would happen if a James Joyce burst upon the scene today, Anthony Burgess assumes that 'an American academic community would cosset him, look forward to his death, and indulge in no carping at even his most fantastic experiments. Ireland, old faithful, would still reject him. England would be, as before, indifferent'.[29] That Joyce can still at times arouse strong feelings in his homeland is perhaps indicated by an untypical incident : a version of 'Clay' being filmed for the BBC in 1972 in Dublin under the direction of Jonathan Miller had to be finished in London because of the crew's reactions to a telephoned threat.[30]

Joyce's work, as a matter of fact, *is* still dangerous and revolutionary, and is likely to remain so, as young readers have realised for half a century. It is true that for a while it may have seemed to older people that Stephen Dedalus' brand of rebellion, say, had gone out of style : after all Stephen joins no movements, refuses to sign petitions, reads books and assumes they matter. But my experience anyway has been that despite the expectations of their elders young readers have continued to relate to Joyce's portrait and to be profoundly moved by it, and are no more eager to form a new Stephen-hating school than I am.

The characters of *Dubliners* and *A Portrait of the Artist as a Young Man* do not overlap – until, that is, many of them meet one another when they reappear in *Ulysses,* which had its inception as an idea for a short story to be included in *Dubliners,* and which was written while Joyce was in 'exile' : for he had left Dublin and Ireland in 1904, and except for short visits – the last in 1912 – he never returned. In a sense he never had to, never having really left. Marcel Proust has observed that all the works of any artist can be regarded as a single work.[31] Novelists have occasionally recognised this truth and have even provided us with an appropriate title, as Balzac did with *La Comédie humaine*. And Proust's own lifework – whether ostensibly part of his long novel or not – could easily be called *A la recherche du temps perdu*. In the same way we might call all of Dostoevsky's books *Crime and Punishment*, all of Conrad's *Heart of Darkness*, all of F. Scott Fitzgerald's *The Beautiful and Damned*, all of Kafka's *The Trial*.

The reader could if he wished supply other examples, but my point is that there is not the slightest doubt that the inevitable title for James Joyce's lifework would be *Dubliners*.

MORRIS BEJA

NOTES

1. Patrick Kavanagh, *Collected Poems* (MacGibbon & Kee, 1964) p. 117.

2. *A Wake Newslitter*, a quite useful forum for those especially interested in *Finnegans Wake*. For all I know, it is the only long-standing critical journal concentrating on not merely one author, but on one work by that author. The possibilities are, however, intriguing : *The Scarlet Newsletter, The Bleak House Organ, The Remembrance of Things Past Memo. . . .*

3. *Travels in Greece* (*Journey to the Morea*), trans. F. A. Reed (Bruno Cassirer, 1966) pp. 171–2.

4. Quoted in Richard Ellmann, *James Joyce* (Oxford, 1959) p. 169.

5. *Letters of James Joyce,* ed. Stuart Gilbert (London : Faber; New York : Viking, 1957) p. 60.

6. James S. Atherton, 'The Joyce of *Dubliners*', in *James Joyce Today : Essays on the Major Works,* ed. Thomas F. Staley (Indiana University, 1966) pp. 29–30.

7. *Letters of James Joyce,* ed. Richard Ellmann (London : Faber; New York : Viking, 1966), vol. ii, pp. 313–14.

8. John Eglinton (W. K. Magee), in *The Workshop of Daedalus: James Joyce and the Raw Materials for A Portrait of the Artist as a*

Young Man, ed. Robert Scholes and Richard M. Kain (Northwestern University, 1965) p. 200.

9. *Letters*, vol. ii, p. 311 (22 August 1912). In the context he associates himself in that struggle with William Butler Yeats and John Millington Synge.

10. Ed. Theodore Spencer, Rev. John J. Slocum and Herbert Cahoon (London : Jonathan Cape, 1956; Norfolk : New Directions, 1963).

11. Morris Beja, *Epiphany in the Modern Novel* (London : Peter Owen; Seattle : University of Washington, 1971) p. 18. The definition is of course an expansion upon Stephen's : see below, p. 50.

12. See the *Workshop*, pp. 11–51.

13. Letter to James B. Pinker, 30 January 1916, in *Pound/Joyce: The Letters of Ezra Pound to James Joyce, with Pound's Essays on Joyce*, ed. Forrest Read (New Directions, 1967) p. 67.

14. It has been argued that the final report may actually represent a re-working by someone else of what Garnett himself had written. See *A Portrait of the Artist as a Young Man: Text, Criticism, and Notes*, ed. Chester G. Anderson (Viking, 1968) p. 319.

15. See *Pound/Joyce*, pp. 104, 118.

16. 'A Dyspeptic Portrait', *Freeman's Journal*, 7 April 1917, in *James Joyce: The Critical Heritage*, ed. Robert H. Deming (Routledge & Kegan Paul, 1970) p. 99.

17. *Age of Yeats*, ed. George Brandon Saul (Dell, 1963) p. 370.

18. See, notably, Marvin Magalaner and Richard M. Kain, *Joyce: The Man, the Work, the Reputation* (New York University, 1956), and the two volumes of Deming's *James Joyce: The Critical Heritage*, including the editor's Introduction, vol. i, pp. 1–31.

19. Joyce, *Letters*, vol. iii, p. 95 and vol. i, p. 412.

20. 'Joyce and Ethics', *The Complete Poems and Selected Letters and Prose*, ed. Brom Weber (Liveright, 1966) p. 200.

21. Joyce, *Letters*, vol. ii, pp. 388, 356.

22. 'The Artist on the Giant's Grave', in *A Bash in the Tunnel: James Joyce by the Irish*, ed. John Ryan (Clifton, 1970) p. 237.

23. In *James Joyce: Two Decades of Criticism*, ed. Seon Givens (Vanguard, 1948, rev. edn 1963) pp. 47–94.

24. *Irish Times*, 12 September 1949, quoted in David Powell, 'An Annotated Bibliography of Myles Na Gopaleen's (Flann O'Brien's) "Cruiskeen Lawn" Commentaries on James Joyce', *James Joyce Quarterly*, 9 (Fall 1971) p. 53.

25. 'The Nineteenth Century and After' in *A Literary History of England*, ed. Albert C. Baugh (Routledge & Kegan Paul, 1948) p. 1560.

26. See below, p. 101. Ghiselin's essay was originally published in two parts, the second of which (not reprinted in this volume) is an elaborate and detailed survey of the stories in geographical-symbolic terms.

27. *Urgent Copy: Literary Studies* (Norton, 1968) p. 78.

28. Ibid. p. 75.

29. Ibid. p. 82.

30. *Irish Times*, 10 October 1972, p. 10. Of course, other films based on Joyce material have been produced in Dublin with no such trouble, including other stories in the same BBC series.

31. See *The Captive*, in *Remembrance of Things Past*, trans. C. K. Scott Moncrieff (Random House, 1934), pp. 640–7.

PART ONE

Background and Early Responses

LETTERS FROM JOYCE (1904-1906)

TO CONSTANTINE P. CURRAN

N.D. (?) 1904   *The Rain, Friday* [*sic*]

Dear Curran : . . . I am writing a series of epicleti – ten – for a
paper. I have written one. I call the series *Dubliners* to betray the
soul of that hemiplegia or paralysis which many consider a city.
Look out for an edition de luxe of all my limericks instantly.
More anon   S.D.

                                                   S D [*sic*]

TO STANISLAUS JOYCE

[*About 24 September 1905*]

                           Via S. Nicolò 30, II°, Trieste Austria

Dear Stannie   Please send me the information I ask you for as
follows :

The Sisters: Can a priest be buried in a habit?

Ivy Day in the Committee Room – Are Aungier St and Wicklow
  in the Royal Exchange Ward? Can a municipal election take
  place in October?

A Painful Case – Are the police at Sydney Parade of the *D* division? Would the city ambulance be called out to Sydney Parade
  for an accident? Would an accident at Sydney Parade be
  treated at Vincent's Hospital?

After the Race – Are the police supplied with provisions by
  government or private contracts?

Kindly answer these questions as quickly as possible. I sent my story *The Clay* (which I had slightly rewritten) to *The LITER-ARY World* but the cursedly stupid ape that conducts that journal neither acknowledged it nor sent it back. This kind of thing is maddening. . . .

It is possible that the delusion I have with regard to my power to write will be killed by adverse circumstances. But the delusion which will never leave me is that I am an artist by temperament. Newman and Renan, for example, are excellent writers but they seem to have very little of the temperament I mean. Whereas Rimbaud, who is hardly a writer at all, has it. Of course Renan is an artist and must have the temperament but it is balanced by the temperament of a philo[lo]gist. Newman must have it too but balanced by the temperament of a theologian. I am neither *savant* nor saint. Grant Richards wrote to me, saying how much he admired *Chamber Music* but adding that, with the present public taste, he could not take more than part of the risk. I wrote back thanking him (I daresay he has no money himself) and saying I had no money. I wrote to Heinemann telling him about *Dubliners* and asking would he read it and consider it. I shall send you on Wednesday or Thursday the tenth story *A Mother* and the book will be finished by the first of November. You might let me know what you think of it as I intend to dedicate it to you. You are a long time sitting on my novel. I wish you'd say what you think of it. The only book I know like it is Lermontoff's *Hero of Our Days*. Of course mine is much longer and Lermontoff's hero is an aristocrat and a tired man and a brave animal. But there is a like-ness in the aim and title and at times in the acid treatment. . . . The book impressed me very much. It is much more interesting than any of Turgénieff's.

Will you read some English 'realists' I see mentioned in the papers and see what they are like – Gissing, Arthur Morrison and a man named [Charles Francis] Keary. I can read very little and am as dumb as a stockfish. But really I think that the two last stories I sent you are very good. Perhaps they will be refused by Heinemann. The order of the stories is as follows. *The Sisters, An Encounter* and another story [*Araby*] which are stories of my childhood : *The Boarding-House, After the Race* and *Eveline,* which are stories of adolescence : *The Clay, Counterparts,* and *A Painful Case* which are stories of mature life : *Ivy Day in the Committee Room, A Mother* and the last story of the book [*Grace*] which are stories of public life in Dublin. When you remember that Dublin has been a capital for thousands of years, that it is the 'second' city of the British Empire, that it is nearly three times as big as Venice it seems strange that no artist has given it to the world. I read that silly, wretched book of Moore's 'The Untilled Field' which the Americans found so remarkable for its 'craftsmanship'. O, dear me! It is very dull and flat, indeed : and ill written. JIM

TO GRANT RICHARDS

15 October 1905 *Via S. Nicolò 30, II° Trieste, Austria*

Dear Mr Grant Richards . . .
The second book which I have ready is called *Dubliners.* It is a collection of twelve short stories. It is possible that you would consider it to be of a commercial nature. I would gladly submit it to you before sending it to Messrs Constable and, if you could promise to publish it soon, I would gladly agree. Unfortunately I am in such circumstances that it is necessary for me to have either of the books published as soon as possible.

I do not think that any writer has yet presented Dublin to the world. It has been a capital of Europe for thousands of years, it is supposed to be the second city of the British Empire and it is nearly three times as big as Venice. Moreover, on account of many circumstances which I cannot detail here, the expression 'Dubliner' seems to me to have some meaning and I doubt whether the same can be said for such words as 'Londoner' and 'Parisian' both of which have been used by writers as titles. From time to time I see in publishers' lists announcements of books on Irish subjects, so that I think people might be willing to pay for the special odour of corruption which, I hope, floats over my stories. Faithfully yours

JAS A. JOYCE

TO GRANT RICHARDS

5 May 1906   *Via Giovanni Boccaccio 1, II°, Trieste, Austria*

Dear Mr Grant Richards, I am sorry you do not tell me why the printer, who seems to be the barometer of English opinion, refuses to print *Two Gallants* and makes marks in the margin of *Counterparts*. . . .

As for my part and share in the book I have already told all I have to tell. My intention was to write a chapter of the moral history of my country and I chose Dublin for the scene because that city seemed to me the centre of paralysis. I have tried to present it to the indifferent public under four of its aspects : childhood, adolescence, maturity and public life. The stories are arranged in this order. I have written it for the most part in a style of scrupulous meanness and with the conviction that he is a very bold man who dares to alter in the presentment, still more to deform, whatever he has seen and heard. I cannot do any more than this. I cannot alter what I have written. All these objections of which the printer is now the mouthpiece arose in my mind when I was writing the book, both as to the themes of the stories and their manner of treatment. Had I listened to them I would not have written the book. I have come to the conclusion that I cannot write without offending people. The printer denounces *Two Gallants* and *Counterparts*. A Dubliner would denounce *Ivy Day in the Committee Room*. The more subtle inquisitor will denounce *An Encounter*, the enormity of which the printer cannot see because he is, as I said, a plain blunt man. The Irish priest will denounce *The Sisters*. The Irish boarding-house keeper will denounce *The Boarding-House*. Do not let the printer imagine, for goodness' sake, that he is going to have all the barking to himself. . . . JAS A. JOYCE

TO GRANT RICHARDS

13 May 1906 Via Giovanni Boccaccio 1, II°, Trieste, Austria

Dear Mr Grant Richards, . . .

The appeal to my pocket has not much weight with me. Of course I would gladly see the book in print and of course I would like to make money by it. But, on the other hand, I have very little intention of prostituting whatever talent I may have to the public. (This letter is not for publication). . . .

JAS A. JOYCE

TO GRANT RICHARDS

23 June 1906 Via Giovanni Boccaccio 1, Trieste

Dear Mr Grant Richards : . . .

Your suggestion that those concerned in the publishing of *Dubliners* may be prosecuted for indecency is in my opinion an extraordinary contribution to the discussion. I know that some amazing imbecilities have been perpetrated in England but I really cannot see how any civilised tribunal could listen for two minutes to such an accusation against my book. I care little or nothing whether what I write is indecent or not but, if I understand the meaning of words, I have written nothing whatever indecent in *Dubliners*.

I send you a Dublin paper by this post. It is the leading satirical paper of the Celtic nations, corresponding to *Punch* or *Pasquino*.

I send it to you that you may see how witty the Irish are as all the world knows. The style of the caricaturist will show you how artistic they are : and you will see for yourself that the Irish are the most spiritual race on the face of the earth. Perhaps this may reconcile you to *Dubliners*. It is not my fault that the odour of ashpits and old weeds and offal hangs round my stories. I seriously believe that you will retard the course of civilisation in Ireland by preventing the Irish people from having one good look at themselves in my nicely polished looking-glass.

S o u r c e : *Letters of James Joyce,* vol. i, ed. Stuart Gilbert (1957) pp. 55, 63–4, and vol. ii, ed. Richard Ellmann (1966) pp. 109–11, 122–3, 132–5, 137.

SELECTIONS FROM JOYCE'S MANUSCRIPTS

I 'A PORTRAIT OF THE ARTIST' (1904)[1]

The features of infancy are not commonly reproduced in the adolescent portrait for, so capricious are we, that we cannot or will not conceive the past in any other than its iron memorial aspect. Yet the past assuredly implies a fluid succession of presents, the development of an entity of which our actual present is a phase only. Our world, again, recognises its acquaintance chiefly by the characters of beard and inches and is, for the most part, estranged from those of its members who seek through some art, by some process of the mind as yet untabulated, to liberate from the personalised lumps of matter that which is their individuating rhythm, the first or formal relation of their parts. But for such as these a portrait is not an identificative paper but rather the curve of an emotion.

Use of reason is by popular judgment antedated by some seven years and so it is not easy to set down the exact age at which the natural sensibility of the subject of this portrait awoke to the ideas of eternal damnation, the necessity of penitence and the efficacy of prayer. <His training had early developed a very lively sense of spiritual obligations at the expense of what is called 'common sense'. He ran through his measure like a spendthrift saint, astonishing many by ejaculatory fervours, offending many by airs of the cloister. One day in a wood near Malahide a labourer had marvelled to see a boy of fifteen praying in an ecstasy of Oriental posture. It was indeed a long time before this boy understood the nature of that most marketable goodness which makes it possible

to give comfortable assent to propositions without ordering one's life in accordance with them. The digestive value of religion he never appreciated and he chose, as more fitting his case, those poorer humbler orders in which a confessor did not seem anxious to reveal himself, in theory at least, a man of the world. In spite, however, of continued shocks, which drove him from breathless flights of zeal shamefully inwards, he was still soothed by devotional exercises when he entered the University.

About this period the enigma of a manner was put up at all comers to protect the crisis. He was quick enough now to see that he must disentangle his affairs in secrecy and reserve had ever been a light penance. His reluctance to debate scandal, to seem curious of others, aided him in his real indictment and was not without a satisfactory flavour of the heroic. It was part of that ineradicable egoism which he was afterwards to call redeemer that he imagined converging to him the deeds and thoughts of the microcosm. Is the mind of boyhood medieval that it is so divining of intrigue? Field sports (or their correspondents in the world of mentality) are perhaps the most effective cure, but for this fantastic idealist, eluding the grunting booted apparition with a bound, the mimic hunt was no less ludicrous than unequal in a ground chosen to his disadvantage. But behind the rapidly indurating shield the sensitive answered. Let the pack of enmities come tumbling and sniffing to the highlands after their game; there was his ground : and he flung them disdain from flashing antlers.> There was evident self-flattery in the image but a danger of complacence too. Wherefore, neglecting the wheezier bayings in that chorus which no leagues of distance could make musical, he began loftily diagnosis of the younglings. His judgment was exquisite, deliberate, sharp; his sentence sculptural. <These young men saw in the sudden death of a dull French novelist [Emile Zola, d. 1902] the hand of Emmanuel God with us; they admired Gla[d]stone, physical science and the tragedies of Shakespeare; and they believed in the adjustment of Catholic teaching to every day

needs, in the Church diplomatic. In their relations among themselves and towards their superiors they displayed a nervous and (wherever there was question of authority) a very English liberalism.> He remarked the half-admiring, half-reproving demeanour of a class, implicitly pledged to abstinences towards <others among whom (the fame went) wild living was not unknown. Though the union of faith and fatherland was ever sacred in that world of easily inflammable enthusiasms a couplet from [Thomas] Davis, accusing the least docile of tempers, never failed of its applause and the memory of [Terence Bellew] McManus was hardly less revered than that of Cardinal Cullen.> They had many reasons to respect authority; and even if <a student were forbidden to go to *Othello* ('There are some coarse expressions in it' he was told) what a little cross was that? Was it not rather an evidence of watchful care and interest, and were they not assured that in their future lives this care would continue, this interest be maintained? The exercise of authority might be sometimes (rarely) questionable, its intention, never. Who therefore readier than these young men to acknowledge gratefully the sallies of some genial professor or the surliness of some door-porter, who more sollicitous to cherish in every way and to advance in person the honour of Alma Mater? For his part he was at the difficult age, dispossessed and necessitous, sensible of all that was ignoble in such matters who, in revery at least, had been acquainted with nobility. An earnest Jesuit had prescribed a clerkship in Guinness's : and doubtless the clerk-designate of a brewery would not have had scorn and pity only for an admirable community had it not been that he desired (in the language of the schoolmen) an arduous good. It was impossible that he should find solace in societies for the encouragement of thought among laymen or any other than bodily comfort in the warm sodality amid so many foolish or grotesque virginities. Moreover, it was impossible that a temperament ever trembling towards its ecstasy should submit to acquiesce, that a soul should decree servitude for its portion

over which the image of beauty had fallen as a mantle. One night in early spring, standing at the foot of the staircase in the library, he said to his friend 'I have left the Church.'> And as they walked home through the streets arm-in-arm he told, in words that seemed an echo of their closing, how he had left it through the gates of Assisi.

Extravagance followed. The simple history of the Poverello [Saint Francis of Assisi] was soon out of mind and he established himself in the maddest of companies. Joachim Abbas [Giordano], Bruno the Nolan, Michael Sendivogius, all the hierarchs of initiation cast their spells upon him. He descended among the hells of Swedenborg and abased himself in the gloom of Saint John of the Cross. His heaven was suddenly illuminated by a horde of stars, the signatures of all nature, the soul remembering ancient days. Like an alchemist he bent upon his handiwork, bringing together the mysterious elements, separating the subtle from the gross. For the artist the rhythms of phrase and period, the symbols of word and allusion, were paramount things. And was it any wonder that out of this marvellous life, wherein he had annihilated and rebuilt experience, laboured and despaired, he came forth at last with a single purpose – to reunite the children of the spirit, jealous and long-divided, to reunite them against fraud and principality. A thousand eternities were to be reaffirmed, divine knowledge was to be re-established. Alas for fatuity! as easily might he have summoned a regiment of the winds. They pleaded their natural pieties – social limitations, inherited apathy of race, an adoring mother, the Christian fable. Their treasons were venial only. Wherever the social monster permitted they would hazard the extremes of heterodoxy, reason of an imaginative determinant in ethics, of anarchy (the folk), of blue triangles, of the fish-gods, proclaiming in a fervent moment the necessity for action. His revenge was a phrase and isolation. He lumped the emancipates together – Venomous Butter – and set away from the sloppy neighborhood.

Isolation, he had once written, is the first principle of artistic economy but traditional and individual revelations were at that time pressing their claims and self-communion had been but shyly welcomed. But in the intervals of friendships (for he had outridden three) he had known the sisterhood of meditative hours and now the hope began to grow up within him of finding among them that serene emotion, that certitude, which among men he had not found. An impulse had led him forth in the dark season to silent and lonely places where the mists hung streamerwise among the trees; and as he had passed there amid the subduing night, in the secret fall of leaves, the fragrant rain, the mesh of vapours moon-transpierced, he had imagined an admonition of the frailty of all things./In summer it had led him seaward. Wandering over the arid, grassy hills or along the strand, avowedly in quest of shellfish, he had grown almost impatient of the day. Waders, into whose childish or girlish hair, girlish or childish dresses, the very wilfulness of the sea had entered – even they had not fascinated. But as day had waned it had been pleasant to watch the last few figures islanded in distant pools; and as evening deepened the grey glow above the sea he had gone out, out among the shallow waters, the holy joys of solitude uplifting him, singing passionately to the tide, sceptically, cynically, mystically, he had sought for an absolute satisfaction and now little by little he began to be conscious of the beauty of mortal conditions. He remembered a sentence in Augustine – 'It was manifested unto me that those things be good which yet are corrupted; which neither if they were supremely good, nor unless they were good could be corrupted : for had they been supremely good they would have been incorruptible but if they were not good there would be nothing in them which could be corrupted.' A philosophy of reconcilement. . . possible. . .as eve. . .The. . .of the. . .at lef. . .bor. . .lit up with dolphin lights but the lights in the chambers of the heart were unextinguished, nay, burning as for espousal.

Dearest of mortals! In spite' of tributary verses and of the comedy of meetings here and in the foolish society of sleep the fountain of being (it seemed) had been interfused. Years before, in boyhood, <the energy of sin opening a world before him,> he had been made aware of thee. <The yellow gaslamps arising in his troubled vision, against an autumnal sky, gleaming mysteriously there before the violet altar – the groups gathered at the doorways arranged as for some rite – the glimpses of revel and fantasmal mirth – the vague face of some welcomer seeming to awaken from a slumber of centuries under his gaze – the blind confusion (iniquity! iniquity!) suddenly overtaking him – in all that ardent adventure of lust didst thou not even then communicate?> Beneficent one! (the shrewdness of love was in the title) thou camest timely, as a witch to the agony of the self-devourer, an envoy from the fair courts of life. How could he thank thee for that enrichment of soul by thee consummated? Mastery of art had been achieved in irony; asceticism of intellect had been a mood of indignant pride : but who had revealed him to himself but thou alone? In ways of tenderness, simple, intuitive tenderness, thy love had made to arise in him the central torrents of life. Thou hadst put thine arms about him and, intimately prisoned as thou hadst been, in the soft stir of thy bosom, the raptures of silence, the murmured words, thy heart had spoken to his heart. Thy disposition could refine and direct his passion, holding mere beauty at the cunningest angle. Thou wert sacramental, imprinting thine indelible mark, of very visible grace. A litany must honour thee; Lady of the Apple Trees, Kind Wisdom, Sweet Flower of Dusk. In another phase it had been not uncommon to devise dinners in white and purple upon the actuality of stirabout but here, surely, is sturdy or delicate food to hand; no need for devising. His way (abrupt creature!) lies out now to the measurable world and the broad expanses of activity. The blood hurries to a gallop in his veins; his nerves accumulate an electric force; he is footed with flame. A kiss : and they leap together, indivisible, upwards, radiant lips and eyes, their bodies sounding with the triumph of harps! Again, beloved! Again, thou bride! Again, ere life is ours!

In calmer mood the critic in him could not but remark a strange prelude to the new crowning era in a season of melancholy and unrest. He made up his tale of losses – a dispiriting tale enough even were there no comments. The air of false Christ was manifestly the mask of a physical decrepitude, itself the brand and sign of vulgar ardours; whence ingenuousness, forbearance, sweet amiability and the whole tribe of domestic virtues. Sadly mindful of the worst [,] the vision of his dead, the vision (far more pitiful) of congenital lives shuffling onwards between yawn and howl, starvelings in mind and body, visions of which came as temporary failure of his olden, sustained manner, darkly beset him. The cloud of difficulties about him allowed only peeps of light; even his rhetoric proclaimed transition. He could convict himself at least of a natural inability to prove everything at once and certain random attempts suggested the need for regular campaigning. His faith increased. It emboldened him to say to a patron of the fine arts 'What advance upon spiritual goods?' and to a capitalist 'I need two thousand pounds for a project.' He had interpreted for orthodox Greek scholarship the living doctrine of the *Poetics* and, out of the burning bushes of excess, had declaimed to a night policeman on the true status of public women : but there was no budge of those mountains, no perilous cerebration. In a moment of frenzy he called for the elves. Many in our day, it would appear, cannot avoid a choice between sensitiveness and dulness; they recommend themselves by proofs of culture to a like-minded minority or dominate the huger world as lean of meat. But he saw between camps his ground of vantage, opportunities for the mocking devil in an isle twice removed from the mainland, under joint government of Their Intensities and Their Bullockships. His Nego, therefore, written amid a chorus of peddling Jews' gibberish and Gentile clamour, was drawn up valiantly while true believers

prophesied fried atheism and was hurled against the obscene hells
of our Holy Mother : but, that outburst over, it was urbanity in
warfare. Perhaps his state would pension off old tyranny – a mercy
no longer hopelessly remote – in virtue of that mature civilization
to which (let all allow) it had in some way contributed. Already the
messages of citizens were flashed along the wires of the world,
already the generous idea had emerged from a thirty years' war
in Germany and was directing the councils of the Latins. To those
multitudes, not as yet in the wombs of humanity but surely engen-
derable there, he would give the word : Man and woman, out of
you comes the nation that is to come, the lightning of your masses
in travail; the competitive order is employed against itself, the
aristocracies are supplanted; and amid the general paralysis of an
insane society, the confederate will issues in action.

JAS A. JOYCE
7/1/1904

SOURCE: *The Workshop of Daedalus: James Joyce and the
Raw Materials for A Portrait of the Artist as a Young Man,*
ed. Robert Scholes and Richard M. Kain (1965) pp. 60–8.

NOTE

1. [*Editor's note.*] I have identified or completed a few allusions
within square brackets. Passages which Joyce crossed out as he used
or adapted them for *Stephen Hero* have been placed between
pointed brackets (< >) by the editors of the manuscript, Robert
Scholes and Richard M. Kain. Ellipses indicate passages lost due to
the flaking of the original manuscript.

II   STEPHEN ON EPIPHANY

. . . The general attitude of women towards religion puzzled and
often maddened Stephen. His nature was incapable of achieving

such an attitude of insincerity or stupidity. By brooding constantly upon this he ended by anathemising [*sic*] Emma as the most deceptive and cowardly of marsupials. He discovered that it was a menial fear and no spirit of chastity which had prevented her from granting his request. Her eyes, he thought, must look strange when upraised to some holy image and her lips when poised for the reception of the host. He cursed her burgher cowardice and her beauty and he said to himself that though her eyes might cajole the half-witted God of the Roman Catholics they would not cajole him. In every stray image of the streets he saw her soul manifest itself and every such manifestation renewed the intensity of his disapproval. It did not strike him that the attitude of women towards holy things really implied a more genuine emancipation than his own and he condemned them out of a purely suppositious [*sic*] conscience. He exaggerated their iniquities and evil influence and returned them their antipathy in full measure. He toyed also with a theory of dualism which would symbolise the twin eternities of spirit and nature in the twin eternities of male and female and even thought of explaining the audacities of his verse as symbolical allusions. It was hard for him to compel his head to preserve the strict temperature of classicism. More than he had ever done before he longed for the season to lift and for spring – the misty Irish spring – to be over and gone. He was passing through Eccles' St. one evening, one misty evening, with all these thoughts dancing the dance of unrest in his brain when a trivial incident set him composing some ardent verses which he entitled a 'Vilanelle of the Temptress'. A young lady was standing on the steps of one of those brown brick houses which seem the very incarnation of Irish paralysis. A young gentlemen was leaning on the rusty railings of the area. Stephen as he passed on his quest heard the following fragment of colloquy out of which he received an impression keen enough to afflict his sensitiveness very severely.

The Young Lady – (drawling discreetly) . . . O, yes . . . I was . . . at the . . . cha . . . pel . . .

The Young Gentleman – (inaudibly) . . . I . . . (again inaudibly)
. . . I . . .

The Young Lady – (softly) . . . O . . . but you're . . . ve . . . ry
. . . wick . . . ed . . .

This triviality made him think of collecting many such moments together in a book of epiphanies. By an epiphany he meant a sudden spiritual manifestation, whether in the vulgarity of speech or of gesture or in a memorable phase of the mind itself. He believed that it was for the man of letters to record these epiphanies with extreme care, seeing that they themselves are the most delicate and evanescent of moments. He told Cranly that the clock of the Ballast Office was capable of an epiphany. Cranly questioned the inscrutable dial of the Ballast Office with his no less inscrutable countenance :

– Yes, said Stephen. I will pass it time after time, allude to it, refer to it, catch a glimpse of it. It is only an item in the catalogue of Dublin's street furniture. Then all at once I see it and I know at once what it is : epiphany.

– What?

– Imagine my glimpses at that clock as the gropings of a spiritual eye which seeks to adjust its vision to an exact focus. The moment the focus is reached the object is epiphanised. It is just in this epiphany that I find the third, the supreme quality of beauty.

– Yes? said Cranly absently.

– No esthetic theory, pursued Stephen relentlessly, is of any value which investigates with the aid of the lantern of tradition. What we symbolise in black the Chinaman may symbolise in yellow : each has his own tradition. Greek beauty laughs at Coptic beauty and the American Indian derides them both. It is almost impossible to reconcile all tradition whereas it is by no means impossible to find the justification of every form of beauty which has ever been adored on the earth by an examination into the mechanism of esthetic apprehension whether it be dressed in red, white, yellow or black. We have no reason for thinking that the

Chinaman has a different system of digestion from that which we have though our diets are quite dissimilar. The apprehensive faculty must be scrutinised in action.

– Yes . . .

– You know what Aquinas says : The three things requisite for beauty are, integrity, a wholeness, symmetry and radiance. Some day I will expand that sentence into a treatise. Consider the performance of your own mind when confronted with any object, hypothetically beautiful. Your mind to apprehend that object divides the entire universe into two parts, the object, and the void which is not the object. To apprehend it you must lift it away from everything else : and then you perceive that it is one integral thing, that is *a* thing. You recognise its integrity. Isn't that so?

– And then?

– That is the first quality of beauty : it is declared in a simple sudden synthesis of the faculty which apprehends. What then? Analysis then. The mind considers the object in whole and in part, in relation to itself and to other objects, examines the balance of its parts, contemplates the form of the object, traverses every cranny of the structure. So the mind receives the impression of the symmetry of the object. The mind recognises that the object is in the strict sense of the word, a *thing*, a definitely constituted entity. You see?

– Let us turn back, said Cranly.

They had reached the corner of Grafton St. and as the footpath was overcrowded they turned back northwards. Cranly had an inclination to watch the antics of a drunkard who had been ejected from a bar in Suffolk St. but Stephen took his arm summarily and led him away.

– Now for the third quality. For a long time I couldn't make out what Aquinas meant. He uses a figurative word (a very unusual thing for him) but I have solved it. *Claritas* is *quidditas*. After the analysis which discovers the second quality the mind makes the only logically possible synthesis and discovers the third quality. This is the moment which I call epiphany. First we recognise that the object is *one* integral thing, then we recognise that it is an organised composite structure, a *thing* in fact : finally, when the relation of the parts is exquisite, when the parts are adjusted to the special point, we recognise that it is *that* thing which it is. Its soul, its whatness, leaps to us from the vestment of its appearance. The soul of the commonest object, the structure of which is so adjusted, seems to us radiant. The object achieves its epiphany.

Having finished his argument Stephen walked on in silence. He felt Cranly's hostility and he accused himself of having cheapened the eternal images of beauty. For the first time, too, he felt slightly awkward in his friend's company and to restore a mood of flippant familiarity he glanced up at the clock of the Ballast Office and smiled :

– It has not epiphanised yet, he said. . . .

SOURCE: *Stephen Hero,* ed. Theodore Spencer, Rev. John J. Slocum and Herbert Cahoon (1956) pp. 215–16.

III   TWELVE 'EPIPHANIES'

1

                        [Bray : in the parlour of the house
                        in Martello Terrace]
Mr Vance – *(comes in with a stick)* . . . O, you know, he'll have to apologise, Mrs Joyce.
Mrs Joyce – O yes . . . Do you hear that, Jim?
Mr Vance – Or else – if he doesn't – the eagle'll come and pull out his eyes.
Mrs Joyce – O, but I'm sure he will apologise.
Joyce – *(under the table, to himself)*
     – Pull out his eyes,
     Apologise,
     Apologise,
     Pull out his eyes.

Apologise,
Pull out his eyes,
Pull out his eyes,
Apologise.

3

The children who have stayed latest are getting on their things to go home for the party is over. This is the last tram. The lank brown horses know it and shake their bells to the clear night, in admonition. The conductor talks with the driver; both nod often in the green light of the lamp. There is nobody near. We seem to listen, I on the upper step and she on the lower. She comes up to my step many times and goes down again, between our phrases, and once or twice remains beside me, forgetting to go down, and then goes down. . . . Let be; let be. . . . And now she does not urge her vanities – her fine dress and sash and long black stockings – for now (wisdom of children) we seem to know that this end will please us better than any end we have laboured for.

5

High up in the old, dark-windowed house : firelight in the narrow room : dusk outside. An old woman bustles about, making tea; she tells of the changes, her odd ways, and what the priest and the doctor said . . . . . I hear her words in the distance. I wander among the coals, among the ways of adventure . . . . Christ! What is in the doorway? . . . . . A skull – a monkey; a creature drawn hither to the fire, to the voices : a silly creature.
– Is that Mary Ellen? –
– No, Eliza, it's Jim –
– O . . . . . . O, goodnight, Jim –
– D'ye want anything, Eliza? –
– I thought it was Mary Ellen . . . . . I thought you were Mary Ellen, Jim –

6

A small field of still weeds and thistles alive with confused forms, half-men, half-goats. Dragging their great tails they move hither and thither, aggressively. Their faces are lightly bearded, pointed and grey as india-rubber. A secret personal sin directs them, holding them now, as in reaction, to constant malevolence. One is clasping about his body a torn flannel jacket; another complains monotonously as his beard catches in the stiff weeds. They move about me, enclosing me, that old sin sharpening their eyes to cruelty, swishing through the fields in slow circles, thrusting upwards their terrific faces. Help!

24

Her arm is laid for a moment on my knees and then withdrawn and her eyes have revealed her – secret, vigilant, an enclosed garden – in a moment. I remember a harmony of red and white that was made for one like her, telling her names and glories, bidding her arise, as for espousal, and come away, bidding her look forth, a spouse, from Amana and from the mountains of the leopards. And I remember that response whereto the perfect tenderness of the body and the soul with all its mystery have gone : Inter ubera mea commorabitur.

25

The quick light shower is over but tarries, a cluster of diamonds, among the shrubs of the quadrangle where an exhalation arises from the black earth. In the colonnade are the girls, an April company. They are leaving shelter, with many a doubtful glance, with the prattle of trim boots and the pretty rescue of petticoats, under umbrellas, a light armoury, upheld at cunning angles. They are returning to the convent – demure corridors and simple dormitories, a white rosary of hours – having heard the fair promises of Spring, that well-graced ambassador.......

Amid a flat rain-swept country stands a high plain building, with windows that filter the obscure daylight. Three hundred boys, noisy and hungry, sit at long tables eating beef fringed with green fat and vegetables that are still rank of the earth.

26

She is engaged. She dances with them in the round – a white dress lightly lifted as she dances, a white spray in her hair; eyes a little averted, a faint glow on her cheek. Her hand is in mine for a moment, softest of merchandise.

– You very seldom come here now. –

– Yes I am becoming something of a recluse. –

– I saw your brother the other day ...... He is very like you. –

– Really? –

She dances with them in the round – evenly, discreetly, giving herself to no one. The white spray is ruffled as she dances, and when she is in shadow the glow is deeper on her cheek.

27

Faintly, under the heavy summer night, through the silence of the town which has turned from dreams to dreamless sleep as a weary lover whom no carresses [*sic*] move, the sound of hoofs upon the Dublin road. Not so faintly now as they come near the bridge; and in a moment as they pass the dark windows the silence is cloven by alarm as by an arrow. They are heard now far away – hoofs that shine amid the heavy night as diamonds, hurrying beyond the grey, still marshes to what journey's end – what heart – bearing what tidings?

28

A moonless night under which the waves gleam feebly. The ship is entering a harbour where there are some lights. The sea is uneasy, charged with dull anger like the eyes of an animal which is about to spring, the prey of its own pitiless hunger. The land is flat and thinly wooded. Many people are gathered on the shore to see what ship it is that is entering their harbour.

29

A long curving gallery : from the floor arise pillars of dark vapours. It is peopled by the images of fabulous kings, set in stone. Their hands are folded upon their knees, in token of weariness, and their eyes are darkened for the errors of men go up before them for ever as dark vapours.

30

The spell of arms and voices – the white arms of roads, their promise of close embraces and the black arms of tall ships that stand against the moon, their tale of distant nations. They are held out to say : We are alone, – come. And the voices say with them : We are your people. And the air is thick with their company as they call to me their kinsman, making ready to go, shaking the wings of their exultant and terrible youth.

31

Here are we come together, wayfarers; here are we housed, amid intricate streets, by night and silence closely covered. In amity we rest together, well content, no more remembering the deviousness of the ways that we have come. What moves upon me from the darkness subtle and murmurous as a flood, passionate and fierce with an indecent movement of the loins? What leaps, crying in answer, out of me, as eagle to eagle in mid air, crying to overcome, crying for an iniquitous abandonment?

S o u r c e : *The Workshop of Daedalus: James Joyce and the Raw Materials for A Portrait of the Artist as a Young Man,* ed. Robert Scholes and Richard M. Kain (1965) pp. 11, 13, 15, 16, 34, 35, 36, 37, 38, 39, 40, 41.

iv the pola notebook (1904)

Bonum est in quod tendit appetitus. St Thomas Aquinas

The good is that towards the possession of which an appetite tends : the good is the desirable. The true and the beautiful are the most persistent orders of the desirable. Truth is desired by the intellectual appetite which is appeased by the most satisfying relations of the intelligible; beauty is desired by the aesthetic appetite which is appeased by the most satisfying relations of the sensible. The true and the beautiful are spiritually possessed; the true by intellection, the beautiful by apprehension, and the appetites which desire to possess them, the intellectual and aesthetic appetites, are therefore spiritual appetites. . . . .

J. A. J. Pola, 7 xi 04.

Pulchra sunt quae visa placent. St Thomas Aquinas

Those things are beautiful the apprehension of which pleases. Therefore beauty is that quality of a sensible object in virtue of which its apprehension pleases or satisfies the aesthetic appetite which desires to apprehend the most satisfying relations of the sensible. Now the act of apprehension involves at least two activities, the activity of cognition or simple perception and the activity of recognition. If the activity of simple perception is, like every other activity, itself pleasant, every sensible object that has been apprehended can be said in the first place to have been and to be in a measure beautiful; and even the most hideous object can be said to have been and to be beautiful in so far as it has been apprehended. In regard then to that part of the act of apprehension which is called the activity of simple perception there is no sensible object which cannot be said to be in a measure beautiful.

With regard to the second part of the act of apprehension which is called the activity of recognition it may further be said that there is no activity of simple perception to which there does not succeed in whatsoever measure the activity of recognition. For by the activity of recognition is meant an activity of decision; and in accordance with this activity in all conceivable cases a sensible object is said to be satisfying or dissatisfying. But the activity of recognition is, like every other activity, itself pleasant and therefore every object that has been apprehended is secondly in whatsoever measure beautiful. Consequently even the most hideous object may be said to be beautiful for this reason as it is *a priori* said to be beautiful in so far as it encounters the activity of simple perception.

Sensible objects, however, are said conventionally to be beautiful or not for neither of the foregoing reasons but rather by reason of the nature, degree and duration of the satisfaction resulting from the apprehension of them and it is in accordance with these latter merely that the words 'beautiful' and 'ugly' are used in practical aesthetic philosophy. It remains then to be said that these words indicate only a greater or less measure of resultant satisfaction and that any sensible object, to which the word 'ugly' is practically applied, an object, that is, the apprehension of which results in a small measure of aesthetic satisfaction, is, in so far as its apprehension results in any measure of satisfaction whatsoever, said to be for the third time beautiful. . . .

J. A. J. POLA, 15 xi 04.

The Act of Apprehension

It has been said that the act of apprehension involves at least two activities – the activity of cognition or simple perception and the activity of recognition. The act of apprehension, however, in its most complete form involves three activities – the third being the activity of satisfaction. By reason of the fact that these three activities are all pleasant themselves every sensible object that has been apprehended must be doubly and may be trebly beautiful. In practical aesthetic philosophy the epithets 'beautiful' and 'ugly' are applied with regard chiefly to the third activity, with regard, that is, to the nature, degree and duration of the satisfaction resultant from the apprehension of any sensible object and therefore any sensible object to which in practical aesthetic philosophy the epithet 'beautiful' is applied must be trebly beautiful, must have encountered, that is, the three activities which are involved in the act of apprehension in its most complete form. Practically then the quality of beauty in itself must involve three constituents to encounter each of these three activities . . . .

J. A. J. Pola, 16 xi 04.

Source: *Critical Writing of James Joyce,* ed. Ellsworth Mason and Richard Ellmann (1959) pp. 146–8.

THE EARLY RESPONSE TO
DUBLINERS: REVIEWS

THE TIMES LITERARY SUPPLEMENT (1914)

DUBLINERS (Grant Richards, 3s. 6d.) is a collection of short stories, the scene of which is laid in Dublin. Too comprehensive for the theme, the title is nevertheless typical of a book which purports, we assume, to describe life as it is and yet regards it from one aspect only. The author, Mr James Joyce, is not concerned with all Dubliners, but almost exclusively with those of them who would be submerged if the tide of material difficulties were to rise a little higher. It is not so much money they lack as the adaptability which attains some measure of success by accepting the world as it is. It is in so far that they are failures that his characters interest Mr Joyce. One of them – a capable washerwoman – falls an easy prey to a rogue in a tramcar and is cozened out of the little present she was taking to her family. Another – a trusted cashier – has so ordered a blameless life that he drives to drink and suicide the only person in the world with whom he was in sympathy. A third – an amiable man of letters – learns at the moment he feels most drawn to his wife that her heart was given once and for all to a boy long dead.

Dubliners may be recommended to the large class of readers to whom the drab makes an appeal, for it is admirably written. Mr Joyce avoids exaggeration. He leaves the conviction that his people are as he describes them. Shunning the emphatic, Mr Joyce is less concerned with the episode than with the mood which it suggests. Perhaps for this reason he is more successful with his

shorter stories. When he writes at greater length the issue seems
trivial, and the connecting thread becomes so tenuous as to be
scarcely perceptible. The reader's difficulty will be enhanced if he
is ignorant of Dublin customs; if he does not know, for instance,
that 'a curate' is a man who brings strong waters.

S O U R C E : *The Times Literary Supplement,* No. 648 (18 June
1914) p. 298.

GERALD GOULD (1914)

... It is easy to say of Gorky that he is a man of genius. To say
the same of Mr James Joyce requires more courage, since his
name is little known; but a man of genius is precisely what he is.
He has an original outlook, a special method, a complete reliance
on his own powers of delineation and presentment. Whether his
powers will develop, his scope widen, his sympathies deepen, or
not – whether, in short, his genius is a large one or only a little
one, I cannot pretend to say. Maturity and self-confidence in a
first book (and I believe that, in prose, this is Mr Joyce's first book)
contain a threat as well as a promise. They hint at a set mode of
thought rather than a developing capacity. Certainly the maturity,
the individual poise and force of these stories are astonishing. The
only recent work with which they suggest comparison is *The House
with the Green Shutters,* and even that was very different, for one
heard in it the undertone of human complaint – its horrors were
partly by way of expressing a personal unhappiness; while Mr
Joyce seems to regard this objective and dirty and crawling world
with the cold detachment of an unamiable god.

He has plenty of humour, but it is always the humour of the
fact, not of the comment. He dares to let people speak for themselves with the awkward meticulousness, the persistent incom-
petent repetition, of actual human intercourse. If you have never
realised before how direly our daily conversation needs editing,

you will realise it from Mr Joyce's pages. One very powerful story, called *Grace*, consists chiefly of lengthy talk so banal, so true to life, that one can scarcely endure it – though one can still less leave off reading it. Here is one of the liveliest passages :

'Pope Leo XIII,' said Mr Cunningham, 'was one of the lights of the age. His great idea, you know, was the union of the Latin and Greek churches. This was the aim of his life.'

'I often heard he was one of the most intellectual men in Europe,' said Mr Power. 'I mean apart from his being Pope.'

'So he was,' said Mr Cunningham, 'if not *the* most so. His motto, you know, as Pope was *Lux upon Lux – Light upon Light*.'

'No, no,' said Mr Fogarty eagerly. 'I think you're wrong there. It was *Lux in Tenebris*, I think – *Light in Darkness*.'

'O yes,' said Mr M'Coy, 'Tenebræ.'

'Allow me,' said Mr Cunningham positively, 'it was *Lux upon Lux*. And Pius IX his predecessor's motto was *Crux upon Crux* – that is, *Cross upon Cross* – to show the difference between their two pontificates.'

The inference was allowed. Mr Cunningham continued.

'Pope Leo, you know, was a great scholar and a poet.'

'He had a strong face,' said Mr Kernan.

'Yes,' said Mr Cunningham. 'He wrote Latin poetry.'

'Is that so?' said Mr Fogarty.

You see the method? It is not employed only in conversation. The description of mood, of atmosphere, is just as detailed and just as relentless. Horrible sordid realities, of which you are not spared one single pang, close in upon you like the four walls of a torture-chamber. It is all done quite calmly, quite dispassionately, quite competently. It never bores. You sometimes rather wish it did, as a relief.

The best things in the book are *Araby*, a wonderful magical study of boyish affection and wounded pride, and *The Dead*, a long story (placed at the end) in which we begin with a queer old-fashioned dance, where the principal anxiety is whether a certain guest will arrive 'screwed', and are led on through all the queer breathless banalities of supper and conversation and leave-taking till we find ourselves back with a husband and wife in their hotel bedroom, the husband's emotion stirred, the wife queerly remote and sad, remembering the boy, Michael Furey, whom she had loved and who had died because of her. To quote the end without the innumerable preparatory touches that prepare for it seems unfair; yet it must be quoted for its mere melancholy beauty :

> A few light taps upon the pane made him turn to the window. It had begun to snow again. He watched sleepily the flakes, silver and dark, falling obliquely against the lamplight. The time had come for him to set out on his journey westward. Yes, the newspapers were right : snow was general all over Ireland. It was falling on every part of the dark central plain, on the tree-less hills, falling softly upon the Bog of Allen and, farther west-ward, softly falling into the dark mutinous Shannon waves. It was falling, too, upon every part of the lonely churchyard on the hill where Michael Furey lay buried. It lay thickly drifted on the crooked crosses and headstones, on the spears of the little gate, on the barren thorns. His soul swooned slowly as he heard the snow falling faintly through the universe and faintly falling, like the descent of their last end, upon all the living and the dead.

Frankly, we think it a pity (perhaps we betray a narrow puritanism in so thinking) that a man who can write like this should insist as constantly as Mr Joyce insists upon aspects of life which are ordinarily not mentioned. To do him justice, we do not think it is a pose with him : he simply includes the 'unmentionable' in his persistent regard. . . .

S o u r c e : *New Statesman*, III (27 June 1914) pp. 374–5

THE JOYCE FAMILY

[*1903*]

Jim's character is unsettled; it is developing. New influences are
coming over him daily, he is beginning new practices. He has
come home drunk three or four times within the last month (on
one occasion he came home sick and dirty-looking on Sunday
morning, having been out all night) and he is engaged at present
in sampling wines and liqueurs and at procuring for himself the
means of living. He has or seems to have taken a liking for con-
viviality, even with those whose jealousy and ill-will towards himself he well knows, staying with them a whole night long dancing
and singing and making speeches and laughing and reciting, and
revelling in the same manner all the way home. To say what is
really his character, one must go beneath much that is passing in
these influences and habits and see what it is in them that his mind
really affects; one must compare what he is with what he was,
one must analyse, one must judge him by his moments of exaltation, not by his hours of abasement.[2]

His intellect is precise and subtle, but not comprehensive. He
is no student. His artistic sympathy and judgment are such as
would be expected in one of his kind of intellect – if he were not
more than a critic, I believe, he would be as good a critic of what
interests him as any using English today. His literary talent seems
to be very great indeed, both in prose and in verse.[3] He has, as
Yeats says, a power of very delicate spiritual writing and whether

he writes in sorrow or is young and virginal, or whether (as in 'He travels after the wintry sun')⁴ he writes of what he has seen, the form is always either strong, expressive, graceful or engaging, and his imagination open-eyed and classic. His 'epiphanies' – his prose pieces (which I almost prefer to his lyrics) and his dialogues – are again subtle. He has put himself into these with singular courage, singular memory, and scientific minuteness; he has proved himself capable of taking very great pains to create a very little thing of prose or verse. The keen observation and satanic irony of his character are precisely, but not fully, expressed. Whether he will ever build up anything broad – a drama, an esthetic treatise – I cannot say. His genius is not literary and he will probably run through many of the smaller forms of literary artistic expression. He has made living his end in life, and in the light of this magnificent importance of living, everything else is like a rushlight in the sun. And so he is more interested in the sampling of liqueurs, the devising of dinners, the care of dress, and whoring, than to know if the one-act play – 'the dwarf-drama' he calls it – is an artistic possibility.

Jim is a genius of character. When I say 'genius', I say just the least little bit in the world more than I believe; yet remembering his youth and that I sleep with him, I say it. Scientists have been called great scientists because they have measured the distances of the unseen stars, and yet scientists who have watched the movements in matter scarcely perceptible to the mechanically aided senses have been esteemed as great; and Jim is, perhaps, a genius, though his mind is minutely analytic. He has, above all, a proud, wilful, vicious selfishness, out of which by times now he writes a poem or an epiphany, now commits the meannesses of whim and appetite, which was at first protestant egoism, and had, perhaps, some desperateness in it, but which is now well-rooted – or developed? – in his nature, a very Yggdrasill.⁵ He has extraordinary moral courage – courage so great that I have hopes that he will one day become the Rousseau of Ireland. Rousseau, indeed,

c

might be accused of cherishing the secret hope of turning away the anger of disapproving readers by confessing unto them, but Jim cannot be suspected of this. His great passion is a fierce scorn of what he calls the 'rabblement' – a tiger-like, insatiable hatred. He has a distinguished appearance and bearing and many graces : a musical singing and especially speaking voice (a tenor), a good undeveloped talent in music, and witty conversation. He has a distressing habit of saying quietly to those with whom he is familiar the most shocking things about himself and others, and, moreover, of selecting the most shocking times, saying them, not because they are shocking merely, but because they are true. They are such things that even knowing him well as I do, I do not believe it is beyond his power to shock me or Gogarty[6] with all his obscene rhymes. His manner however is generally very engaging and courteous with strangers, but, though he dislikes greatly to be rude, I think there is little courtesy in his nature. As he sits on the hearth-rug, his arms embracing his knees, his head thrown a little back, his hair brushed up straight off his forehead, his long face red as an Indian's in the reflexion of the fire, there is a look of cruelty in his face. Not that he is not gentle at times, for he can be kind, and one is not surprised to find simpleness in him. (He is always simple and open with those that are so with him.) But few people will love him, I think, in spite of his graces and his genius, and whosoever exchanges kindnesses with him is likely to get the worst of the bargain. (This is coloured too highly, like a penny cartoon.)

[*26 September 1903*]

Jim says it is not moral courage in him but as he phrases it of himself, 'when the Bard begins to write he intellectualizes himself.' Jim's voice, when in good form, has a beautiful flavour, rich and pure, and goes through one like a strong exhilarating wine. He sings well.

Jim has a wolf-like intellect, neither massive nor very strong, but lean and ravenous, tearing the heart out of his subject.

Pappie[7] is very scurrilous.

He scourges the house with his tongue.

Mother kept the house together at the cost of her life.[8]

The Sophists will never be extinct while Jim is alive.

The twelve tribes of Galway are :

Athy,	Blake,	Bodkin
Deane,	D'Arcy,	Lynch
Joyce,	Kirwin,	Martin
Morris,	Skerret,	French

Pappie is the only child of an only child (his father) and therefore the spoiled son of a spoiled son, the spendthrift son of a spendthrift. His temperament was probably Gasconish – gallant and sentimental – and was certainly shallow and without love. If he ever had any self-criticism his inordinate self-love and vanity choked it in his early youth. Yet, strangely enough, he is shrewd in his judgment of others. He takes pride in a family of some refinement, education and some little distinction on one side, and of some wealth on the other. He is domineering and quarrelsome and has in an unusual degree that low, voluble abusiveness characteristic of the Cork people when drunk. He is worse in this respect since we have grown up because even when silent we are an opposition. He is ease-loving and his ambition in life has been to be respected and to keep appearances. However unworthy this may sound, it has been so difficult of attainment and he has struggled for it with such tenacious energy against the effects of his constant drunkenness that it is hard to despise it utterly. He is lying and hypocritical. He regards himself as the victim of circumstances and pays himself with words. His will is dissipated, and his intellect besotted, and he has become a crazy drunkard. He is spiteful like all drunkards who are thwarted, and invents the most cowardly insults that a scandalous mind and a naturally derisive tongue can suggest. He undoubtedly hastened Mother's death. He was an insulting son, and as a husband, a household bully and a bester in money matters. For his children he has no love or care but a peculiar sense of duty arising out of his worship of respectability. He is full of prejudices, which he tries to instil into us, regarding all opposition as impertinent puppyism. He boasts of being a bit of a snob. His idea of the home is a well-furnished house in which he can entertain and his children grow up under their mother's care, and to which, having spent the evening in drinking and story-telling with his friends, he can return to lord it and be obeyed.

He is generous, however, and when he claims to have 'some ideas of a gentleman' he does not seem to be ridiculous. When he has been sober for a few days he is strangely quiet, though irritable and nerve-shaken, with a flow of lively talk. It is difficult to talk tò him even now at 54 for his vanity is easily hurt. Moreover this quietness seems unnatural and to be the reaction of his drunkenness.

He has the remains of the best tenor of the 'light English style I ever heard. His range was unusual and he sings with taste.

Jim's ingenuousness and gentleness are false, and since I pointed this out to him his affectation of false ingenuousness and false gentleness has been false.

I see in his verse and prose self-deception and a desire for display without the redeeming foolishness of vanity.

Jim claims of his friends the right to ruin himself.

Jim has a hardly controlled itch for deceit. He lies without reason and exerts himself to deceive those that know him best, from a contempt of the dullness of morality and right-doing.

When Pappie is sober and fairly comfortable he is easy and pleasant spoken though inclined to sigh and complain and do nothing. His conversation is reminiscent and humourous, ridiculing without malice, and accepting peace as an item of comfort. This phase is regrettably rare and of short duration. It comes at times of dire poverty and does not last till bedtime. The mood is genuine, indeed, but a chance phrase will reveal that it is more an amnesty temporarily agreed to than a peace. Unsettling from his comfortable position before the fire and gathering up his papers to go to bed effect a change in him, and he goes up the stairs complaining and promising changes over which he has no control.

Pappie has for many years regarded his family as an encumbrance which he suffers impatiently while he must, and which he seeks to cast off at the earliest opportunity. Jim and I and Charlie,[9] who naturally do not see matters in this light, he abuses and threatens as wasters. He calls all his children bastards as a habit, and really the treatment he wishes to give them is that enforced by law even to bastards – support until the sixteenth year for a male child.

He is truculent and inflicts a thoughtless selfishness on his children. I have said he has a peculiar sense of duty toward them. It is true, but that sense does not include the office of feeding them regularly. Even tonight when his being was comfortable there was a somewhat vicious hue about his contentment.

My cousin Kathleen Murray (called Katsy)[10] has a luxurious nature and the promise of a magnificent contralto. It has the depth (in tone) of a bass and I flattered myself that I first discovered it in her.

That amongst his innumerable acquaintances, Pappie had a few real friends, is to be remembered to his credit.

At that time which I remember most vividly, Mother had little left of what had once made her a figure in drawing-rooms, little except a very graceful carriage and occasional brilliancy at the piano. She had a small, very feminine head, and was pretty. I remember her intelligent, sparing, very patient in troubles (the normal state) and too patient of insults. When I saw her lying in her brown habit on the bed in the front room, her head a little wearily to one side, I seemed to be standing beside the death-bed of a victim. Now for the first time waking in the quietness and subdued light of the room, beside the candles and the flowers, she had the importance that should always have been hers. An ever-watchful anxiety for her children, a readiness to sacrifice herself to them utterly, and a tenacious energy to endure for their sakes replaced love in a family not given to shows of affection. She was very gentle towards her children though she understood them each. It is understanding and not love that makes the confidence between Mother and children so natural though unacknowledged, so unreserved though nothing is confessed (there is no need of words or looks between them, the confidence surrounds them like the atmosphere). Rather it is this understanding that makes the love so enduring. Pappie, who had no relatives and was free and selfish, demanded of Mother, who had many, alienation from them. I can well believe that she never brought them to his house and that Pappie himself, being weak and inconstant, did; but in heart she was never altogether alienated from them. To have been so for Pappie's sake would have demanded more passionateness than was in Mother's nature. Perhaps if she had done so she would have been just as unloved by one so eminently selfish as Pappie, or if not as unloved certainly as cruelly treated. It is in her favour that in the middle of worries in which it is hard to remain gentle or beautiful or noble Mother's character was refined as much as Pappie's was debased, and she gained a little wisdom. Yet I cannot regard Mother and Pappie as ill-matched, for with Pappie Mother had more than mere Christian patience, seeing in him what only lately and with great difficulty I have seen in him. It is strange, too, that the true friendships Pappie made (with Mr Kelly[11] for instance) were confirmed at home and, I think, under Mother's influence, his friends being scarcely less friendly towards Mother than towards himself. Up to the last Mother had a lively sense of humour and was an excellent mimic of certain people. Though worn and grave, Mother was capable at unusual times of unusual energy. She was a selfish drunkard's unselfish wife.

Mother had seventeen children of whom nine are now living.[12]

Mother's treatment of Poppie was unjust, not nearly so unjust but of the same kind as Pappie's treatment of her, and perhaps due a little unconsciously to that example. These women of Nirvana who accept their greatest trials with resignation, letting worries be heaped like ashes on their heads, and hoping only in one thing – their power to live them down, vent themselves in irritability about ridiculous little annoyances. One of the most difficult things to excuse is a nagging temper, but it must be remembered that Mother's temper was only lately of this kind, that it was due to disease in one who died of cirrhosis[13] of the liver, and that it was directed against Poppie from a habit begun when Poppie was young and very obstinate. Mother, too, saw that the reading of life in our home was unchristian and, constantly, deceived herself to make her life submissive to that Priest-worship in which she was reared. She even asserted her Catholicism that by speaking much she might convince herself, and this is called insincerity. Mother's religion was acquiescence and she had the eye of unbelievers constantly upon her.

Jim has lately become a prig about women, affecting to regard them as dirty animals and frequently quoting an epigram of a Dr Perse's.[14]

Katsy Murray is a type of what the mediaeval schoolmen called 'the pride of the flesh'.

The Murrays don't know the value of kisses.

S O U R C E : *The Complete Dublin Diary of Stanislaus Joyce,* ed. George H. Healey (1971) pp. 1–11.

NOTES

1. [*Editor's note.*] The following notes are by George H. Healey, editor of the manuscript.

2. Written across this paragraph is the word 'rubbish'.

3. MS. note : 'He is not an artist he says. He is interesting himself

in politics – in which he says [he has] original ideas. He says he does not care for art or music though he admits he can judge them. He lives on the excitement of incident.'

4. From 'Tilly', published in *Pomes Penyeach*.

5. The great ash tree symbolic of the universe in Norse mythology.

6. Oliver St John Gogarty, the original of Buck Mulligan in *Ulysses*.

7. John S. Joyce, father of the author.

8. Mrs May Joyce had died on 13 August 1903, at the age of 44.

9. Charles, then 17, was the youngest of the surviving brothers.

10. Though only about 14 years of age, Katsy Murray had previously attracted the passing interest of James and was now receiving the shy attentions of Stanislaus. Her mother (Aunt Josephine) was a favorite of the Joyce boys. Her father (Uncle Willie), brother of Mrs Joyce, is the Richie Goulding of *Ulysses*.

11. John Kelly, of Tralee, the John Casey of *A Portrait of the Artist as a Young Man*.

12. James, b. 1882; Margaret ('Poppie'), b. 1884; Stanislaus, b. 1884; Charles, b. 1886; Eileen, b. 1889; Mary ('May'), b. 1890; Eva, b. 1891; Florence ('Florrie'), b. 1892; and Mabel ('Baby'), b. 1893, George, b. 1887, had died in 1902.

13. The author first wrote 'cancer', but later corrected it.

14. MS. note : 'Woman is an animal that micturates once a day, defecates once a week, menstruates once a month, and parturates once a year.'

II JAMES JOYCE

There was once a lounger named Stephen (1917)

There was a lounger named Stephen
Whose youth was most odd and uneven.
   He throve on the smell
   Of a horrible hell
That a Hottentot wouldn't believe in.

SOURCE: *Letters of James Joyce*, vol. i, ed. Stuart Gilbert (1957) p. 102 [letter to Ezra Pound, 9 April 1917].

III JOHN STANISLAUS JOYCE, LETTER TO HIS
     SON (1931)

31 January 1931   *25 Claude Road, Glasnevin, Dublin*

My dear Jim I wish you a very happy birthday and also a bright
and happy New Year. I wonder do you recollect the old days in
Brighton Square, when you were Babie Tuckoo, and I used to
take you out in the Square and tell you all about the moo-cow
that used to come down from the mountain and take little boys
across?

I will write to Georgio in a few days, when he returns from his
honeymoon. I see by the photo that he too wears glasses? I suppose he needs [them] but if possible he should not use them. I hope
Lucia's sight is all right, give her my fond love and also to Nora.
I often hear from Mr Healy, who's [*sic*] generous gifts I should be
glad if *you* would also acknowledge. Again, my dear boy, may
God bless you is the prayer of Your fond and loving   FATHER

SOURCE: *Letters of James Joyce*, vol. iii, ed. Richard Ellmann
     (1966) p. 212.

THE EARLY RESPONSE TO
A PORTRAIT OF THE ARTIST:
COMMENTS AND REVIEWS

EDWARD GARNETT: READER'S REPORT
(1916?)

Duckworth & Co., Publishers,
3 Henrietta Street,
Covent Garden, London, W.C.

James Joyce's 'Portrait of the Artist as a Young Man' wants
going through carefully from start to finish. There are many
'longueurs'. Passages which, though the publisher's reader may
find them entertaining, will be tedious to the ordinary man among
the reading public. That public will call the book, as it stands at
present, realistic, unprepossessing, unattractive. We call it ably
written. The picture is 'curious', it arouses interest and attention.
But the author must revise it and let us see it again. It is too discursive, formless, unrestrained, and ugly things, ugly words, are
too prominent; indeed at times they seem to be shoved in one's
face, on purpose, unnecessarily. The point of view will be voted
'a little sordid'. The picture of life is good; the period well brought
to the reader's eye, and the types and characters are well drawn,
but it is too 'unconventional'. This would stand against it in
normal times. At the present time, though the old conventions are
in the background, we can only see a chance for it if it is pulled
into shape and made more definite.

In the earlier portion of the MS. as submitted to us, a good deal
of pruning can be done. Unless the author will use restraint and

proportion he will not gain readers. His pen and his thoughts seem to have run away with him sometimes.

And at the end of the book there is a complete falling to bits; the pieces of writing and the thoughts are all in pieces and they fall like damp, ineffective rockets.

The author shows us he has art, strength and originality, but this MS. wants time and trouble spent on it, to make it a more finished piece of work, to shape it more carefully as the product of the craftsmanship, mind and imagination of an artist.

S O U R C E : *Letters of James Joyce,* vol. ii, ed. Richard Ellmann (1957) pp. 371–2.

'THE EGOIST': JAMES JOYCE AND HIS CRITICS – SOME CLASSIFIED COMMENTS (1917)

CAUTION : It is very difficult to know quite what to say about this new book by Mr Joyce – *Literary World.*

DRAINS : Mr Joyce is a clever novelist but we feel he would be really at his best in a treatise on drains. – *Everyman.*

CLEANMINDEDNESS : This pseudo-autobiography of Stephen Dedalus, a weakling and a dreamer, makes fascinating reading. . . . No clean-minded person could possibly allow it to remain within reach of his wife, his sons or daughters. – *Irish Book Lover.*

OPPORTUNITIES OF DUBLIN : If one must accuse Mr Joyce of anything, it is that he too wilfully ignores the opportunities which Dublin offers even to a Stephen Dedalus. . . . He has undoubtedly failed to bring out the undeniable superiority of many features of life in the capital. . . . He is as blind to the charm of its situation as to the stirrings of literary and civic consciousness which give an interest and zest to social and political intercourse. – *New Ireland.*

BEAUTY : There is much in the book to offend a good many

varieties of readers, and little compensating beauty. – *New York Globe.*

The most obvious thing about the book is its beauty. – *New Witness.*

STYLE : It is possible that the author intends to write a sequel to the story. If so, he might acquire a firmer, more coherent and more lucid style by a study of Flaubert, Daudet, Thackeray and Thomas Hardy. – *Rochester (New York) Post-Express.*

The occasional lucid intervals in which one glimpses imminent setting forth of social elements and forces in Dublin, only to be disappointed, are similar to the eye or ear which appears in futurist portraits, but proves the more bewildering because no other recognizable feature is to be discerned among the chaos. – *Bellman* (U.S.A.). [*Editor's Note:* In the sentence quoted above, 'lucid intervals' is to be parsed with 'are similar' and 'eye or ear' with 'proves'. The adjective 'recognizable' is apparently pleonastic.]

REALISM : It is a ruthless, relentless essay in realism. – *Southport Guardian.*

To put the literary form of rude language in a book makes some authors feel realistic. – *Manchester Weekly Times.*

Mr Joyce aims at being realistic, but his method is too chaotic to produce the effect of realism. – *Rochester (New York) Post-Express.*

Its realism will displease many. – *Birmingham Post.*

Mr Joyce is unsparing in his realism, and his violent contrasts – the brothel, the confessional – jar on one's finer feelings. – *Irish Book Lover.*

The description of life in a Jesuit school, and later in a Dublin college, strikes one as being absolutely true to life – but what a life! – *Everyman.*

WISDOM : Is it even wise from a wordly point of view – mercenary, if you will – to dissipate one's talents on a book which can only attain a limited circulation? – *Irish Book Lover.*

ADVANTAGES OF IRISH EDUCATION : One boy from Clongowes School is not a replica of all the other boys. I will reintroduce Mr Wells to half a dozen Irish 'old boys' of whom five – Sir Arthur Conan Doyle is one – were educated at Roman Catholic schools and have nevertheless become most conventional citizens of the Empire. – *Sphere.*

COMPARISON WITH OTHER IRISH AUTHORS : The book is not within a hundred miles of being as fine a work of art as 'Lime-house Nights', the work of another young Irishman. – *Sphere.*

There are a good many talented young Irish writers today, and it will take a fellow of exceptional literary stature to tower above Lord Dunsany, for example, or James Stephens. – *New York Globe.*

IMAGINATION : He shows an astonishingly un-Celtic absence of imagination and humour. – *Bellman* (U.S.A.).

RELIGION : The irreverent treatment of religion in the story must be condemned. – *Rochester (New York) Post-Express.*

TRUTH : It is an accident that Mr Joyce's book should have Dublin as its background. – *Freeman's Journal* (Dublin).

He is justified, in so far as too many Dubliners are of the calibre described in this and the preceding volume. – *New Ireland.*

S O U R C E : *The Egoist*, IV (June 1917) p. 74

'EVERYMAN': A STUDY IN GARBAGE (1917)

Mr James Joyce is an Irish edition of Mr Caradoc Evans. These writers, that is to say, have made it their business in life to portray the least estimable features of their respective contrymen, Irish or Welsh. Mr Joyce's new book, A PORTRAIT OF AN ARTIST AS A YOUNG MAN (The Egoist Ltd. 6s.), is an astonishingly powerful and extraordinarily dirty study of the upbringing of a young man by Jesuits, which ends – so far as we have been at all able to unravel the meaning of the impressionist ending – with his

insanity. The description of life in a Jesuit school, and later in a
Dublin college, strikes one as being absolutely true to life – but
what a life! Parts of the book are perhaps a little too allusive to be
readily understood by the English reader. On pp. 265–6, there
is an account of what happened at the Abbey Theatre, Dublin,
when 'The Countess Cathleen', by Mr W. B. Yeats, was put on,
but the fact is darkly hidden. Mr Joyce is a clever novelist, but
we feel he would be really at his best in a treatise on drains.

SOURCE: *Everyman* (23 February 1917) p. 398.

'THE LITERARY WORLD AND READER': REVIEW
OF 'A PORTRAIT OF THE ARTIST AS A YOUNG
MAN' (1917)

For some reason which we shall not try to fathom the publishers
enclose a leaflet of Press notices of a volume of short stories by Mr
Joyce. All the critics, big and small, seem to have tumbled over
themselves in their haste to acclaim a genius. It is, of course, very
impressive, and it behoves us to be cautious and to remember that
in a review there are often reservations that liberally discount the
praise. We confess that it is very difficult to know quite what to say
about this new book by Mr Joyce. It is rather a study of a temperament than a story in the ordinary sense. Whether it is self-
portraiture we do not know, but it has the intimate veracity, or
appearance of veracity, of the great writers of confessions. It is
concerned mainly with the school and college life – a Jesuit school
and Trinity College – of a youth who has no home life to balance
him. Stephen Dedalus is not only real, he is like every artistic projection, a type. He is an artist with all the artist's vices and virtues,
exquisite sensibility, moral perversity, Christian mysticism and
Pagan sensualism, the refinement of human nature at its best and
a bestial coarseness. At times the analysis of emotions reminds us
of Andreyev in the brutal probing of the depths of uncleanliness;

at others the writing is pure lyrical beauty. It is not a book we can recommend to anyone; it has the coarseness in places of a young man who is wilfully coarse. But people who stand Mr Masefield's exploitation of the vulgarity of the farm labourer will not find much to hurt them in the brutal language of college students who are mostly good Catholics. The tradition of English fiction, however, is not in the direction of Russian realism, and we cannot say that we regret it.

S O U R C E : *The Literary World and Reader: A Monthly Review of Current Literature,* LXXXIII (March 1917) p. 43.

'THE IRISH BOOK LOVER': REVIEW OF
'A PORTRAIT OF THE ARTIST AS A YOUNG MAN'
(1 9 1 7)

In spite of the serious drawbacks to be mentioned later, truth compels one to admit that this pseudo autobiography of Stephen Dedalus, a weakling and a dreamer, makes fascinating reading. We read it at a single sitting. The hero's schooldays at Clongowes Wood, and later at Belvedere, are graphically and doubtless, faithfully portrayed, as is the visit to Cork in company with his father, a clever ne'er-do-well, gradually sinking in the social scale. One of the strongest scenes in the book is the description of the Christmas dinner party during the black year of 1891, when Nationalist Ireland was riven to the centre over the Parnell 'split'. Mr Joyce is unsparing in his realism, and his violent contrasts – the brothel, the confessional – jar on one's finer feelings. So do the quips and jeers of the students, in language unprinted in literature since the days of Swift and Sterne, following on some eloquent and orthodox sermons! That Mr Joyce is a master of a brilliant descriptive style and handles his dialogue as ably as any living writer is conceded on all hands, and, oh! the the pity of it. In writing thus is he just to his fine gifts? Is it even wise, from a wordly point of view – mercenary, if you will – to dissipate one's talents on a book which can only attain a limited circulation? – for no clean-minded person could possibly allow it to remain within reach of his wife, his sons or daughters. Above all, is it Art? We doubt it.

SOURCE: *The Irish Book Lover*, 8 (April–May 1917) p. 113.

PART TWO

Critical Studies

Harry Levin

THE ARTIST (1941)

The history of the realistic novel shows that fiction tends toward autobiography. The increasing demands for social and psychological detail that are made upon the novelist can only be satisfied out of his own experience. The forces which make him an outsider focus his observation upon himself. He becomes his own hero, and begins to crowd his other characters into the background. The background takes on a new importance for its influence on his own character. The theme of his novel is the formation of character; its habitual pattern is that of apprenticeship or education; and it falls into that category which has been distinguished, by German criticism at least, as the *Bildungsroman*. The novel of development, when it confines itself to the professional sphere of the novelist, becomes a novel of the artist, a *Künstlerroman*. Goethe's *Wilhelm Meister*, Stendhal's *Vie d'Henri Brulard*, and Butler's *Way of All Flesh* amply suggest the potentialities of the form.

The *Künstlerroman* offered a tentative solution to the dilemma of Joyce's generation, by enabling writers to apply the methods of realism to the subject of art. It enabled Marcel Proust to communicate experience more fully and subtly than had been done before, because it was his own experience that he was communicating, and because he was an artist to his finger-tips. *A la recherche du temps perdu* has been described as a novel that was written to explain why it was written. But, having come to be written, it offers other novelists little stimulus toward self-portraiture. It is singularly fitting that *Ulysses* should have appeared in the year of Proust's death. The perverse logic of André Gide

can still present, in his *Journal des faux-monnayeurs*, the diary of
a novelist who is writing a novel about a novelist who is keeping
a diary about the novel he is writing. Of course, the *Künstlerroman*
has no logical limit; but, like the label on the box of Quaker Oats,
it has a vanishing-point. Already it is beginning to look as old-
fashioned as Murger's *Vie de Bohême*.

The *Künstlerroman*, though it reverses the more normal pro-
cedure of applying the methods of art to the subject of reality, is
the only conception of the novel that is specialized enough to
include *A Portrait of the Artist as a Young Man*. In 1913, the
year before Joyce finished his book, D. H. Lawrence had published his own portrait of the artist, *Sons and Lovers*. Both books
convey the claustral sense of a young intelligence swaddled in
convention and constricted by poverty, and the intensity of its
first responses to esthetic experience and life at large. The extent
to which Lawrence warms to his theme is the measure of Joyce's
reserve. Characteristically, they may be reacting from the very
different institutions behind them – evangelical English protest-
antism and Irish Catholic orthodoxy – when Lawrence dwells
on the attractions of life, and Joyce on its repulsions. The respective mothers of the two artists play a similar role, yet May Dedalus
is a wraith beside the full-bodied realization of Mrs Morel. The
characters in *Sons and Lovers* seem to enjoy an independent
existence; in the *Portrait of the Artist* they figure mainly in the
hero's reveries and resentments. Joyce's treatment of childhood
is unrelieved in its sadness : endless generations of choirs of children sounded, for Stephen Dedalus, the same note of pain and
weariness that Newman had heard in Vergil. 'All seemed weary
of life even before entering upon it.'

The attitude of the novelist toward his subject is one of the
critical questions considered by Joyce's subject. Stephen expounds
his own esthetic theory, which he designates as 'applied Aquinas',
during a walk in the rain with his irreverent friend, Lynch. *Solvitur
ambulando*. It should be noted that the principal action of the

Portrait of the Artist, whether in conversation or revery, is walking. The lingering images of *Dubliners* are those of people – often children – in the streets. And it was reserved for Joyce to turn the wanderings of Ulysses into a peripatetic pilgrimage through Dublin. He was, in that respect, a good Aristotelian. But he added a personal touch to the critical theory of Aristotle and Aquinas, when he based the distinction between the various literary forms on the relation of the artist to his material. In the lyric, it is immediate; in the epic, the artist presents his material 'in mediate relation to himself and others'; in drama it is presented in immediate relation to others.

The lyrical form is in fact the simplest verbal vesture of an instant of emotion, a rhythmical cry such as ages ago cheered on the man who pulled at the oar or dragged stones up a slope. He who utters it is more conscious of the instant of emotion than of himself as feeling emotion. The simplest epical form is seen emerging out of lyrical literature when the artist prolongs and broods upon himself as the centre of an epical event and this form progresses till the centre of emotional gravity is equidistant from the artist himself and from others. The narrative is no longer purely personal. The personality of the artist passes into the narration itself, flowing round and round the persons and the action like a vital sea. This progress you will see easily in that old English ballad *Turpin Hero,* which begins in the first person and ends in the third person. The dramatic form is reached when the vitality which has flowed and eddied round each person fills every person with such force that he or she assumes a proper and intangible esthetic life. The personality of the artist, at first a cry or a cadence or a mood and then a fluid and lambent narrative, finally refines itself out of existence, impersonalizes itself, so to speak. The esthetic image in the dramatic form is life purified in and reprojected from the human imagination. The mystery of esthetic like that of the material creation is accomplished. The artist, like the God of creation, remains within or behind or beyond or above his handiwork, invisible, refined out of existence, indifferent, paring his fingernails.

This progress you will see easily in the succession of Joyce's works. The cry becomes a cadence in *Chamber Music*; the mood becomes a *nuance* in *Dubliners*. If *Exiles* is unsuccessful, it is because the epiphany is not manifest to others; the artist has failed to objectify the relations of his characters with each other or with the audience. The narrative of the *Portrait of the Artist* has scarcely emerged from the lyrical stage. Whereas *Dubliners* began in the first person and ended in the third, the *Portrait of the Artist* takes us back from an impersonal opening to the notes of the author at the end. The personality of the artist, prolonging and brooding upon itself, has not yet passed into the narration. The shift from the personal to the epic will come with *Ulysses,* and the center of emotional gravity will be equidistant from the artist himself and from others. And with *Finnegans Wake,* the artist will have retired within or behind, above or beyond his handiwork, refined out of existence.

Except for the thin incognito of its characters, the *Portrait of the Artist* is based on a literal transcript of the first twenty years of Joyce's life. If anything, it is more candid than other autobiographies. It is distinguished from them by its emphasis on the emotional and intellectual adventures of its protagonist. If we can trust the dates at the end of the book, Joyce started to write in Dublin during 1904, and continued to rewrite until 1914 in Trieste. There is reason to believe that he had accumulated almost a thousand pages – and brought Stephen to the point of departure for Paris – when the idea of *Ulysses* struck him, and he decided to reserve those further adventures for the sequel. His provisional title, *Stephen Hero,* with its echo of the ballad of Dick Turpin, marks the book as an early point in his stages of artistic impersonality. As the hero of a pedagogical novel, Stephen is significantly baptized. Saint Stephen Protomartyr was patron of the green on which University College was located, and therefore of the magazine with which Joyce had had his earliest literary misadventures.

Stephen is ever susceptible to the magic of names – particularly of his own last name. Names and words, copybook phrases and schoolboy slang, echoes and jingles, speeches and sermons float through his mind and enrich the restricted realism of the context. His own name is the wedge by which symbolism enters the book. One day he penetrates its secret. Brooding on the prefect of studies, who made him repeat the unfamiliar syllables of 'Dedalus', he tells himself that it is a better name than Dolan. He hears it shouted across the surf by some friends in swimming, and the strangeness of the sound is for him a prophecy : 'Now, at the name of the fabulous artificer, he seemed to hear the noise of dim waves and to see a winged form flying above the waves and slowly climbing the air. What did it mean? Was it a quaint device opening a page of some medieval book of prophecies and symbols, a hawklike man flying sunward above the sea, a prophecy of the end he had been born to serve and had been following through the mists of childhood and boyhood, a symbol of the artist forging anew in his workshop out of the sluggish matter of the earth a new soaring impalpable imperishable being?'

The *Portrait of the Artist,* as we have it, is the result of an extended process of revision and refinement. The original version – if an *Ur-Portrait* can be remotely discerned – must have been securely founded upon the bedrock of naturalistic narrative. It must have been a human document, virtually a diary, to which Joyce confided his notions and reactions not very long after they occurred. In turning from a reproductive to a selective method, he has foreshortened his work. A fragmentary manuscript, now in the Harvard College Library, touches only the period covered by the last chapter of the printed book, and yet it is nearly as long as the book itself. What is obliquely implied in the final version is explicitly stated in this early draft. The economic situation, for example, as the Dedalus household declines from the genteel to the shabby, is attested by a series of moving vans. In the book there is just one such episode, when Stephen arrives home to hear from his brothers and sisters that the family is looking for another house. Even then the news is not put in plain English, but in evasive pig-

Latin. And the book leaves us with only the vaguest impression of the brothers and sisters; Stephen himself is not sure how many there are.

With revision, the other characters seem to have retreated into the background. Stephen's mother, because of the tension between her love and his disbelief, should be the most poignant figure in the book, just as her memory is the most unforgettable thing in *Ulysses*. But the actual conflict is not dramatized; it is coldly analyzed by Stephen in the course of one of his interminable walks and talks – this time with the serious-minded Cranly. In the manuscript it gives rise to a powerful scene, on the death of Stephen's sister, when his mother's orthodox piety is humbled before the mysteries of the body. The heroine of the book has been refined out of existence; she survives only in veiled allusions and the initials E— C—. Emma Clery, in the manuscript, is an enthusiastic young lady with whom Stephen attends a Gaelic class. Their prolonged and pallid romance comes to an unexpected climax when he sees her mackintosh flashing across the green, and abruptly leaves his lesson to confront her with the proposal that they spend the night together and say farewell in the morning. Her reaction explains the interview so cryptically reported in the book, when Stephen turns on the 'spiritual-heroic refrigerating apparatus, invented and patented in all countries by Dante Alighieri'.

The esthetic theory plays a more active part in the earlier version. Instead of being dogmatically expounded to Lynch, it is sounded in the debating society, where it occasions a bitter argument. As Joyce rewrote his book he seems to have transferred the scene of action from the social to the psychological sphere. As he recollected his 'conflicts with orthodoxy' in the comparative tranquility of exile, he came to the conclusion that the actual struggles had taken place within the mind of Stephen. Discussions gave way to meditations, and scenes were replaced by *tableaux*. Evasion and indirection were ingrained in Joyce's narrative technique. The final effect is that which Shakespearean actors achieve by cutting out all the scenes in *Hamlet* where the hero does not appear. The continuity of dynastic feuds and international issues is obscured by the morbid atmosphere of introspection. Drama has retired before soliloquy.

The Stephen we finally meet is more sharply differentiated from his environment than the figure Joyce set out to describe. How can he be a poet – the other boys have asked him – and not wear long hair? The richness of his inner experience is continually played off against the grim reality of his external surroundings. He is trying 'to build a breakwater of order and elegance against the sordid tide of life without him'. He is marked by the aureole of the romantic hero, like Thomas Mann's outsiders, pressing their noses against the window panes of a bourgeois society from which they feel excluded. 'To merge his life in the common tide of other lives was harder for him than any fasting or prayer, and it was his constant failure to do this to his own satisfaction which caused in his soul at last a sensation of spiritual dryness together with a growth of doubts and scruples.' At school he takes an equivocal position, 'a free boy, a leader afraid of his own authority, proud and sensitive and suspicious, battling against the squalor of his life and against the riot of his mind'. At home he feels 'his own futile isolation'. He feels that he is scarcely of the same blood as his mother and brother and sister, but stands to them 'rather in the mystical kinship of fosterage, foster child and foster brother'.

Joyce's prose is the register of this intellectual and emotional cleavage. It preserves the contrast between his rather lush verse and his rather dry criticism, between the pathetic children and the ironic politicians of *Dubliners*. All his sensibility is reserved for himself; his attitude towards others is consistently caustic. The claims to objectivity of a subjective novel, however, must be based on its rendering of intimate experience. If Joyce's treatment of Stephen is true to himself, we have no right to interpose any other criteria. Mr Eliot has made the plausible suggestion that Joyce's two masters in prose were Newman and Pater. Their alternating influence would account for the oscillations of style in the *Portrait of the Artist*. The sustaining tone, which it adopts toward the outside world, is that of precise and mordant description. Interpolated, at strategic points in Stephen's development, are a number of purple passages that have faded considerably.

Joyce's own contribution to English prose is to provide a more fluid medium for refracting sensations and impressions through the author's mind – to facilitate the transition from photographic realism to esthetic impressionism. In the introductory pages of the *Portrait of the Artist,* the reader is faced with nothing less than the primary impact of life itself, a presentational continuum of the tastes and smells and sights and sounds of earliest infancy. Emotion is integrated, from first to last, by words. Feelings, as they filter through Stephen's sensory apparatus, become associated with phrases. His conditioned reflexes are literary. In one of the later dialogues of the book, he is comparing his theory to a trimmed lamp. The dean of studies, taking up the metaphor, mentions the lamp of Epictetus, and Stephen's reply is a further allusion to the stoic doctrine that the soul is like a bucketful of water. In his mind this far-fetched chain of literary associations becomes attached to the sense impressions of the moment : 'A smell of molten tallow came up from the dean's candle butts and fused itself in Stephen's consciousness with the jingle of the words, bucket and lamp and lamp and bucket'.

This is the state of mind that confers upon language a magical potency. It exalts the habit of verbal association into a principle for the arrangement of experience. You gain power over a thing by naming it; you become master of a situation by putting it into words. It is psychological need, and not hyperfastidious taste, that goads the writer on to search for the *mot juste,* to loot the thesaurus. Stephen, in the more explicit manuscript, finds a treasure-house in Skeat's *Etymological Dictionary.* The crucial moment of the book, which leads to the revelation of his name and calling, is a moment he tries to make his own by drawing forth a phrase of his treasure :

– A day of dappled seaborne clouds. –
The phrase and the day and the scene harmonised in a chord.
Words. Was it their colours? He allowed them to glow and fade,
hue after hue : sunrise gold, the russet and green of apple
orchards, azure of waves, the greyfringed fleece of clouds. No,
it was not their colours : it was the poise and balance of the
period itself. Did he then love the rhythmic rise and fall of
words better than their associations of legend and colour? Or
was it that, being as weak of sight as he was shy of mind, he drew
less pleasure from the reflection of the glowing sensible world
through the prism of a language manycoloured and richly
storied than from the contemplation of an inner world of individual emotions mirrored perfectly in a lucid supple periodic
prose.

The strength and weakness of his style, by Joyce's own diagnosis,
are those of his mind and body. A few pages later he offers a cogent
illustration, when Stephen dips self-consciously into his word-
hoard for suitable epithets to describe a girl who is wading along
the beach. We are given a paragraph of word-painting which is
not easy to visualize. 'Her bosom was as a bird's, soft and slight,
slight and soft as the breast of some dark-plumaged dove,' it concludes. 'But her long fair hair was girlish : and girlish, and touched
with the wonder of mortal beauty, her face.' This is incantation,
and not description. Joyce is thinking in rhythms rather than meta-
phors. Specification of the bird appeals to the sense of touch rather
than to the sense of sight. What is said about the hair and face is
intended to produce an effect without presenting a picture. The
most striking effects in Joyce's imagery are those of coldness, whiteness, and dampness, like the bodies of the bathers who shout
Stephen's name.

The most vital element in Joyce's writing, in the *Portrait of the
Artist* as in *Dubliners,* is his use of conversation. As a reporter of
Irish life, for all his reservations, Joyce is a faithful and apprecia-
tive listener. It is a tribute to Stephen's ear that, in spite of the
antagonism between father and son, Simon Dedalus is such a ripe

and congenial character. Like Sean O'Casey's *Paycock,* with all
his amiable failings, he is Ireland itself. Though he takes pride in
showing Cork to Stephen, and in showing off his son to his own
native city, he is really the embodiment of Dublin : 'A medical
student, an oarsman, a tenor, an amateur actor, a shouting
politician, a small landlord, a small investor, a drinker, a good
fellow, a storyteller, somebody's secretary, something in a distil-
lery, a taxgatherer, a bankrupt and at present a praiser of his own
past.' The improvident worldliness of John Stanislaus Joyce had
made him, in the unforgiving eyes of his son, a foster-parent. So
young Charles Dickens, hastening from the blacking-factory to the
Marshalsea, came to look upon his father as a horrible example of
good-fellowship, a Mr Micawber.

This disorder, 'the misrule and confusion of his father's house',
comes to stand in Stephen's mind for the plight of Ireland. Like
Synge's *Playboy,* he must go through the motions of parricide to
make good his revolt. Religion and politics, to his adult perception, are among the intimations of early childhood : harsh words
and bitter arguments that spoil the taste of the Christmas turkey.
Again, as in 'Ivy Day in the Committee Room', or in Lennox
Robinson's *Lost Leader* on the stage, it is the ghost of Parnell that
turns conversation into drama. 'Dante', the devout Mrs Riordan,
is true to the Catholic Church in denouncing the disgraced
nationalist leader. Mr Casey, the guest of honor, is of the anti-
clerical faction. Mr Dedalus is by no means a neutral, and some
of his mellowest profanity is enlisted in the cause of his dead hero.
Mrs Dedalus softly rebukes him :

> – Really Simon, you should not speak that way before
> Stephen. It's not right.
> – O, he'll remember all this when he grows up, said Dante
> hotly – the language he heard against God and religion and
> priests in his own home.
> – Let him remember too, cried Mr Casey to her from across
> the table, the language with which the priests and the priests'

pawns broke Parnell's heart and hounded him into his grave.
Let him remember that too when he grows up.

The *Portrait of the Artist,* as Joyce's remembrance finally
shaped it, is a volume of three hundred pages, symmetrically constructed around three undramatic climaxes, intimate crises of
Stephen's youth. The first hundred pages, in two chapters, trace
the awakening of religious doubts and sexual instincts, leading up
to Stephen's carnal sin at the age of sixteen. The central portion, in
two more chapters, continues the cycle of sin and repentance to the
moment of Stephen's private apocalypse. The external setting for
the education of the artist is, in the first chapter, Clongowes Wood
College; in the second, third, and fourth, Belvedere College,
Dublin. The fifth and final chapter, which is twice as long as the
others, develops the theories and projects of Stephen's student
days in University College, and brings him to the verge of exile.
As the book advances, it becomes less sensitive to outside impressions, and more intent upon speculations of its own. Friends figure
mainly as interlocutors to draw Stephen out upon various themes.
Each epiphany – awakening of the body, literary vocation, farewell to Ireland – leaves him lonelier than the last.

A trivial episode at Clongowes Wood seems fraught for Joyce
with a profoundly personal meaning. Young Stephen has been
unable to get his lessons, because his glasses were broken on the
playing-field. Father Dolan, the prefect of studies, is unwilling to
accept this excuse, and disciplines Stephen with the boys who have
shirked their books. Smarting with pain and a sense of palpable
injustice, Stephen finally carries his case to the rector, who shows
a humane understanding of the situation. Many years later Father
Conmee, the rector, takes a walk through a chapter of *Ulysses;*
and Father Dolan – who was actually a Father Daly – pops up
with his 'pandybat' in Stephen's nightmare. This schoolboy incident lays down a pattern for Joyce's later behavior. When he
cabled Lloyd George, who had other things on his mind during

the First World War, *re* a pair of trousers and *The Importance of Being Earnest,* he was behaving like an aggrieved schoolboy unjustly pandied.

The physical handicap, the public humiliation, the brooding sensibility, the sense of grievance, the contempt for convention, the desire for self-justification, and the appeal to higher authority – these are all elements of Joyce's attitude toward society and toward himself. He had begun his education by questioning the Jesuit discipline; he would finish by repudiating the Catholic faith. Having responded to the urgent prompting of his senses, he would be treated as a sinner; he would refer the ensuing conflict, over the head of religious authority, to the new light of his scientific and naturalist studies; he would seek, in the end, to create his own authority by the light of his senses. In turning away from Ireland toward the world at large, he would appeal from the parochial Daly to the enlightened Conmee. That miserable day at Clongowes Wood, like that long evening at Combray when M. Swann's visit kept Marcel's mother downstairs, had unforeseen consequences.

Adolescence complicates the second chapter. Stephen is beginning to appreciate beauty, but as something illicit and mysterious, something apart from the common walks of life. Literature has begun to color his experience, and to stimulate his mind and his senses. His untimely enthusiasm for Lord Byron – 'a heretic and immortal too' – provokes a beating at the hands of his classmates. Now in jest and again in earnest, he is forced to repeat the *confiteor.* One of his essays had been rewarded with the taunt of heresy from his English master, and he takes rueful consolation in the self-conscious part of the Byronic hero. He will not agree that Lord Tennyson is a poet, though he gives tacit consent to the assertion that Newman has the best prose style. But it is his other master, Pater, whose influence is felt at the climax of the chapter. Stephen's sexual initiation is presented in empurpled prose, as an esthetic ritual for which his literary heresies have been preparing him. In trying to find a cadence for his cry, he harks back to the lyricism of *Chamber Music* and the anguish of the small boy in *Dubliners:*

> He stretched out his arms in the street to hold fast the frail swooning form that eluded him and incited him : and the cry that he had strangled for so long in his throat issued from his lips. It broke from him like a wail of despair from a hell of sufferers and died in a wail of furious entreaty, a cry for an iniquitous abandonment, a cry which was but the echo of an obscene scrawl which he had read on the oozing wall of a urinal.

The unromantic reader is prone to feel that a scrawl would have been more adequate to the occasion. The incidence of the word 'swoon' is a humorless symptom of the Pateresque influence on Joyce's early writing. There is many 'A swoon in shame' in *Chamber Music* and 'a slowly swooning soul' in the last paragraph of *Dubliners.* 'His soul was swooning' at the end of the fourth chapter of the *Portrait of the Artist,* having been darkened by 'the swoon of sin' at the end of the second chapter. Though the scene is clouded with decadent incense, it is clear that Stephen is still a child, and that the woman plays the part of a mother. Joyce's heroes are sons and lovers at the same time; his heroines are always maternal. It is like him to lavish his romantic sensibility on an encounter with a prostitute and to reserve his acrid satire for the domain of the church. In Stephen's mind a symbolic association between art and sex is established, and that precocious revelation helps him to decide his later conflict between art and religion.

Meanwhile, the third chapter is devoted to his remorse. It embodies at formidable length a sermon on hell, suffered by Stephen and his classmates during a retreat. The eloquent Jesuit preacher takes as his object-lesson the sin of Lucifer, pride of the intellect, his great refusal and his terrible fall. Stephen's repentant imagination is harrowed by the torments of the damned. This powerful discourse provides an ethical core for the book, as Father Mapple's sermon on Jonah does for *Moby-Dick,* or Ivan's legend of the Grand Inquisitor for *The Brothers Karamazov.*

Joyce is orthodox enough to go on believing in hell, and – as
Professor Curtius recognized – to set up his own *Inferno* in
Ulysses. Like another tormented apostate, Christopher Marlowe,
he lives in a world where there is still suffering, but no longer the
prospect of salvation. Like Blake's Milton, he is a true poet, and
of the devil's party. Stephen's ultimate text is the defiance of the
fallen archangel : *'Non serviam!'*

Temporarily, there is confession and absolution. When Stephen
sees the eggs and sausages laid out for the communion breakfast,
life seems simple and beautiful after all. For a time his restlessness
seems to be tranquilized by church and satisfied by school.
Seeking to order his existence, he contemplates the possibilities of
the Jesuit order itself : the Reverend Stephen Dedalus, S.J. After
a conference with a member of that order, he is fascinated and
terrified by the awful assumption of powers which ordination
involves. In the fourth chapter the call comes unexpectedly – the
call to another kind of priesthood. Stephen dedicates himself to art,
and enters upon his peculiar novitiate. The church would have
meant order, but it would also have meant a denial of the life of the
senses. A walk along the strand brings him his real vocation – an
outburst of profane joy at the bird-like beauty of a girl, a realization of the fabulous artificer whose name he bears, a consciousness
of the power of words to confer an order and life of their own.
Like the birds that circle between the sea and the sky, his soul soars
in 'an ecstasy of flight', in a metaphor of sexual fulfilment and
artistic creation. 'To live, to err, to fall, to triumph, to recreate
life out of life !'

The fifth chapter is the discursive chronicle of Stephen's rebellion. He moves among his fellow-students, an aloof and pharasaic
figure, unwilling to share their indignation at the first performance
of the *Countess Cathleen*, or their confidence in a petition to ensure
world peace. His own struggle comes when his mother requests
him to make his Easter duty and his diabolic pride of intellect
asserts itself. Cranly, with the sharpest instruments of casuistry,

tries to probe his stubborn refusal. It is less a question of faith than of observance. Stephen will not, to please his mother, do false homage to the symbols of authority, yet he is not quite unbeliever enough to take part in a sacrilegious communion. If he cannot accept the eucharist, he must be anathema; he respects the forms by refusing to observe them. 'I will not serve that in which I no longer believe, whether it call itself my home, my fatherland or my church : and I will try to express myself in some mode of life or art as freely as I can and as wholly as I can, using for my defence the only arms I allow myself to use, silence, exile and cunning.'

With this peremptory gesture, emancipating himself from his petty-bourgeois family, and from Ireland and Catholicism at the same time, Stephen stands ready to take his solitary way wherever the creative life engages him. In a previous argument with other friends, he abandoned the possibility of fighting these issues out at home. 'Ireland is the old sow that eats her farrow.' Davin, the nationalist, is willing to admit that Stephen's position is thoroughly Irish, all too typical of their gifted countrymen. 'In your heart you are an Irishman but your pride is too powerful.' Stephen is unwilling to compromise : 'When the soul of a man is born in this country there are nets flung at it to hold it back from flight. You talk to me of nationality, language, religion. I shall try to fly by those nets.' In exile, silence, and cunning he trusts to find substitutes for those three forms of subjection.

On his way to and from Belvedere College, his soul was 'disquieted and cast down by the dull phenomenon of Dublin'. With his realization of the end he was soon to serve, a new vista of 'the slowflowing Liffey' became visible 'across the timeless air'. Nomadic clouds, dappled and seaborne, voyaging westward from Europe, suggested strange tongues and marshalled races. 'He heard a confused music within him as of memories and names. . . .' At University College, the time-worn texts of Ovid and Horace have filled him with awe for the past and contempt of the present : '. . . it wounded him to think that he would never be but a shy

D

guest at the feast of the world's culture and that the monkish learning, in terms of which he was striving to forge out an esthetic philosophy, was held no higher by the age he lived in than the subtle
and curious jargons of heraldry and falconry.'

English is as strange a tongue as Latin. 'His language, so familiar
and so foreign, will always be for me an acquired speech,' Stephen
reflects, while conversing with the dean of studies, an English con-
vert to Catholicism. 'I have not made or accepted its words. My
voice holds them at bay. My soul frets in the shadow of his language.' The last pages are fragments from Stephen's notebook,
duly recording his final interviews with teachers and friends, with
his family and 'her'. Spring finds him setting down 'vague words
for a vague emotion', his farewell to Dublin, and to sounds of the
city which will never stop echoing in his ears :

> *April 10.* Faintly, under the heavy night, through the silence
> of the city which has turned from dreams to dreamless sleep as
> a weary lover whom no caresses move, the sound of hoofs upon
> the road.

Toward the end, his purpose stiffens into a flourish of blank verse :

> *April 26.* Mother is putting my new secondhand clothes in
> order. She prays now, she says, that I may learn in my own life
> and away from home and friends what the heart is and what it
> feels. Amen. So be it. Welcome, O life ! I go to encounter for the
> millionth time the reality of experience and to forge in the
> smithy of my soul the uncreated conscience of my race.

On the eve of departure he makes his final entry :

> *April 27.* Old father, old artificer, stand me now and ever
> in good stead.

The mythical and priestly figure of Dædalus is known for more
than one work of genius – for a pair of wings, as well as a labyrinth.

Stephen invokes his namesake under both aspects, the hawklike man and the fabulous artificer. Sometimes it is the cunning of the craftsman, the smithy of the artist, that is symbolized. At other times, soaring, falling, flying by the nets of Ireland, it is life itself. Yet these images of aspiration can also be associated with Icarus, the son of Dædalus. That ill-fated and rebellious spirit, who borrowed his father's wings and flew too near the sun, is an equally prophetic symbol : in a classical drama, *Icaro,* the young anti-fascist poet, Lauro de Bosis, adumbrated the heroism of his own death. The epigraph of Joyce's book is a quotation from Ovid – or rather a misquotation (the correct reference is to the *Metamorphoses,* viii, 188). Here we are told that Dædalus abandoned his mind to obscure arts, '*et ignotas animum dimittit in artes.*' But Joyce does not tell us Ovid's reason :

> . . . *longumque perosus*
> *exsilium, tractusque soli natalis amore* . . .

The artificer was weary of his long exile and lured by the love of his natal soil, the Roman poet and exile goes on to say, and the rest of his myth rehearses the filial tragedy. The father cries out for the son; Joyce's confused recollection, in *Ulysses,* makes the son cry out for the father : '*Pater, ait.*' On the brink of expatriation, poised for his trial flight, Stephen, in the *Portrait of the Artist,* is more nearly akin to the son. His natural father, Simon Dedalus, is left standing in the mystical kinship of fosterage. The Jesuit fathers, who supervised his education, no longer call him son. He has appealed from Father Dolan to Father Conmee; now he appeals from the church to another paternity. His wings take him from the fatherland. The labyrinth leads toward a father.

S o u r c e : *James Joyce: A Critical Introduction* (1941; rev. edn 1960) pp. 41–62.

Brewster Ghiselin

THE UNITY OF *DUBLINERS* (1956)

The idea is not altogether new that the structure of James Joyce's
Dubliners, long believed to be loose and episodic, is really unitary.
In 1944, Richard Levin and Charles Shattuck made it clear that
the book is 'something more than a collection of discrete sketches'.
In their essay 'First Flight to Ithaca : A New Reading of Joyce's
Dubliners', they demonstrated that like the novel *Ulysses* the
stories of *Dubliners* are integrated by a pattern of correspondence
to the *Odyssey* of Homer. To this first demonstration of a latent
structural unity in *Dubliners* must be added the evidence of its
even more full integration by means of a symbolic structure so
highly organized as to suggest the most subtle elaborations of
Joyce's method in his maturity.

So long as *Dubliners* was conceived of only as 'a straight work
of Naturalistic fiction', the phrase of Edmund Wilson character-
izing the book in *Axel's Castle,* its unity could appear to be no
more than thematic. The work seemed merely a group of brilliant
individual stories arranged in such a way as to develop effectively
the import which Joyce himself announced, but did not fully
reveal, in describing the book as 'a chapter of the moral history of
my country' and in suggesting that his interest focused upon
Dublin as 'the centre of paralysis'. As Harry Levin explained in
his introduction to *The Portable Joyce,* 'The book is not a systematic canvas like *Ulysses;* nor is it integrated, like the *Portrait,* by
one intense point of view; but it comprises, as Joyce explained,
a series of chapters in the moral history of his community; and
the episodes are arranged in careful progression from childhood
to maturity, broadening from private to public scope.'

So narrow an understanding of *Dubliners* is no longer acceptable. Recent and steadily increasing appreciation of the fact that there is much symbolism in the book has dispelled the notion that it is radically different in technique from Joyce's later fiction. During the past six or eight years a significant body of critics, among them Caroline Gordon, Allen Tate, and W. Y. Tindall, have published their understanding that the naturalism of *Dubliners* is complicated by systematic use of symbols, which establish relationships between superficially disparate elements in the stories. Discussion of 'The Dead', for example, has made it obvious that the immobility of snowy statues in that story is symbolically one with the spiritual condition of Gabriel Conroy turned to the wintry window at the very end of *Dubliners* and with the deathly arrest of paralysis announced on the first page of the book. In the light of this insight other elements of the same pattern, such as the stillness of the girl frozen in fear at the end of the fourth story, virtually declare themselves.

Such images, significantly disposed, give a firm symbolic texture and pattern to the individual stories of *Dubliners* and enhance the integrity of the work as a whole. But no constellation, zodiac, or whole celestial sphere of symbols is enough in itself to establish in the fifteen separate narratives, each one in its realistic aspect a completely independent action, the embracing and inviolable order of full structural unity. That is achieved, however, by means of a single development, essentially of action, organized in complex detail and in a necessary, meaningful sequence throughout the book. Because this structure is defined partly by realistic means, partly by symbols, much of it must remain invisible until the major symbols in which it defines itself are recognized, as too few of them have been, and displayed in their more significant relationships. When the outlines of the symbolic pattern have been grasped, the whole unifying development will be discernible as a sequence of events in a moral drama, an action of the human spirit struggling for survival under peculiar conditions of deprivation, enclosed and disabled by a degenerate environment that provides none of the primary necessities of spiritual life. So understood, *Dubliners* will be seen for what it is, in effect, both a group of short stories and a novel, the separate histories of its protagonists composing one essential history, that of the soul of a people which has confused and weakened its relation to the source of spiritual life and cannot restore it.

In so far as this unifying action is evident in the realistic elements of the book, it appears in the struggle of certain characters to escape the constricting circumstances of existence in Ireland, and especially in Dublin, 'the centre of paralysis'. As in *A Portrait of the Artist as a Young Man,* an escape is envisaged in traveling eastward from the city, across the seas to the freedom of the open world. In *Dubliners,* none of Joyce's protagonists moves very far on this course, though some aspire to go far. Often their motives are unworthy, their minds are confused. Yet their dreams of escape and the longing of one of them even to 'fly away to another country' are suggestive of the intent of Stephen Dedalus in *A Portrait* to 'fly by those nets', those constrictions of 'nationality, language, religion', which are fully represented in *Dubliners* also. Thus, in both books, ideas of enclosure, of arrest, and of movement in space are associated with action of moral purport and with spiritual aspiration and development.

In *Dubliners,* the meaning of movement is further complicated by the thematic import of that symbolic paralysis which Joyce himself referred to, an arrest imposed from within, not by the 'nets' of external circumstance, but by a deficiency of impulse and power. The idea of a moral paralysis is expressed sometimes directly in terms of physical arrest, even in the actual paralysis of the priest Father Flynn, whose condition is emphasized by its appearance at the beginning of the book and is reflected in the behavior of Father Purdon, in the penultimate story 'observed to be struggling up into the pulpit' as if he were partially paralyzed. But sheer physical inaction of any kind is a somewhat crude means of indicating moral paralysis. Joyce has used it sparingly. The frustrations and degradations of his moral paralytics are rarely defined in physical stasis alone, and are sometimes concomitant with vigorous action. Their paralysis is more often expressed in a weakening of their impulse and ability to move forcefully, effectually, far, or in the right direction, especially by their frustration in ranging eastward in the direction of release or by their complete lack of orientation, by their failure to pass more than a little way beyond the outskirts of Dublin, or by the restriction of their movement altogether to the city or to some narrow area within it.

The case of the boy in the first story, 'The Sisters', is representative. Restive under the surviving influence of his dead mentor Father Flynn, yet lost without him, and resentful of the meager life of the city, he only dreams vaguely and disturbingly of being in a far country in the East, and wakes to wander in the city that still encloses him. At the end of the story he sits among hapless women, all immobile and disconsolate, in the dead priest's own room, in the very house where the priest has died, near the center of the center of paralysis. His physical arrest and his enclosure are expressive, even apart from a knowledge of the rich symbolism which qualifies them in ways too complicated to consider at this stage in discussion. Bereft of spiritual guidance, and deprived of the tension of an interest that has been primary in his life, he sits confused and in isolation, unstained by the secular world about him, unstirred by anything in the natural world, moved only by a fleeting sense of life still in the coffin in the room overhead, a doubt and a hope like a faint resurgence of faith, instantly dispelled.

It should be no surprise to discover in a book developing the theme of moral paralysis a fundamental structure of movements and stases, a system of significant motions, countermotions, and arrests, involving every story, making one consecutive narrative of the surge and subsidence of life in Dublin. In the development of the tendency to eastward movement among the characters of

Dubliners, and in its successive modifications, throughout the
book, something of such a system is manifest. It may be characterized briefly as an eastward trend, at first vague, quickly becoming dominant, then wavering, weakening, and at last reversed.
Traced in rough outline, the pattern is as follows : in a sequence
of six stories, an impulse and movement eastward to the outskirts
of the city or beyond; in a single story, an impulse to fly away
upward out of a confining situation near the center of Dublin;
in a sequence of four stories, a gradual replacement of the impulse
eastward by an impulse and movement westward; in three stories,
a limited activity confined almost wholly within the central area
of Dublin; and in the concluding story a movement eastward to
the heart of the city, the exact center of arrest, then, in vision only,
far westward into death.

Interpreted realistically, without recourse to symbol, this pattern
may show at most the frustration of Dubliners unable to escape
eastward, out of the seaport and overseas, to a more living world.
An orientation so loosely conceived seems quite unsuited to determine a powerful organization of form and meaning. Understood
in its symbolic import, however, the eastward motion or the desire
for it takes on a much more complicated and precise significance.

Orientation and easting are rich in symbolic meanings of which
Joyce was certainly aware. An erudite Catholic, he must have
known of the ancient though not invariable custom of building
churches with their heads to the east and placing the high altar
against the east wall or eastward against a reredos in the depths
of the building, so that the celebrant of the mass faced east, and
the people entered the church and approached the altar from
the west and remained looking in the same direction as the priest.
He knew that in doing so they looked toward Eden, the earthly
paradise, and he may have felt, like Gregory of Nyssa, that the
force of the sacramental orientation was increased by that fact.
Perhaps he did not know that the catechumens of the fourth century turned to the west to renounce Satan and to the east to recite

the creed before they stepped into the baptismal font, to receive the sacrament that opens the door of spiritual life. Probably he did know that Christ returning for the Last Judgment was expected to come from the east. And he must have shared that profound human feeling, older than Christianity, which has made the sunrise immemorially and all but universally an emblem of the return of life and has made the east, therefore, an emblem of beginning and a place of rebirth. Many times Joyce must have seen the sun rise out of the Irish Sea, washed and brilliant. He could not have failed to know that washing and regeneration are implicit in the sacrament of baptism, and he may have known that in the earlier ages of Christianity baptism was called Illumination. He could not have failed, and the evidence of his symbolism in *Dubliners* shows that he did not fail, to see how a multitude of intimations of spiritual meaning affected the eastward aspirations and movements of characters in his book, and what opportunity it afforded of giving to the mere motion of his characters the symbolic import of moral action.

In constructing *Dubliners,* Joyce must have responded to the force of something like the whole body of insights of which these are representative. For these insights, with some others closely associated with them, are the chief light by which we shall be enabled to follow the development of what I have called the unifying action of *Dubliners* and, through understanding the structure of the book, to penetrate to its central significance. The unity of *Dubliners* is realized, finally, in terms of religious images and ideas, most of them distinctively Christian.

Among these the most important for the immediate purpose of understanding are the symbols, sacraments, and doctrines of the Catholic Church, especially its version of the ancient sacraments of baptism and the sacrificial meal and its concepts of the soul's powers, its perils, and its destiny. In terms of the religious ideas with which Joyce was most familiar the basic characteristics of his structural scheme are readily definable, and some of them are not definable otherwise. The unifying action may be conceived of, oversimply yet with essential accuracy, as a movement of the human soul, in desire of life, through various conditions of Christian virtue and stages of deadly sin, toward or away from the font and the altar and all the gifts of the two chief sacraments provided for its salvation, toward or away from God. In these ideas all the most essential determinants of the spiritual action which makes of *Dubliners* one consecutive narrative are represented : its motivation, its goal and the means of reaching it, and those empowering or disempowering states of inmost being which define the moral conditions under which the action takes place.

The states of being, of virtue and sin, are doubly important. For in *Dubliners* the primary virtues and sins of Christian tradition function both in their intrinsic character, as moral manifestations and determinants of behavior, and structurally in defining the order of the separate stories and in integrating them in a significant sequence. Thus they are one means of establishing the unity of the book, a simple but not arbitrary or wholly superficial means, supplementing with structural reinforcement and with a deepening of import that more fundamental pattern of motions and arrests already touched upon.

Like the booklong sequence of movements and stases, the various states of the soul in virtue and sin form a pattern of strict design traceable through every story. Each story in *Dubliners* is an action defining amid different circumstances of degradation and difficulty in the environment a frustration or defeat of the soul in a different state of strength or debility. Each state is related to the preceding by conventional associations or by causal connections or by both, and the entire sequence represents the whole course of moral deterioration ending in the death of the soul. Joyce's sense of the incompatibility of salvation with life in Dublin is expressed in a systematic display, one by one in these stories, of the three theological virtues and the four cardinal virtues in suppression, of the seven deadly sins triumphant, and of the

deathly consequence, the spiritual death of all the Irish. Far more
than his announced intention, of dealing with childhood, adolescence, maturity, and public life, this course of degenerative
change in the states of the soul tends to determine the arrangement
of the stories in a fixed order and, together with the pattern of
motions and arrests, to account for his insistence upon a specific,
inalterable sequence.

Although Joyce's schematic arrangement of virtues and sins in
Dubliners does not conform entirely to the most usual order in
listing them, it does so in the main. In the first three stories, in
which the protagonists are presumably innocent, the theological
virtues faith, hope, and love, in the conventional order, are successively displayed in abeyance and finally in defeat. In the fourth
story, the main character, Eveline, lacking the strength of faith,
hope, and love, wavers in an effort to find a new life and, failing
in the cardinal virtue of fortitude, remains in Dublin, short of her
goal and weakened in her spiritual powers and defenses against
evil. In the fifth through the eleventh stories the seven deadly sins,
pride, covetousness, lust, envy, anger, gluttony, and sloth, are
portrayed successively in action, usually in association with other
sins adjacent in the list. The seven stories devoted to the sins
occupy exactly the central position in the book. The sequence
of their presentation is the most conventional one except for the
placing of anger before gluttony, a slight and not unique devia-
tion. Gluttony is strongly represented, moreover, in the usual
position, the fifth place, by means of the drunkenness of the central
character Farrington, as well as in the sixth. And in the sixth place
gluttony is defined in the attitudes and behavior of others than
the main character, Maria, who is interested in food and much
concerned with it rather than avid of it. Her quiet depression is
more truly expressive of her essential state of soul; and in it another
sin that appears rarely in lists of the seven is apparent, the sin of
tristitia, or gloominess, sometimes substituted for the similar sin
of sloth. Joyce's intent seems to have been to create here a

palimpsest, incribing three sins in the space afforded for two. The effect has been to reduce gluttony to secondary importance while giving it full recognition in both of its aspects as over-indulgence in drinking as well as in eating. The sequence of sins completes Joyce's representation of the defeat of the soul in its most inward strength and prepares for its failure in the exercise of rational powers. Alienated wholly from God, it cannot act now even in expression of the natural or cardinal virtues, in the words of Aquinas 'the good as defined by reason'. In the twelfth through the fourteenth stories, the subversion of the cardinal virtues of justice, temperance, and prudence, and the contradiction of reason, upon which they are based, is displayed in those narratives that Joyce intended to represent 'public life' in Ireland. Justice, the social virtue regulating the others, comes first in the group. The placing of prudence or wisdom last instead of first, the commonest position, is perhaps influenced by the sequence of appearance in these stories of those hindrances of the spirit in Ireland, the 'nets' of 'nationality, language, religion'. The order, moreover, is climactic. Certainly the culminating subversion of the three virtues is represented in the third story of this group, 'Grace', in the sermon of 'a man of the world' recommending worldly wisdom for the guidance of 'his fellowmen'. In the fifteenth and last story of *Dubliners,* no virtue or sin is given such attention as to suggest its predominance. Perhaps that virtue of magnanimity which Aristotle added to the group of four named by the Greeks is displayed in abeyance in Gabriel Conroy's self-concern, but recovered at last in his final self-abnegation and visionary acceptance of the communion of death. Perhaps merely the consequences of moral degeneration are to be discerned in the final story, the completion of spiritual disintegration, death itself.

The pattern of virtues and sins and the spatial pattern of motions and arrests in *Dubliners* are of course concomitant, and they express one development. As sin flourishes and virtue withers, the force of the soul diminishes, and it becomes more and more disorientated, until at the last all the force of its impulse toward the vital east is confused and spent and it inclines wholly to the deathly west. All this development is embodied, realistically or symbolically, in the experience of the principal characters as they search for vital satisfaction either in spiritual wholeness or in personal willfulness, apprehending the nature of their goal and their immediate needs truly or falsely, moving effectually toward the means of spiritual enlargement or faltering into meanness and withdrawing into a meager and spurious safety, seeking or avoiding the sacred elements of the font and the altar, those ancient Christian and pre-Christian means of sustaining the life of the spirit through lustration, regeneration, illumination, and communion. The unifying pattern of motions and arrests is manifested, story by story, in the action of the principal figure in each, as he moves in relation to the orient source and to the sacramental resources of spiritual life, expressing in physical behavior his moral condition of virtue or sin and his spiritual need and desire. His activity, outwardly of the body, is inwardly that of the soul, either advancing more or less freely and directly eastward or else confined and halted or wandering disoriented, short of its true goal and its true objects the water of regeneration and the wine and bread of communion, the means of approach to God, and often in revulsion from them, accepting plausible substitutes or nothing whatever.

In *Dubliners* from first to last the substitutes are prominent, the true objects are unavailable. The priest in the first story, 'The Sisters', has broken a chalice, is paralyzed, and dies; he cannot offer communion, and an empty chalice lies on his breast in death. The food and drink obtained by the boy whose friend he has been are unconsecrated: wine and crackers are offered to him solemnly, but by secular agents. Again and again throughout *Dubliners* such substitutes for the sacred elements of the altar recur, always in secular guise: 'musty biscuits' and 'raspberry lemonade', porter and 'a caraway seed'. Suggestions less overt are

no less pointed. The abundant table in 'The Dead', loaded with
food and with bottled water and liquors but surrounded by human
beings gathered together in imperfect fellowship, emphasizes the
hunger of the soul for bread and wine that can nourish it, rather
than the body, and assuage its loneliness through restoring it to
the communion of love. The symbolism of baptismal water like-
wise enforces the fact of spiritual privation. In 'The Sisters' the
secular baptism of a cold bath is recommended by the boy's
uncle as the source of his strength. Less certainly symbolic, but
suggestive in the context, is the fact that the body of the priest
is washed by a woman, a point that Joyce thought important
enough to define by explicit statements in two passages. In the
house where the priest has lived and died, his sisters keep a shop
where umbrellas, devices for rejecting the rain of heaven, are
sold and re-covered. The open sea, the great symbol of the font
in *Dubliners,* is approached by many of the central characters,
longed for, but never embarked upon, never really reached. Canal,
river, and estuary are crossed; Kingstown Harbor is attained,
but the vessel boarded in the harbor is lying at anchor. When, in
fear of drowning, the reluctant protagonist of the fourth story,
'Eveline', hangs back refusing to embark on an ocean voyage,
she may be understood to have withdrawn as at the brink of the
baptismal font, for by her action she has renounced that new life
which she had looked forward to attaining through moving eastward out of Dublin Bay on the night sea. The idea of her deprivation is reinforced by her final condition, of insenate terror, the
reverse of spiritual refreshment and illumination.

Though the spiritual objects that are imaged in these substitutes represent the gifts of the two chief sacraments of the Church,
baptism, the first in necessity, and the Eucharist, the first in
dignity, there is no suggestion in *Dubliners* that the soul's needs
can be supplied by the Church, in its current condition. The only
scene in a church, in the story 'Grace', implies exactly the opposite, for the sermon of Father Purdon is frankly designed to serve

the purposes of those who 'live in the world, and, to a certain
extent, for the world'. The Church is secularized, and it shares
in the general paralysis. Its failure in the lives of Joyce's Dubliners
is emphasized by the irony that although the nature of the soul
has not altered and the means of its salvation retain their old
aspects, its needs must be satisfied in entire dissociation from the
Church.

Since those needs cannot be satisfied in Ireland, as Joyce represents it in *Dubliners,* the soul's true satisfaction cannot be exhibited
in the experience of those who remain in Ireland. It can only be
simulated and suggested, either in their relation to those secular
substitutes for spiritual things that intimate the need for baptism
and communion or in their turning toward the soul's orient, the
symbolic east, variously imaged. Some of Joyce's dissatisfied
characters, such as Little Chandler, suppose that they can change
their condition by escaping from Ireland eastward across the sea
to another life in a different place. Physically their goal must be
another country; spiritually it has the aspect of a new life. The
association functions symbolically. Throughout *Dubliners,* one
of the symbolic images of the spiritual goal is a far country. Like
the symbols of water, wine and bread, the far country images the
soul's need for life that cannot be attained in Ireland.

Apparently it is not easily attainable outside of Ireland either.
Those Dubliners who have reached England or the Continent,
characters such as Gabriel Conroy or Ignatius Gallaher, the
journalist whom Little Chandler envies because he has made a
life for himself in London, show by their continuing to behave
like other Dubliners that to be transported physically overseas is
not necessarily to find a new life, or to be changed essentially at
all. No doubt their failure to change means that the whole of
Europe is secularized, perhaps the whole world. Still more, it
emphasizes the subjective nature of the attainment symbolized by
arrival in a far country. A new condition of inward life is the
goal; not a place, but what the place implies, is the true east of

the soul. The far countries reached by the boy in 'The Sisters' and sought by the boy in 'Araby', perhaps the same boy, are not in the world. In one story he dreams of being in an eastern land which he thinks, not very confidently, is Persia. In the other he goes to a bazaar bearing the 'magical name' *Araby,* a word casting 'an Eastern enchantment'. In both stories the far country is probably the same, that fabulous Arabia which is associated with the Phoenix, symbol of the renewal of life in the resurrection of the sun. To the dreamer it suggests a journey and strange customs, but he cannot conceive its meaning. The meaning is plain, however, to the reader aware of the symbols : the boy has looked inward toward the source of his own life, away from that civilization which surrounds him but does not sustain him. The same import, with further meaning, is apparent in the later story. The response of the boy to the name *Araby* and his journey eastward across the city define his spiritual orientation, as his response to the disappointing reality of the bazaar indicates his rejection of a substitute for 'the true object of the soul's desire.

The sea too, like the image and idea of a far country, symbolizes the orient goal of life. It may of itself, as water, suggest the baptismal font. And in any case it must tend strongly to do so because of the sacramental import of water established by other water symbolism throughout *Dubliners.* The element itself is highly significant, and the great image of it is the sea, the water of liberating voyage and of change and danger, of death and resurrection. The sheer physical prominence of the sea eastward from Dublin colors the east with the significance of baptismal water. In turn the sea is colored by the significance of the east. The altar, even more immediately than the font, is implied in the concept of orientation.

Perhaps in the symbol of the sea in *Dubliners* the identification of the two chief sacraments should be understood. Their identification would not be altogether arbitrary. For the close relationship and even the essential similarity of the two sacraments is

suggested in several ways, apart from their association with the
east : by their interdependence in fulfillment of a spiritual purpose;
by the invariable mixture of a few drops of water with the wine
in the chalice; and above all by the concept of rebirth, in which
the font is profoundly associated with the altar, the place where
Christ is believed to be reborn at the consecration of the divine
sacrifice. That Joyce could make the identification is plain from
his having merged font with altar in *Finnegans Wake,* in the
conception of the 'tubbathaltar' of Saint Kevin Hydrophilos.
Going 'westfrom' toward a suitable supply of water, and showing
his sense of the importance of orientation by genuflecting seven
times eastward, Saint Kevin fills up his device of dual function, in
'ambrosian eucharistic joy of heart', and sits in it. Though Joyce
may not have been ready, so early as in *Dubliners,* to identify font
with altar, he has developed a body of symbolism which intimately
involves them, and possibly merges them, in the symbol of the
orient sea.

In that spatial pattern in which the unity of *Dubliners* is expressed as an action, the orient goal is no one simple thing. It is a
rich complex of associated ideas and images, only outwardly a
place of places, intrinsically a vital state of being, a condition of
grace conferred and sustained, presumably, by all the means of
grace. Perhaps the main aspect of the symbolic orient, however,
is of the eastward sea, its richest and most constantly represented
image. The sea is the image most clearly opposable to that deadly
contrary of the symbolic orient in all its import of spiritual life, that
death state of moral disability, which Joyce conceived to be dominant in Ireland and centered in Dublin. The opposition is basic
and clear in *Dubliners* of the eastward sea to the westward land,
of ocean water to earth, of movement to fixation, of vital change
to passivity in the status quo, of the motion toward a new life to
the stasis of paralysis in old life ways.

Lesser symbols in *Dubliners* are understandable largely in terms
of this opposition, the symbols of water, of color, of music, of

clothing, and the various symbols of enclosure. Not even the predominant element of the sea, water itself, always implies the sea or its vital freedom. No doubt in its basic symbolic meaning water is conceivable truly enough in conventional terms as the water of life. But in *Dubliners* it is distinctly this only in a general sense, as it is also the natural water of the globe of earth and sky. For full understanding it must be viewed more exactly in terms of specific symbolism and associations. In the eastern sea, it is the water of the font and the chalice, toward which the soul is oriented. Sluggish in a canal beside which a wastrel walks with his tart, or as the ooze on the lavatory floor where a drunkard lies, at the opening of the story 'Grace', it loses virtue. At the end of 'Eveline', as the water of voyage which can carry the frightened girl from Ireland to a new life and to fulfilling love, it retains its basic meaning and values as well as those given it by its place in the symbolic complex of the sea.

The colors associated with the sea are established very emphatically in 'An Encounter' by the boy narrator's finding to his surprise that none of the foreign sailors has the green eyes that he expected; their eyes are only blue, grey, or 'even black'. Truly green eyes, 'bottle-green', appear to him only when he encounters the demonic gaze of the pervert on the bank in Ringsend near the Dodder. Thus green is dissociated from the sea and associated with degeneracy in Ireland, with crippling spiritual limitations, and with the physical limitation of enclosure in a bottle, an image suggesting water, but not the water of the open sea. The symbols of the bottle and of green are effectively combined later in the book in the symbolic complex of the bottled water on the table in 'The Dead', pure water appropriately 'white', but precisely marked with 'transverse green sashes', the cancelling strokes that declare the contents to be spiritually without virtue. Among the ten colors mentioned in description of the table, and the many more only suggested by the foods and drinks and the dishes and bottles that are described, blue and grey do not appear, black is mentioned once, and brown is markedly predominant. Brown, like green, is associated with the limitations of life in Ireland, but much more emphatically. It recurs many times in the stories. It is mentioned as the tint of Dublin streets and is found in the freckled face and in the eyes of Miss Ivors, in 'The Dead', who wears a brooch with 'an Irish device and motto' and is militantly Irish. Yellow and red, the colors of fire, are variable in meaning, being associable at one extreme with the vital orient, at another with the punishments of the pit, as at the end of 'A Painful Case'.

The symbol of music is more clearly related to the east than to the land, but it takes its meaning very largely from the context of association and symbol in which it is represented. In 'Eveline', where it is associated with far countries and the sea, an Italian air played on a street organ, the singing of a sailor about a sailor, and the quayside whistle and bell of departure on an ocean voyage, music symbolizes the motion of the soul toward life or the call of life to the soul. As the remembered singing of Michael Furey in 'The Dead', it is the call to the past life, to communion with the dead.

Since clothing is an expression of character or of personal preference, or an indication of occupation or other circumstance, its symbolic use is restricted by the requirements of naturalism, the need to conform to objective fact. Its symbolic meaning is given unequivocally only in images associated with it at the free will of the artist. The blackness of Father Flynn's clothing is less certainly symbolic than its green discoloration, but the 'suit of greenish-black' worn by the pervert in 'An Encounter' is indubitably symbolic in both its hues, since Joyce was free in his choice of both. The 'brown-clad' girl worshipped by the boy in 'Araby' is a madonna emphatically Irish. Lenehan, in 'Two Gallants', is clothed in unmistakable contradictions. His 'light waterproof' and 'white rubber shoes' express an aversion to water, as W. Y. Tindall has pointed out. It must be noted, however, that he is also wearing a yachting cap, a suggestion of inclination toward the

water of the sea. His waterproof, moreover, is 'slung over one
shoulder in toreador fashion,' suggesting the far country of Spain,
another symbol of the soul's orient. The symbolism precisely defines his position as a vagrant, a drifter in the city, neither committed to the ways of life in Dublin nor free of them. Generally
regarded as a 'leech', he seems to be a creature of the pools and
streams of the earth, not of the sea. He belongs to the dregs of the
established world.

Certain images in *Dubliners,* of closed or circumscribed areas,
such as coffin, confession-box, rooms, buildings, the city and its
suburbs, become symbolic when they are presented in any way
suggesting enclosure, as they frequently are; and by recurrence
many of them are early established as conventional symbols. In
general they express the restrictions and fixations of life in Ireland.
Except for the city itself and its suburbs, the commonest of these
symbolic images are the houses of the people of Dublin, which are
so well characterized in *Stephen Hero* as 'those brown brick
houses which seem the very incarnation of Irish paralysis'. Such is
the home, no doubt, of Little Chandler in the story 'A Little
Cloud', who supposes himself to be a prisoner simply in the external circumstances of his existence, though really he is afflicted with
the prevailing paralysis, the psychic limitation of his commitment
to the ways of a society without vitality. Like Eveline of the story
that bears her name, who leaves for a while the 'little brown
houses of her neighborhood', in one of which she lives, Chandler
cannot escape the constriction which those houses symbolize.
Surely his house too must be of symbolically brown brick, situ-
ated somewhere near those houses referred to in *Stephen Hero,*
which are in Eccles Street, in the north central part of Dublin, at
the very center of paralysis. . . .

SOURCE: *Accent: A Quarterly of New Literature,*
XVI (Summer 1956) pp. 75–88.

Frank O'Connor

JOYCE AND DISSOCIATED METAPHOR (1956)

Proust and Joyce were the heroes of my youth, but while Proust's work has continued to grow on me, Joyce's has lost its charm. The reason may be that I know too much about it. The reason for that may be that there is far too much to know. . . .

Sir Desmond MacCarthy describes in one of his essays how I first came to notice the peculiar cast of Joyce's mind. The incident concerned a picture of Cork in his hallway. I could not detect what the frame was made of. 'What is that?' I asked. 'Cork,' he replied. 'Yes,' I said, 'I know it's Cork, but what's the frame?' 'Cork,' he replied with a smile. 'I had the greatest difficulty in finding a French frame-maker who would make it.'

Whether or not this indicated, as I thought, that he was suffering from associative mania, it proved a valuable key in my efforts to understand his work.

It also proved a necessary one, for though in his years of fame Joyce had interpreters galore who propounded his work to the public even before it was completed, we have no such interpreters for the early stories and *A Portrait of the Artist as a Young Man*.

This seems to me an exceedingly difficult book. The first thing to notice is that the peculiar style used in the opening of *Two Gallants* is now a regular device. It can best be described as 'mechanical prose', for certain key words are repeated deliberately and mechanically to produce a feeling of hypnosis in the reader.

> The soft beauty of the Latin word *touched* with an enchanting
> *touch* the *dark* of the evening, with a *touch* fainter and more

persuading than the *touch* of music or of a *woman's* hand. The strife of their minds was quelled. The figure of a *woman* as she appears in the liturgy of the church *passed* silently through the *darkness:* a white-robed figure, small and slender as a boy, and with a falling girdle. Her *voice,* frail and high as a boy's, was heard intoning from a distant choir the first words of a *woman* which pierce the gloom and clamour of the first chanting of the passion :

Et tu cum Jesu Galilæo eras –

And all hearts were *touched* and turned to her *voice,* shining like a young star, shining clearer as the *voice* intoned the proparoxyton, and more faintly as the cadence died.

I have italicized a few of the principal words to show how a chain of association is built up, but the reader can see for himself that other words are similarly repeated. The whole structure of the book is probably lost unless Joyce's notebooks give some indication of what it was, but I have an impression that Joyce wrote with a list of a couple of hundred words before him, each representing some association, and that at intervals the words were dropped in, like currants in a cake and a handful at a time, so that their presence would be felt rather than identified. I suspect that a number of those words, like the spotlighted word 'touch' in the passage I have quoted, are of sensory significance, and are intended to maintain in our subconscious minds the metaphor of the Aristotelian scheme of psychology, while others, like the word 'passed', seem to have a general significance in relation to the movement of the individual through time and space. Whenever the emotion overflows, it is represented by inversion and repetition. The whole subject should be studied in a few paragraphs like the following :

He was *alone.* He was unheeded, happy and near to the *wild heart* of life. He was *alone* and young and wilful and *wildhearted, alone* amid a waste of *wild air* and blackish waters and the *sea*harvest of shells and tangle and veiled grey sunlight and gayclad, lightclad figures of *children* and *girls* and voices *childish* and *girlish* in the *air.*

A *girl* stood before him in mid*stream; alone* and *still, gazing* out to *sea.* She seemed like one whom magic had changed into the likeness of a strange and beautiful *seabird.* Her *long* slender *bare* legs were delicate as a *crane's* and pure save where an emerald trail of *sea*weed had fashioned itself as a sign upon the flesh. Her thighs, fuller and *soft*hued as ivory, were *bared* almost to the hips where the *white* fringes of her drawers were like *feathering* of *soft white down.* Her slate-blue skirts were kilted boldly about her waist and *dovetailed* behind her. Her bosom was as a *bird's, soft and slight, slight and soft,* as the breast of some dark *plumaged* dove. But her *long* fair hair was *girlish:* and *girlish* and *touched* with the wonder of mortal beauty, her face.

She was *alone and still, gazing* out to *sea:* and when she felt his presence and the worship of his *eyes,* her *eyes* turned to him in quiet *sufferance* of his *gaze,* without shame or wantonness. *Long, long* she *suffered* his *gaze* and then quietly withdrew her *eyes* from his and bent them towards the *stream.* The first *faint* noise of gently moving water broke the silence, low and *faint* and whispering, *faint* as the bells of sleep; hither and thither, hither and thither; and a *faint* flame trembled on her cheek.

I find it difficult to transcribe, let alone analyze, the passage because it seems to me insufferably self-conscious, as though Walter Pater had taken to business and commercialized his style for the use of schools and colleges, but those who admire such prose should, I feel, be compelled to consider how it is constructed. I suspect there are at least two movements in a passage of this sort, one a local movement that seems to rise and fall within the framework of the paragraph in relation to the dominant image, and which produces words like 'crane', 'feathering', 'down', 'dovetailed', and 'plumaged'; and another, over-all movement in which key words, particularly words of sensory significance like 'touch', 'eyes', and 'gazed', are repeated and varied. I fancy that these could be traced right through the book, and that the study of them would throw considerable light on Joyce's intentions.

It is important to note that this is something new in literature, and it represents the point, anticipated in Flaubert, at which style ceases to be a relationship between author and reader and becomes a relationship of a magical kind between author and object. Here *le mot juste* is no longer *juste* for the reader, but for the object. It is not an attempt at communicating the experience to the reader, who is supposed to be present only by courtesy, but at equating the prose with the experience. Indeed, one might say that it aims at replacing the experience by the prose, and the process may be considered complete when Joyce and his interpreters refer to one chapter in *Ulysses* as a canon fugue or, as they prefer to describe it in their idiomatic way, a *fuga per canonem,* which it is not and, by the nature of prose and of canon fugues, could not possibly be.

So far as I understand it, which is not very far, *A Portrait* is a study in differentiation based on Aristotle's *De Anima* and St Thomas's *Commentary.* The first page, which looks like a long passage of baby talk, is an elaborate construct that relates the development of the senses to the development of the arts, a device later used in *Ulysses,* when we find the transmigration of souls discussed over an underlying metaphor of the transmutation of matter. 'Once upon a time,' the words with which the book opens, represent story-telling, the primary form of art. This whole passage is a fascinating piece of exposition. The first external person identified by the child is his father, whom he identifies first by sight, then by touch. Himself he identifies with a character in the story his father tells him, and from the abstract 'road' of the bedtime story constructs a real road containing a real character whom he identifies by the sense of taste – 'she sold lemon platt'. He learns a song, the second of the arts, which contains the key words 'rose' and 'green', and he unconsciously identifies these with 'hot' and 'cold'. When, instead 'O, the wild rose blosssoms in the little green place', he remembers 'O the green wothe botheth', we know that he has wet the bed because he has linked the symbols for hot and cold. From this episode the unconscious images become conscious, and the sense of touch, the primary sense, according to Aristotle, is clearly differentiated. 'When you wet the bed first it is warm then it gets cold.' The metaphor is carried through into the divided politics of the home, for 'Dante had two brushes in her press. The brush with the maroon velvet back was for Michael Davitt and the brush with the green velvet gack was for Parnell.'

As the first chapter develops, we find the boy at school with a high temperature that causes him to feel hot and cold by turn. This is illustrated in the prose by alternations of metaphor. The boy remembers washing his hands in the Wicklow Hotel where there were two taps, hot and cold. At school his class is divided into two groups, York and Lancaster, red and white. When he goes to bed, we know he is shivering violently because he is thinking of ghost stories, of black dogs and white cloaks, of old people and of strange people. We know the bed is warming up when he begins to think of the holidays, of warm colors and familiar faces. Eventually, when delirium overtakes him, the civil war between Davitt and Parnell is also used as a metaphor. The little drama is played out against a background of other antitheses: big, small; nasty, nice; damp, dry. There are not mental or moral antitheses because the boy knows of 'right' and 'wrong' only in terms of answers to schoolbook questions. He cannot think. As he can only feel, the only quality that can be attributed to him is 'heart', the organ to which Aristotle ascribes sensation, and so we get, casually tossed in, the phrase 'He was sick in his heart if you could be sick in that place.'

In the next section we get a repetition of the words 'good' and 'bad', 'right' and 'wrong', which still have no true meaning for the boy because mind has not yet been born in him. Mind emerges only when he has been unjustly punished, and once more Joyce tosses the casual reference in – 'before he could make up his mind,' to indicate that the miracle of differentiation has taken place. The soul, though born in all women with menstruation, is born in males only with mortal sin, so that it is scarcely mentioned until the boy has been with a prostitute. Then it overflows the pages. The differentiation is marked also in the literary forms. Its æsthetic is propounded to Lynch in the final pages of the book.

> Art necessarily divides itself into three forms progressing from one to the next. These forms are : the lyrical form, the form wherein the artist presents his image in immediate relation to himself : the epical form, the form wherein he presents his image in mediate relation to himself and to others : the dramatic form, the form wherein he presents his image in immediate relation to others.

This progress is also used as part of the metaphorical structure of the book to illustrate the differentiation taking place in Stephen's character. It begins with lyrical forms; when he goes to college, it turns into epic; and, finally, when he makes up his mind to leave home (action), it becomes dramatic – the diary form. 'The lyrical form,' says Stephen, 'is in fact the simplest verbal vesture of an instant of emotion, a rhythmical cry such as ages ago cheered on the man who pulled at the oar or dragged stone up a slope.' Accordingly, each of the early sections represents an 'instant of emotion' and ends with a cry, though the cries seem to be differentiated according to the stage of self-consciousness which the individual has reached. Thus, the first cry, 'Parnell! Parnell! He is dead', though supposed to come from a crowd of imaginary figures on a shore, is the impersonal, unindividualized cry of the sick child in a state of delirium, attributing his own suffering to dream figures. In the next section, when Mr Casey cries : 'Poor Parnell! My dead king!' the cry, though impersonal, is individualized and is followed by tears, though the tears are not Stephen's own. It is not until he himself has been punished unjustly that he gives a scream of pain and his tears flow. Again he cries when he goes to the prostitute, but this time with lust, and his tears are tears of relief. He cries once more when terrified by the thought of his sins, and his tears are tears of repentance.

Finally, in the scene with the bird-girl, he cries again, but there are no tears, for the artistic emotion is not kinetic.

In reading Joyce, one is reading Literature – Literature with a capital L. The tide rises about the little figures islanded here and there in a waste of waters, and gradually they disappear till nothing is left but the blank expanse of Literature, mirroring the blank face of the sky.

SOURCE: *The Mirror in the Roadway* (1956) pp. 295, 301–8.

Hugh Kenner

THE *PORTRAIT* IN PERSPECTIVE
(1955)

LINKING THEMES

In the reconceived *Portrait* Joyce abandoned the original intention of writing the account of his own escape from Dublin. One cannot escape one's Dublin. He recast Stephen Dedalus as a figure who could not even detach himself from Dublin because he had formed himself on a denial of Dublin's values. He is the egocentric rebel become an ultimate. There is no question whatever of his regeneration. 'Stephen no longer interests me to the same extent [as Bloom],' said Joyce to Frank Budgen one day. 'He has a shape that can't be changed.'[1] His shape is that of aesthete. The Stephen of the first chapter of *Ulysses* who 'walks wearily', constantly 'leans' on everything in sight, invariably sits down before he has gone three paces, speaks 'gloomily', 'quietly', 'with bitterness', and 'coldly', and 'suffers' his handkerchief to be pulled from his pocket by the exuberant Mulligan, is precisely the priggish, humourless Stephen of the last chapter of the *Portrait* who cannot remember what day of the week it is, P206/201,[2] sentimentalizes like Charles Lamb over the 'human pages' of a second-hand Latin book, P209/204, conducts the inhumanly pedantic diaglogue with Cranly on mother-love, P281/271, writes Frenchified verses in bed in an erotic swoon, and is epiphanized at full length, like Shem the Penman beneath the bedclothes, F176, shrinking from the 'common noises' of daylight :

> Shrinking from that life he turned towards the wall, making a cowl [!] of the blanket and staring at the great overblown

scarlet flowers of the tattered wall-paper. He tried to warm his
perishing joy in their scarlet glow, imaging a roseway from
where he lay upwards to heaven all strewn with scarlet flowers.
Weary! Weary! He too was weary of ardent ways. P260/252.

This new primrose path is a private Jacob's ladder let down to
his bed now that he is too weary to do anything but go to heaven.

To make epic and drama emerge naturally from the intrinsic
stresses and distortions of the lyric material meant completely new
lyric techniques for a constation exact beyond irony. The *Portrait*
concentrates on stating themes, arranging apparently transparent
words into configurations of the utmost symbolic density. Here is
the director proposing that Stephen enter the priesthood :

> The director stood in the embrasure of the window, his back
> to the light, leaning an elbow on the brown crossblind, and, as he
> spoke and smiled, slowly dangling and looping the cord of the
> other blind, Stephen stood before him, following for a moment
> with his eyes the waning of the long summer daylight above the
> roofs or the slow deft movements of the priestly fingers. The
> priest's face was in total shadow, but the waning daylight from
> behind him touched the deeply grooved temples and the curves
> of the skull. P178/175.

The looped cord, the shadow, the skull, none of these is accidental.
The 'waning daylight', twice emphasized, conveys that denial of
nature which the priest's office represented for Stephen; 'his back
to the light' co-operates toward a similar effect. So 'crossblind' :
'blind to the cross',[3] 'blinded by the cross'. 'The curves of the skull'
introduces another death-image; the 'deathbone' from Lévy-
Bruhl's Australia, pointed by Shaun in *Finnegans Wake,* F193,
is the dramatic version of an identical symbol. But the central
image, the epiphany of the interview, is contained in the movement of the priest's fingers : 'slowly dangling and looping the
cord of the other blind'. That is to say, coolly proffering a noose.
This is the lyric mode of *Ulysses'* epical hangman, 'The lord of

things as they are whom the most Roman of Catholics call *dio
boia,* hangman god', U210/201.

THE CONTRAPUNTAL OPENING

According to the practice inaugurated by Joyce when he rewrote
'The Sisters' in 1906, the *Portrait,* like the two books to follow,
opens amid elaborate counterpoint. The first two pages, terminat-
ing in a row of asterisks, enact the entire action in microcosm. An
Aristotelian catalogue of senses, faculties, and mental activities is
played against the unfolding of the infant conscience.

> Once upon a time and a very good time it was there was a
> moocow coming down along the road and this moocow that was
> down along the road met a nicens little boy named baby
> tuckoo. . . .
> His father told him that story : his father looked at him
> through a glass : he had a hairy face.
> He was baby tuckoo. The moocow came down along the road
> where Betty Byrne lived : she sold lemon platt.

> *O, the wild rose blossoms
> On the little green place.*

He sang that song. That was his song.

> *O, the green wothe botheth.*

> When you wet the bed, first it is warm then it gets cold. His
> mother put on the oilsheet. That had the queer smell.

This evocation of holes in oblivion is conducted in the mode of
each of the five senses in turn; hearing (the story of the moocow),
sight (his father's face), taste (lemon platt), touch (warm and
cold), smell (the oil-sheet). The audible soothes : the visible dis-
turbs. Throughout Joyce's work, the senses are symbolically disposed. Smell is the means of discriminating empirical realities

('His mother had a nicer smell than his father', is the next sentence), sight corresponds to the phantasms of oppression, hearing to the imaginative life. Touch and taste together are the modes of sex. Hearing, here, comes first, via a piece of imaginative literature. But as we can see from the vantage-point of *Finnegans Wake,* the whole book is about the encounter of baby tuckoo with the moocow : the Gripes with the mookse.[4] The father with the hairy face is the first Mookse-avatar, the Freudian infantile analogue of God the Father.

In the *Wake*

> Derzherr, live wire, fired Benjermine Funkling outa th'Empyre, sin right hand son.   F289.

Der Erzherr (arch-lord), here a Teutonic Junker, is the God who visited his wrath on Lucifer; the hairy attribute comes through via the music-hall refrain, 'There's hair, like wire, coming out of the Empire'.

Dawning consciousness of his own identity ('He was baby tuckoo') leads to artistic performance ('He sang that song. That was his song.') This is hugely expanded in chapter IV :

> Now, as never before, his strange name seemed to him a prophecy . . . of the end he had been born to serve and had been following through the mists of childhood and boyhood, a symbol of the artist forging anew in his workshop out of the sluggish matter of the earth a new soaring impalpable imperishable being.   P196/192.

By changing the red rose to a green and dislocating the spelling, he makes the song his own ('But you could not have a green rose. But perhaps somewhere in the world you could.' P8/13)

> His mother had a nicer smell than his father. She played on the piano the sailor's hornpipe for him to dance. He danced :
>
> > *Tralala lala,*
> > *Tralala tralaladdy,*

Tralala lala,
Tralala lala.

Between this innocence and its Rimbaudian recapture through
the purgation of the *Wake* there is to intervene the hallucination
in Circe's sty :

THE MOTHER
(*With the subtle smile of death's madness.*) I was once the
beautiful May Goulding. I am dead. . . .

STEPHEN
(*Eagerly.*) Tell me the word, mother, if you know it now. The
word known to all men. . . .

THE MOTHER
(*With smouldering eyes.*) Repent ! O, the fire of hell ! U565/
547.

This is foreshadowed as the overture to the *Portrait* closes :

He hid under the table. His mother said :
– O, Stephen will apologise.
Dante said :
– O, if not, the eagles will come and pull out his eyes. –
      Pull out his eyes,
      Apologise,
      Apologise,
      Pull out his eyes.

      Apologise,
      Pull out his eyes,
      Pull out his eyes,
      Apologise.

The eagles, eagles of Rome, are emissaries of the God with the
hairy face : the punisher. They evoke Prometheus and gnawing
guilt : again-bite. So the overture ends with Stephen hiding under
the table awaiting the eagles. He is hiding under something most
of the time : bedclothes, 'the enigma of a manner', an indurated
rhetoric, or some other carapace of his private world.

THEME WORDS

It is through their names that things have power over Stephen.

> – The language in which we are speaking is his before it is
> mine. How different are the words *home, Christ, ale, master,* on
> his lips and on mine! I cannot speak or write these words with-
> out unrest of spirit. His language, so familiar and so foreign,
> will always be for me an acquired speech. I have not made or
> accepted its words. My voice holds them at bay. My soul frets
> in the shadow of his language.   P221/215.

Not only is the Dean's English a conqueror's tongue; since the
loss of Adam's words which perfectly mirrored things, all language
has conquered the mind and imposed its own order, askew from
the order of creation. Words, like the physical world, are imposed
on Stephen from without, and it is in their canted mirrors that he
glimpses a physical and moral world already dyed the colour
of his own mind since absorbed, with language, into his personality.

> Words which he did not understand he said over and over
> to himself till he had learnt them by heart; and through them
> he had glimpses of the real world about him.   P68/70.

Language is a Trojan horse by which the universe gets into the
mind. The first sentence in the book isn't something Stephen sees
but a story he is told, and the overture climaxes in an insistent
brainless rhyme, its jingle corrosively fascinating to the will. It
has power to terrify a child who knows nothing of eagles, or of
Prometheus, or of how his own grown-up failure to apologise will
blend with gathering blindness.

It typifies the peculiar achievement of the *Portrait* that Joyce
can cause patterns of words to make up the very moral texture of
Stephen's mind :

> Suck was a queer word. The fellow called Simon Moonan
> that name because Simon Moonan used to tie the prefect's false

E

sleeves behind his back and the prefect used to let on to be
angry. But the sound was ugly. Once he had washed his hands
in the lavatory of the Wicklow hotel and his father pulled the
stopper up by the chain after and the dirty water went down
through the hole in the basin. And when it had all gone down
slowly the hole in the basin had made a sound like that : suck.
Only louder.

To remember that and the white look of the lavatory made
him feel cold and then hot. There were two cocks that you turned
and the water came out : cold and hot. He felt cold and then
a little hot : and he could see the names printed on the cocks.
That was a very queer thing.   P6/12.

'Suck' joins two contexts in Stephen's mind : a playful sinner
toying with his indulgent superior, and the disappearance of dirty
water. The force of the conjunction is felt only after Stephen has
lost his sense of the reality of the forgiveness of sins in the confessional. The habitually orthodox penitent tangles with a God
who pretends to be angry; after a reconciliation the process is
repeated. And the mark of that kind of play is disgraceful servility.
Each time the sin disappears, the sinner is mocked by an impersonal voice out of nature : 'Suck !'

This attitude to unreal good and evil furnishes a context for the
next conjunction : whiteness and coldness. Stephen finds himself,
like Simon Moonan,[5] engaged in the rhythm of obedience to
irrational authority, bending his mind to a meaningless act, the
arithmetic contest. He is being obediently 'good'. And the appropriate colour is adduced : 'He thought his face must be white
because it felt so cool.'

The pallor of lunar obedient goodness is next associated with
damp repulsiveness : the limpness of a wet blanket and of a
servant's apron :

> He sat looking at the two prints of butter on his plate but
> could not eat the damp bread. The table-cloth was damp and
> limp. But he drank off the hot weak tea which the clumsy
> scullion, girt with a white apron, poured into his cup. He

wondered whether the scullion's apron was damp too or whether
all white things were cold and damp. P8/13.

Throughout the first chapter an intrinsic linkage, white-cold-
damp-obedient, insinuates itself repeatedly. Stephen after saying
his prayers, 'his shoulders shaking', 'so that he might not go to hell
when he died', 'curled himself together under the cold white
sheets, shaking and trembling. But he would not go to hell when
he died, and the shaking would stop.' P16/20. The sea, mysterious
as the terrible power of God, 'was cold day and night, but it was
colder at night', P14/19; we are reminded of Anna Livia's gesture
of submission : 'my cold father, my cold mad father, my cold
mad feary father', F628. 'There was a cold night smell in the
chapel. But it was a holy smell', P14/19. Stephen is puzzled by the
phrase in the Litany of the Blessed Virgin : Tower of Ivory.
'How could a woman be a tower of ivory or a house of gold?' He
ponders until the revelation comes :

> Eileen had long white hands. One evening when playing tig
> she had put her hands over his eyes : long and white and thin
> and cold and soft. That was ivory : a cold white thing. That was
> the meaning of *Tower of Ivory.* P36/40.

This instant of insight depends on a sudden reshuffling of associations, a sudden conviction that the Mother of God, and the
symbols appropriate to her, belong with the cold, the white, and
the unpleasant in a blindfold morality of obedience. Contemplation focussed on language is repaid :

> *Tower of Ivory, House of Gold.* By thinking of things you
> could understand them. P45/48.

The white-damp-obedient association reappears when Stephen
is about to make his confession after the celebrated retreat; its
patterns provide the language in which he thinks. Sin has been

associated with fire, while the prayers of the penitents are epiphanized as 'soft whispering cloudlets, soft whispering vapour, whispering and vanishing'. P164/163. And having been absolved :

> White pudding and eggs and sausages and cups of tea. How
> simple and beautiful was life after all! And life lay all before
> him. . . .
>   The boys were all there, kneeling in their places. He knelt
> among them, happy and shy. The altar was heaped with fragrant
> masses of white flowers : and in the morning light the pale flames
> of the candles among the white flowers were clear and silent as
> his own soul. P168/166.

We cannot read *Finnegans Wake* until we have realized the significance of the way the mind of Stephen Dedalus is bound in by
language. He is not only an artist : he is a Dubliner.

THE PORTRAIT AS LYRIC

The 'instant of emotion', P251/244, of which this 300-page lyric
is the 'simplest verbal vesture' is the exalted instant, emerging at
the end of the book, of freedom, of vocation, of Stephen's destiny,
winging his way above the waters at the side of the hawklike man :
the instant of promise on which the crushing ironies of *Ulysses*
are to fall. The epic of the sea of matter is preceded by the lyric
image of a growing dream : a dream that like Richard Rowan's
in *Exiles* disregards the fall of man; a dream nourished by a sensitive youth of flying above the sea into an uncreated heaven :

> The spell of arms and voices : the white arms or roads, their
> promise of close embraces and the black arms of tall ships that
> stand against the moon, their tale of distant nations. They are
> held out to say : We are alone – come. And the voices say with
> them : We are your kinsmen. And the air is thick with their
> company as they call to me, their kinsman, making ready to go,

shaking the wings of their exultant and terrible youth.   P298/
288.

The emotional quality of this is continuous with that of the *Count
of Monte Cristo,* that fantasy of the exile returned for vengeance
(the plot of the *Odyssey*) which kindled so many of Stephen's
boyhood dreams :

> The figure of that dark avenger stood forth in his mind for
> whatever he had heard or divined in childhood of the strange
> and terrible. At night he built up on the parlour table an image
> of the wonderful island cave out of transfers and paper flowers
> and strips of the silver and golden paper in which chocolate
> is wrapped. When he had broken up this scenery, weary of its
> tinsel, there would come to his mind the bright picture of Mar-
> seilles, of sunny trellises and of Mercedes.   P68/70.

The prose surrounding Stephen's flight is empurpled with trans-
fers and paper flowers too. It is not immature prose, as we might
suppose by comparison with *Ulysses.* The prose of 'The Dead'
is mature prose, and 'The Dead' was written in 1908. Rather, it
is a meticulous pastiche of immaturity. Joyce has his eye constantly on the epic sequel.

> He wanted to meet in the real world the unsubstantial image
> which his soul so constantly beheld. He did not know where to
> seek it or how, but a premonition which led him on told him
> that this image would, without any overt act of his, encounter
> him. They would meet quietly as if they had known each other
> and had made their tryst, perhaps at one of the gates or in some
> more secret place. They would be alone, surrounded by dark-
> ness and silence : and in that moment of supreme tenderness he
> would be transfigured.   P71/73.

As the vaginal imagery of gates, secret places, and darkness implies, this is the dream that reaches temporary fulfilment in the
plunge into profane love, P113/114. But the ultimate 'secret

place' is to be Mabbot Street, outside Bella Cohen's brothel; the unsubstantial image of his quest, that of Leopold Bloom, advertisement canvasser – Monte Cristo, returned avenger, Ulysses; and the transfiguration, into the phantasmal dead son of a sentimental Jew :

> *Against the dark wall a figure appears slowly, a fairy boy of eleven, a changeling, kidnapped, dressed in an Eton suit with glass shoes and a little bronze helmet, holding a book in his hand. He reads from right to left inaudibly, smiling, kissing the page.* U593/574.

That Dedalus the artificer did violence to nature is the point of the epigraph from Ovid, *Et ignotas animum dimittit in artes;* the Icarian fall is inevitable.

> In tedious exile now too long detain'd
> Dedalus languish'd for his native land.
> The sea foreclos'd his flight; yet thus he said,
> Though earth and water in subjection laid,
> O cruel Minos, thy dominion be,
> We'll go through air; for sure the air is free.
> *Then to new arts his cunning thought applies,*
> *And to improve the work of nature tries.*

Stephen does not, as the careless reader may suppose, become an artist by rejecting church and country. Stephen does not become an artist at all. Country, church, and mission are an inextricable unity, and in rejecting the two that seem to hamper him, he rejects also the one on which he has set his heart. Improving the work of nature is his obvious ambition ('But you could not have a green rose. But perhaps somewhere in the world you could'), and it logically follows from the aesthetic he expounds to Lynch. It is a neo-platonic aesthetic; the crucial principle of epiphanization has been withdrawn. He imagines that 'the loveliness that has not yet come into the world', P297/286, is to be found in his own soul. The earth is gross, and what it brings forth is cowdung; sound and shape and colour are 'the prison gates of our soul'; and beauty is something mysteriously gestated within. The genuine artist reads signatures, the fake artist forges them, a process adumbrated in the obsession of Shem the Penman (from *Jim the Penman,* a forgotten drama about a forger) with 'Macfearsome's Ossean', the most famous of literary forgeries, studying 'how cutely to copy all their various styles of signature so as one day to utter an epical forged cheque on the public for his own private profit'. F181.

One can sense all this in the first four chapters of the *Portrait,* and *Ulysses* is unequivocal :

> Fabulous artificer, the hawklike man. You flew. Whereto? Newhaven-Dieppe, steerage passenger. Paris and back.   U208/ 199.

The Stephen of the end of the fourth chapter, however, is still unstable; he had to be brought into a final balance, and shown at some length as a being whose development was virtually ended. Unfortunately, the last chapter makes the book a peculiarly difficult one for the reader to focus, because Joyce had to close it on a suspended chord. As a lyric, it is finished in its own terms; but the themes of the last forty pages, though they give the illusion of focusing, don't really focus until we have read well into *Ulysses.* The final chapter, which in respect to the juggernaut of *Ulysses* must be a vulnerable flank, in respect to what has gone before must be a conclusion. This problem Joyce didn't wholly solve; there remains a moral ambiguity (how seriously are we to take Stephen?) which makes the last forty pages painful reading.

Not that Stephen would stand indefinitely if *Ulysses* didn't topple him over; his equilibrium in chapter v, though good enough to give him a sense of unusual integrity in University College, is precarious unless he can manage, in the manner of so many permanent undergraduates, to prolong the college context for the rest of his life. Each of the preceding chapters, in fact, works toward an equilibrium which is dashed when in the next chapter Stephen's world becomes larger and the frame of reference more complex. The terms of equilibrium are always stated with disquieting accuracy; at the end of chapter i we find

> He was alone. He was happy and free : but he would not be any- way proud with Father Dolan. He would be very quiet and obedient : and he wished that he could do something kind for him to show him that he was not proud.   P64/66.

And at the end of chapter iii :

> He sat by the fire in the kitchen, not daring to speak for happiness. Till that moment he had not known how beautiful and peaceful life could be. The green square of paper pinned round the lamp cast down a tender shade. On the dresser was a plate of sausages and white pudding and on the shelf there were eggs. They would be for the breakfast in the morning after the communion in the college chapel. White pudding and eggs and sausages and cups of tea. How simple and beautiful was life after all! And life lay all before him.   P168/166.

Not 'irony' but simply the truth : the good life conceived in terms of white pudding and sausages is unstable enough to need no underlining.

The even-numbered chapters make a sequence of a different sort. The ending of iv, Stephen's panting submission to an artistic vocation :

> Evening had fallen when he woke and the sand and arid grasses of his bed glowed no longer. He rose slowly and, recal- ling the rapture of his sleep, sighed at its joy. . . .   P201/197.

– hasn't quite the finality often read into it when the explicit parallel with the ending of ii is perceived :

> . . . He closed his eyes, surrendering himself to her, body and mind, conscious of nothing in the world but the dark pressure

of her softly parting lips. They pressed upon his brain as upon
his lips as though they were the vehicle of a vague speech; and
between them he felt an unknown and timid pressure, darker
than the swoon of sin, softer than sound or odour.   P114/115.

When we link these passages with the fact that the one piece of
literary composition Stephen actually achieves in the book comes
out of a wet dream ('Towards dawn he awoke. O what sweet
music! His soul was all dewy wet', P254) we are in a position to
see that the concluding 'Welcome, O life!' has an air of finality
and balance only because the diary-form of the last seven pages
disarms us with an illusion of auctorial impartiality.

CONTROLLING IMAGES: CLONGOWES
AND BELVEDERE

Ego *vs.* authority is the theme of the three odd-numbered chapters, Dublin *vs.* the dream that of the two even-numbered ones.
The generic Joyce plot, the encounter with the alter ego, is consummated when Stephen at the end of the book identifies himself
with the sanctified Stephen who was stoned by the Jews after
reporting a vision (Acts 7:56) and claims sonship with the classical Daedalus who evaded the ruler of land and sea by turning his
soul to obscure arts. The episodes are built about adumbrations
of this encounter : with Father Conmee, with Monte Cristo, with
the whores, with the broad-shouldered moustached student who
cut the word 'Foetus' in a desk, with the weary mild confessor, with
the bird-girl. Through this repeated plot intertwine controlling
emotions and controlling images that mount in complexity as
the book proceeds.

In chapter 1 the controlling emotion is fear, and the dominant
image Father Dolan and his pandybat; this, associated with the
hangman–god and the priestly denial of the senses, was to become
one of Joyce's standard images for Irish clericalism – hence the

jack-in-the-box appearance of Father Dolan in Circe's nightmare imbroglio, his pandybat cracking twice like thunder, U547/531. Stephen's comment, in the mode of Blake's repudiation of the God who slaughtered Jesus, emphasizes the inclusiveness of the image : 'I never could read His handwriting except His criminal thumbprint on the haddock.'

Chapter II opens with a triple image of Dublin's prepossessions : music, sport, religion. The first is exhibited via Uncle Charles singing sentimental ballads in the outhouse; the second via Stephen's ritual run around the park under the eye of a super-annuated trainer, which his uncle enjoins on him as the whole duty of a Dubliner; the third via the clumsy piety of Uncle Charles, kneeling on a red handkerchief and reading above his breath 'from a thumb-blackened prayerbook wherein catchwords were printed at the foot of every page'. P67/69. This trinity of themes is unwound and entwined throughout the chapter, like a net woven round Stephen; it underlies the central incident, the Whitsuntide play in the Belvedere chapel (religion), which opens with a display by the dumb-bell team (sport) precluded by sentimental waltzes from the soldier's band (music).

While he is waiting to play his part, Stephen is taunted by fellow-students, who rally him on a fancied love-affair and smiting his calf with a cane bid him recite the *Confiteor*. His mind goes back to an analogous incident, when a similar punishment had been visited on his refusal to 'admit that Byron was no good'. The further analogy with Father Dolan is obvious; love, art, and personal independence are thus united in an ideogram of the prepossessions Stephen is determined to cultivate in the teeth of persecution.

The dream-world Stephen nourishes within himself is played against manifestations of music, sport, and religion throughout the chapter. The constant ironic clash of Dublin *vs.* the Dream animates chapter II, as the clash of the ego *vs.* authority did chapter I. All these themes come to focus during Stephen's visit

with his father to Cork. The dream of rebellion he has silently
cultivated is externalized by the discovery of the word *Foetus*
carved in a desk by a forgotten medical student :

> It shocked him to find in the outer world a trace of what he
> had deemed till then a brutish and individual malady of his
> own mind. His monstrous reveries came thronging into his
> memory. They too had sprung up before him, suddenly and
> furiously, out of mere words. . . .   P101/102.

The possibility of shame gaining the upper hand is dashed,
however, by the sudden banal intrusion of his father's conversation ('When you kick out for yourself, Stephen, as I daresay you
will one of these days, remember, whatever you do, to mix with
gentlemen . . .'). Against the standards of Dublin his monstrous
reveries acquire a Satanic glamour, and the trauma is slowly
diverted into a resolution to rebel. After his father has expressed
a resolve to 'leave him to his Maker' (religion), and offered to
'sing a tenor song against him' (music) or 'vault a fivebarred gate
against him' (sport), Stephen muses, watching his father and two
cronies drinking to the memory of their past :

> An abyss of fortune or of temperament sundered him from
> them. His mind seemed older than theirs : it shone coldly on
> their strifes and happiness and regrets like a moon upon a
> younger earth. No life or youth stirred in him as it had stirred
> in them. He had known neither the pleasure of companion-
> ship with others nor the vigour of rude male health nor filial
> piety. Nothing stirred within his soul but a cold and cruel and
> loveless lust.   P107/108.

After one final effort to compromise with Dublin on Dublin's
terms has collapsed into futility ('The pot of pink enamel paint
gave out and the wainscot of his bedroom remained with its un-
finished and illplastered coat', P110/111), he fiercely cultivates
his rebellious thoughts, and moving by day and night 'among

distorted images of the outer world', P111/112, plunges at last
into the arms of whores. 'The holy encounter he had then imagined
at which weakness and timidity and inexperience were to fall from
him', P112/113, finally arrives in inversion of Father Dolan's and
Uncle Charles' religion : his descent into night-town is accompanied by lurid evocations of a Black Mass (Cf. *Ulysses, 583/
565*) :

> The yellow gasflames arose before his troubled vision against
> the vapoury sky, burning as if before an altar. Before the doors
> and in the lighted halls groups were gathered arrayed as for
> some rite. He was in another world : he had awakened from
> a slumber of centuries. P113/114.

CONTROLLING IMAGES: SIN AND REPENTANCE

Each chapter in the *Portrait* gathers up the thematic material of
the preceding ones and entwines them with a dominant theme
of its own. In chapter III the fear-pandybat motif is present in
Father Arnall's crudely materialistic hell, of which even the thickness of the walls is specified; and the Dublin-*vs.*-dream motif
has ironic inflections in Stephen's terror-stricken broodings, when
the dream has been twisted into a dream of holiness, and even
Dublin appears transfigured :

> How beautiful must be a soul in the state of grace when God
> looked upon it with love!
> Frowsy girls sat along the curbstones before their baskets.
> Their dank hair trailed over their brows. They were not beauti-
> ful to see as they crouched in the mire. But their souls were seen
> by God; and if their souls were in a state of grace they were
> radiant to see; and God loved them, seeing them. P162/160.

A *rapprochement* in these terms between the outer world and
Stephen's desires is too inadequate to need commentary; and it
makes vivid as nothing else could the hopeless inversion of his

attempted self-sufficiency. It underlines, in yet another way, his persistent sin : and the dominant theme of chapter III is Sin. A fugue-like opening plays upon the Seven Deadly Sins in turn; gluttony is in the first paragraph ('Stuff it into you, his belly counselled him'), followed by lust, then sloth ('A cold lucid indifference reigned in his soul'), pride ('His pride in his own sin, his loveless awe of God, told him that his offence was too grievous to be atoned for'), anger ('The blundering answer stirred the embers of his contempt for his fellows'); finally, a recapitulation fixes each term of the mortal catalogue in a phrase, enumerating how 'from the evil seed of lust all the other deadly sins had sprung forth', P120/120.

Priest and punisher inhabit Stephen himself as well as Dublin : when he is deepest in sin he is most thoroughly a theologian. A paragraph of gloomy introspection is juxtaposed with a list of theological questions that puzzle Stephen's mind as he awaits the preacher :

> . . . Is baptism with mineral water valid? How comes it that while the first beatitude promises the kingdom of heaven to the poor of heart, the second beatitude promises also to the meek that they shall possess the land? . . . If the wine changes into vinegar and the host crumble into corruption after they have been conscrated, is Jesus Christ still present under their species as God and as man?
> — Here he is! Here he is!
> A boy from his post at the window had seen the rector come from the house. All the catechisms were opened and all heads bent upon them silently.   P120/120.

Wine changed into vinegar and the host crumbled into corruption fits exactly the Irish clergy of 'a church which was the scullery-maid of Christendom'. The excited 'Here he is! Here he is!' following hard on the mention of Jesus Christ and signalling nothing more portentous than the rector makes the point as dramatically as anything in the book, and the clinching sentence,

with the students suddenly bending over their catechisms, places
the rector as a vehicle of pandybat morality.

The last of the theological questions is the telling question.
Stephen never expresses doubt of the existence of God nor of the
essential validity of the priestly office – his *Non serviam* is not a
non credo, and he talks of a 'malevolent reality' behind these
appearances P287/277 – but the wine and bread that were offered
for his veneration were changed into vinegar and crumbled into
corruption. And it was the knowledge of that underlying validity
clashing with his refusal to do homage to vinegar and rot that
evoked his ambivalent poise of egocentric despair. The hell of
Father Arnall's sermon, so emotionally overwhelming, so picayune
beside the horrors that Stephen's imagination can generate, had
no more ontological content for Stephen than had 'an eternity
of bliss in the company of the dean of studies', P282/273.

The conflict of this central chapter is again between the phantasmal and the real. What is real – psychologically real, because
realized – is Stephen's anguish and remorse, and its context in
the life of the flesh. What is phantasmal is the 'heaven' of the
Church and the 'good life' of the priest. It is only fear that makes
him clutch after the latter at all; his reaching out after orthodox
salvation is, as we have come to expect, presented in terms that
judge it :

> The wind blew over him and passed on to the myriads and
> myriads of other souls, on whom God's favour shone now more
> and now less, stars now brighter and now dimmer, sustained
> and failing. And the glimmering souls passed away, sustained
> and failing, merged in a moving breath. One soul was lost; a
> tiny soul; his. It flickered once and went out, forgotten, lost.
> The end : black cold void waste.
> Consciousness of place came ebbing back to him slowly over
> a vast tract of time unlit, unfelt, unlived. The squalid scene
> composed itself around him; the common accents, the burning
> gasjets in the shops, odours of fish and spirits and wet sawdust,
> moving men and women. An old woman was about to cross the

street, an oilcan in her hand. He bent down and asked her was
there a chapel near. P162/160.

That wan waste world of flickering stars is the best Stephen has
been able to do towards an imaginative grasp of the communion
of Saints sustained by God; 'unlit, unfelt, unlived' explains suc-
cinctly why it had so little hold on him, once fear had relaxed.
Equally pertinent is the vision of human temporal occupations
the sermon evokes :

> What did it profit a man to gain the whole world if he lost his
> soul? At last he had understood : and human life lay around
> him, a plain of peace whereon antlike men laboured in brother-
> hood, their dead sleeping under quiet mounds. P144/143.

To maintain the life of grace in the midst of nature, sustained
by so cramped a vision of the life of nature, would mean maintaining an intolerable tension. Stephen's unrelenting philosophic
bias, his determination to understand what he is about, precludes
his adopting the double standard of the Dubliners; to live both
the life of nature and the life of grace he must enjoy an imaginative grasp of their relationship which stunts neither. 'No one doth
well against his will,' writes Saint Augustine, 'even though what
he doth, be well;' and Stephen's will is firmly harnessed to his
understanding. And there is no one in Dublin to help him achieve
understanding. Father Arnall's sermon precludes rather than
secures a desirable outcome, for it follows the modes of pandybat
morality and Dublin materiality. Its only possible effect on
Stephen is to lash his dormant conscience into a frenzy. The
description of Hell as 'a strait and dark and foul smelling prison,
an abode of demons and lost souls, filled with fire and smoke',
with walls four thousand miles thick, its damned packed in so
tightly that 'they are not even able to remove from the eye the
worm that gnaws it', is childishly grotesque beneath its sweeping
eloquence; and the hair-splitting catalogues of pains – pain of

loss, pain of conscience (divided into three heads), pain of extension, pain of intensity, pain of eternity – is cast in a brainlessly
analytic mode that effectively prevents any corresponding Heaven
from possessing any reality at all.

Stephen's unstable pact with the Church, and its dissolution,
follows the pattern of composition and dissipation established by
his other dreams : the dream for example of the tryst with 'Mercedes', which found ironic reality among harlots. It parallels
exactly his earlier attempt to 'build a breakwater of order and
elegance against the sordid tide of life without him', P110/111,
whose failure, with the exhaustion of his money, was epiphanized
in the running-dry of a pot of pink enamel paint. His regimen
at that time :

> He bought presents for everyone, overhauled his rooms, wrote
> out resolutions, marshalled his books up and down their shelves,
> pored over all kinds of price lists. . . .

is mirrored by his searching after spiritual improvement :

> His daily life was laid out in devotional areas. By means of
> ejaculations and prayers he stored up ungrudgingly for the souls
> in purgatory centuries of days and quarantines and years. . . .
> He offered up each of his three daily chaplets that his soul
> might grow strong in each of the three theological virtues. . . .
> On each of the seven days of the week he further prayed that
> one of the seven gifts of the Holy Ghost might descend upon his
> soul. P170/167.

The 'loan bank' he had opened for the family, out of which he had
pressed loans on willing borrowers 'that he might have the pleasure
of making out receipts and reckoning the interests on sums lent'
finds its counterpart in the benefits he stored up for souls in purga-
tory that he might enjoy the spiritual triumph of 'achieving with
ease so many fabulous ages of canonical penances'. Both projects
are parodies on the doctrine of economy of grace; both are

attempts, corrupted by motivating self-interest, to make peace with Dublin on Dublin's own terms; and both are short-lived.

As this precise analogical structure suggests, the action of each of the five chapters is really the same action. Each chapter closes with a synthesis of triumph which the next destroys. The triumph of the appeal to Father Conmee from lower authority, of the appeal to the harlots from Dublin, of the appeal to the Church from sin, of the appeal to art from the priesthood (the bird-girl instead of the Virgin) is always the same triumph raised to a more comprehensive level. It is an attempt to find new parents; new fathers in the odd chapters, new objects of love in the even. The last version of Father Conmee is the 'priest of the eternal imagination'; the last version of Mercedes is the 'lure of the fallen seraphim'. But the last version of the mother who said, 'O, Stephen will apologise' is the mother who prays on the last page 'that I may learn in my own life and away from home and friends what the heart is and what it feels'. The mother remains.

THE DOUBLE FEMALE

As in *Dubliners* and *Exiles,* the female role in the *Portrait* is less to arouse than to elucidate masculine desires. Hence the complex function in the book of physical love : the physical is the analogue of the spiritual, as St Augustine insisted in his *Confessions* (which, with Ibsen's *Brand,* is the chief archetype of Joyce's book). The poles between which this affection moves are those of St Augustine and St John : the Whore of Babylon and the Bride of Christ. The relation between the two is far from simple, and Stephen moves in a constant tension between them.

His desire, figured in the visions of Monte Cristo's Mercedes, 'to meet in the real world the unsubstantial image which his soul so constantly beheld' draws him toward the prostitute ('In her arms he felt that he had suddenly become strong and fearless and sure of himself', P114/114) and simultaneously toward the vaguely spiritual satisfaction represented with equal vagueness by the wraithlike E— C—, to whom he twice writes verses. The Emma Clery of *Stephen Hero,* with her loud forced manners and her body compact of pleasure, S66/56, was refined into a wraith with a pair of initials to parallel an intangible Church. She is continually assimilated to the image of the Blessed Virgin and of the heavenly Bride. The torture she costs him is the torture his apostasy costs him. His flirtation with her is his flirtation with Christ. His profane villanelle draws its imagery from religion – the incense, the eucharistic hymn, the chalice – and her heart, following Dante's image, is a rose, and in her praise 'the earth was like a swinging swaying censer, a ball of incense', P256/248.

The woman is the Church. His vision of greeting Mercedes with 'a sadly proud gesture of refusal' :

– Madam, I never eat muscatel grapes.   P68/71

is fulfilled when he refuses his Easter communion. Emma's eyes, in their one explicit encounter, speak to him from beneath a cowl, P76/78. 'The glories of May held his soul captive', P118/118, and a temporary reconciliation of his lust and his spiritual thirst is achieved as he reads the Lesson out of the Song of Solomon. In the midst of his repentance she functions as imagined mediator : 'The image of Emma appeared before him,' and, repenting, 'he imagined that he stood near Emma in a wide land, and, humbly and in tears, bent and kissed the elbow of her sleeve', P132/131. Like Dante's Beatrice, she manifests in his earthly experience the Church Triumphant of his spiritual dream. And when he rejects her because she seems to be flirting with Father Moran, his anger is couched in the anti-clerical terms of his apostasy : 'He had done well to leave her to flirt with her priest, to toy with a church which was the scullery-maid of Christendom', P258/250.

That Kathleen ni Houlihan can flirt with priests is the unforgivable sin underlying Stephen's rejection of Ireland. But he makes

a clear distinction between the stupid clericalism which makes
intellectual and communal life impossible, and his long-nourished
vision of an artist's Church Triumphant upon earth. He rejects
the actual for daring to fall short of his vision.

THE FINAL BALANCE

The climax of the book is of course Stephen's ecstatic discovery
of his vocation at the end of chapter IV. The prose rises in nervous
excitement to beat again and again the tambours of a fin-de-siècle
ecstasy :

> His heart trembled; his breath came faster and a wild spirit
> passed over his limbs as though he were soaring sunward. His
> heart trembled in an ecstasy of fear and his soul was in flight.
> His soul was soaring in an air beyond the world and the body
> he knew was purified in a breath and delivered of incertitude
> and made radiant and commingled with the element of the
> spirit. An ecstasy of flight made radiant his eyes and wild his
> breath and tremulous and wild and radiant his windswept
> limbs.
> —One! Two! . . . Look out!—
> —O, Cripes, I'm drownded!—P196/192.

The interjecting voices of course are those of bathers, but their
ironic appropriateness to Stephen's Icarian 'soaring sunward' is
not meant to escape us : divers have their own 'ecstasy of flight',
and Icarus was 'drownded'. The imagery of Stephen's ecstasy is
fetched from many sources; we recognize Shelley's skylark, Icarus,
the glorified body of the Resurrection (cf. 'His soul had arisen
from the grave of boyhood, spurning her graveclothes', P197/193)
and a tremulousness from which it is difficult to dissociate adolescent sexual dreams (which the Freudians tell us are frequently
dreams of flying). The entire eight-page passage is cunningly
organized with great variety of rhetoric and incident; but we

cannot help noticing the limits set on vocabulary and figures of thought. The empurpled triteness of such a cadence as 'radiant his eyes and wild his breath and tremulous and wild and radiant his windswept face' is enforced by recurrence : 'But her long fair hair was girlish; and girlish, and touched with the wonder of mortal beauty, her face', P199/195. 'Ecstasy' is the keyword, indeed. This riot of feelings corresponds to no vocation definable in mature terms; the paragraphs come to rest on images of irresponsible motion :

> He turned away from her suddenly and set off across the strand. His cheeks were aflame; his body was aglow; his limbs were trembling. On and on and on and on he strode, far out over the sands, singing wildly to the sea, crying to greet the advent of the life that had cried to him.   P200/196.

What 'life' connotes it skills not to ask; the word recurs and recurs. So does the motion onward and onward and onward :

> A wild angel had appeared to him, the angel of mortal youth and beauty, an envoy from the fair courts of life, to throw open before him in an instant of ecstasy the gates of all the ways of error and glory. On and on and on and on!   P200/196.

It may be well to recall Joyce's account of the romantic temper :

> . . . an insecure, unsatisfied, impatient temper which sees no fit abode here for its ideals and chooses therefore to behold them under insensible figures. As a result of this choice it comes to disregard certain limitations. Its figures are blown to wild adventures, lacking the gravity of solid bodies. . . .   S78/66.

Joyce also called *Prometheus Unbound* 'the Schwärmerei of a young jew'.

And it is quite plain from the final chapter of the *Portrait* that we are not to accept the mode of Stephen's 'freedom' as the 'message' of the book. The 'priest of the eternal imagination' turns out to be indigestibly Byronic. Nothing is more obvious than his total lack of humour. The dark intensity of the first four chapters is moving enough, but our impulse on being confronted with the final edition of Stephen Dedalus is to laugh; and laugh at this moment we dare not; he is after all a victim being prepared for a sacrifice. His shape, as Joyce said, can no longer change. The art he has elected is not 'the slow elaborative patience of the art of satisfaction'. 'On and on and on and on' will be its inescapable mode. He does not *see* the girl who symbolizes the full revelation; 'she seemed like one whom magic had changed into the likeness of a strange and beautiful seabird', P199/195, and he confusedly apprehends a sequence of downy and feathery incantations. What, in the last chapter, he does see he sees only to reject, in favour of an incantatory 'loveliness which has not yet come into the world', P197/286.

The only creative attitude to language exemplified in the book is that of Stephen's father :

> —Is it Christy? he said. There's more cunning in one of those warts on his bald head than in a pack of jack foxes.

His vitality is established before the book is thirty pages under way. Stephen, however, isn't enchanted at any time by the proximity of such talk. He isn't, as a matter of fact, even interested in it. Without a backward glance, he exchanges this father for a myth.

S o u r c e : *Dublin's Joyce* (1955) pp. 112–33.

NOTES

1. Frank Budgen, *James Joyce and the Making of Ulysses* (Grayson & Grayson, 1934) p. 112.

2. [*Editor's Note*.] In Professor Kenner's essay, a letter followed by two numbers with a slash between them refers to the American and English editions of Joyce's books current at the publication of *Dublin's*

Joyce. P : *A Portrait of the Artist as a Young Man* (Modern Library/ Jonathan Cape); S : *Stephen Hero* (New Directions/Jonathan Cape); U : *Ulysses* (Modern Library/John Lane, The Bodley Head); F : *Finnegans Wake* (Viking/Faber [identical pagination]).

3. — You want me, said Stephen, to toe the line with those hypocrites and sycophants in the college. I will never do so.

— No. I mentioned Jesus.

— Don't mention him. I have made it a common noun. They don't believe in him; they don't observe his precepts. . . . S141/124.

4. Compare the opening sentence : 'Eins within a space, and a wearywide space it wast, ere wohned a Mookse', F152. Mookse is moocow plus fox plus mock turtle. The German 'Eins' evokes Einstein, who presides over the interchanging of space and time; space is the Mookse's 'spatialty'.

5. Joyce's names should always be scrutinized. Simon Moonan : moon : the heatless (white) satellite reflecting virtue borrowed from Simon Peter. Simony, too, is an activity naturally derived from this casually businesslike attitude to priestly authority.

Maurice Beebe

JOYCE AND AQUINAS: THE THEORY OF AESTHETICS (1957)

While most critics of James Joyce agree that the theory of art presented by Stephen Dedalus in *A Portrait of the Artist as a Young Man* is both a key to the novel in which it appears and a programme for Joyce's later writings, they disagree on the extent of Joyce's alleged indebtedness to Saint Thomas Aquinas. When Stephen has finished expounding his theory, his friend Lynch comments, 'That has the true scholastic stink.'[1] Some critics agree. According to Padraic Colum, for example, Stephen 'is unable to analyze his ideas or shape his life except in terms of the philosophy that the Catholic Church has evolved or adopted.'[2] S. Foster Damon asserts that Stephen 'has mastered Aquinas and Aristotle so well that he saw the whole world through their eyes.'[3] Haskell M. Block, in what is perhaps the most complete and illuminating discussion of the theory, writes : 'The theoretical formulation of Joyce's aesthetic rigidly followed Thomistic principles.'[4] And according to Harry Levin, Joyce 'required the sanction of Saint Thomas Aquinas for his art, though not for his belief.'[5]

If Joyce's art were Thomist, it would be necessary to qualify the usual interpretation of Joyce–Stephen as an exile. Presumably he turned from the religion of his fathers to a religion of art. If his aesthetic remained orthodox, his self-proclaimed revolt from God, Home, and Country would appear to have been only a matter of convenience – and since he insisted that only art justifies alienation, unnecessary. It would follow that Joyce's art is sanctioned and that Joyce the artist, if not Joyce the man, may be claimed for the Church. However, the point is in dispute, and there are critics who argue that Joyce's aesthetic does not follow the Thomist line. William York Tindall, for example, asserts that Joyce diverged considerably from Aquinas, 'who, liberally interpreted and applied, is made to serve other ends than his own.'[6] According to Francis Fergusson, 'the divergence from Aquinas and Aristotle is completely self-conscious and consistent. Joyce must diverge . . . making his Thomism godless, interpreting Aristotle in a neoclassic sense, if the freedom of exile is to have its demonic completeness.'[7]

Neither of these conflicting opinions has thus far been carefully defended or documented by means of a close scrutiny of the exact extent to which Joyce does follow Aquinas. Such an examination, a point-by-point comparison of Joyce's theory with the Thomist sources from which it derives, will reveal that Joyce follows the form of certain scholastic principles, but by denying the premises upon which they are based, distorts the meaning. Aquinas alludes to questions of art and beauty only in passing; his statements must be culled from their context, yet seen in their context. By taking Aquinas's definitions of beauty out of their context and by insisting upon his right to interpret them literally, Joyce draws some conclusions which would be – and have been – the despair of neo-Thomists, who see the theory of art in relation to Thomism in general. For this reason, it seems necessary to compare Stephen's theory not only with the actual text of Aquinas, but also with the explanations of Aquinas provided by such interpreters as Jacques Maritain (from whose *Art and Scholasticism*, first published in 1920, Thomist aesthetics properly dates), Thomas Gilby, and Herbert Ellsworth Cory.

The theory advanced in the *Portrait* appears fragmentarily in two earlier forms : in Joyce's notes, first published in Herbert Gorman's 1940 biography, and in the rejected version of the *Portrait*, published in 1944 as *Stephen Hero*. Since there is only one important difference among these separate versions – one which will be discussed in detail – and since the earlier versions often clarify points passed over quickly or inadequately in the *Portrait*, they may safely be considered as a single unit.

Joyce draws three main principles from two statements by Aquinas; thus, there is some overlapping. An outline of the entire theory may therefore serve as a useful point of reference for discussion of the parts :

I   Art is a *stasis* brought about by the formal rhythms of beauty.

   A   The tragic emotions, pity and terror, arouse and arrest the mind in a condition of *stasis* rather than *kinesis*.

   B   Comedy is proper and perfect when it arouses the static emotion of joy rather than the kinetic emotion of desire or loathing.

   C   The aesthetic *stasis,* an ideal pity, terror, or joy, is awakened or induced by the formal rhythm of beauty.

II   Art or beauty, divorced from good and evil, is akin to truth; therefore, if truth can best be approached through intellection, beauty or art is best approached through the three stages of apprehension.

   A   Beauty is separated from good and evil because good and evil excite the kinetic emotions of desire or loathing.

   B   Beauty is related to truth because both are static.

   C   Just as the first step in the direction of truth is to comprehend the act of intellection, the first step in the direction of beauty is to understand the process of aesthetic comprehension; the stages of apprehension and the qualities of beauty are akin.

III   The three qualities of beauty which correspond to the three stages of apprehension are, in the terms of Aquinas, *integritas, consonantia,* and *claritas.*

   A   *Integritas* is wholeness – *one* thing.

   B   *Consonantia* is harmony – a *thing.*

C   *Claritas* is radiance – *that* thing.
   1   *Claritas* is not to be considered a manifestation of the
     sublime or divine; it is simply the whatness of a thing.
   2   (In *Stephen Hero* only). *Claritas* is revealed through
     the experience of epiphanies.

A fourth main division of the theory is Stephen's explanation of
the three forms of art : the lyrical, the epical, and the dramatic.
But this part is concerned more with the problem of creating art,
the artist's relationship to his materials, than with the problem of
the nature of art and beauty. Stephen claims the authority of
Aquinas only for his discussion of the latter : 'So far as this side of
esthetic philosophy extends Aquinas will carry me all along the
line. When we come to the phenomena of artistic conception,
artistic gestation and artistic reproduction, I require a new termin-
ology and a new personal experience' (pp. 245–6).[8]
    But to what extent does Saint Thomas carry Stephen 'all along
the line'?

I   ART AS STASIS

Stephen bases two main principles of his theory – art as *stasis* and
the separation of beauty from good and evil – upon one sentence
by Aquinas : *Pulchra sunt quoe visa placent,* which he translates
'that is beautiful the apprehension of which pleases' (p. 243).
Slight variations in the Latin text appear in Joyce's several versions. *Pulcra,* the form in both *Stephen Hero* and the *Portrait,* is
pulcera in the original notes, and *quoe* is *quae* in the notes and
Stephen Hero.[9] Although these changes may be typographical
errors, it can be demonstrated that whenever Joyce cited Aquinas
he was anything but meticulous in adhering to the original Latin.
If he deliberately misquoted, we have the first sign of his irreverent
attitude towards the Angelic Doctor. At any rate, the text of the

Summa Theologica has *pulchra enim dicunter quae visa placent.*
A translation by the Dominican Fathers makes it apparent that
Joyce had read the paragraph in which the sentence appears :

> Beauty and goodness are identical fundamentally; for they
> are based upon the same thing, namely, the form. Consequently
> goodness may be rightly praised as beauty. But they differ logic-
> ally, for goodness properly relates to the appetitive faculty
> (goodness being what all men desire); and therefore it has the
> formal aspect of an end (the appetitive faculty being a kind of
> movement towards a thing). Beauty relates to the cognoscitive
> faculty; for *beautiful things are those which please when seen.*
> Hence beauty consists in due proportion; for the senses are satis-
> fied in things duly proportioned, as in what is after their own
> kind – because sense is a sort of reason; and so is every cognos-
> citive faculty.[10]

The complete passage at least partly clears up the mystification of
Stephen's explanation of the one sentence drawn from it : 'He uses
the word *visa* . . . to cover esthetic apprehensions of all kinds,
whether through sight or hearing or through any other avenue of
apprehension. This word, though it is vague, is clear enough to
keep away good and evil, which excite desire and loathing. It
means certainly a stasis and not a kinesis' (p. 243).

On this foundation, the first part of the theory is developed.
Stephen begins by discussing the true nature of tragedy :

> Pity is the feeling which arrests the mind in the presence of what-
> soever is grave and constant in human sufferings and unites it
> with the human sufferer. Terror is the feeling which arrests the
> mind in the presence of whatsoever is grave and constant in
> human sufferings and unites it with the secret cause. . . . You see
> I use the word *arrest.* I mean that the tragic emotion is static.
> Or rather the dramatic emotion is. The feelings excited by
> improper art are kinetic, desire or loathing. Desire urges us to
> possess, to go to something; loathing urges us to abandon, to go
> from something. The arts which excite them, pornographical or
> didactic, are therefore improper arts. (pp. 239–40)

Stephen's ultimate purpose is to establish beauty in the objectivity of the art-work rather than in the subjectivity of the artist. The missing link between *stasis* and formal rhythm is found in Joyce's original notes, in the discussion of comedy :

> An improper art aims at exciting in the way of comedy the feeling of desire but the feeling which is proper to comic art is the feeling of joy. . . . For desire urges us from rest that we may possess something but joy holds us in rest so long as we possess something. . . . this rest is necessary for the apprehension of the beautiful – the end of all art, tragic or comic, – for this rest is the only condition under which the images, which are to excite in us terror or pity or joy, can be properly presented to us and properly seen by us. For beauty is a quality of something seen but terror and pity and joy are states of mind.[11]

If beauty is a quality of something seen, then it is to be found in the rhythm or proportion of the art-object : 'Beauty expressed by the artist . . . awakens, or ought to awaken, or induces, or ought to induce, an esthetic stasis, an ideal pity or an ideal terror, a stasis called forth, prolonged and at last dissolved by what I call the rhythm of beauty. . . . Rhythm . . . is the first formal esthetic relation of part to part in any esthetic whole or of an esthetic whole to its part or parts or of any part to the esthetic whole of which it is a part' (p. 241).

Although Saint Thomas has nothing to say about tragedy and comedy, it would seem that, read literally, he supplies sanction for the main features of this part of Stephen's theory. The separation of beauty, the product of cognition, from goodness, the goal of appetition, and the dependence of beauty on form are found in the paragraph from the *Summa Theologica* cited above. Naturally, neo-Thomists support these aspects of Aquinas's theory. For example, Father Thomas Gilby says that the experience of beauty 'comes as a rest in human activity, as something desirable for its own sake' and that 'it is of the essence of Beauty that with the knowledge of it desire is at rest.'[12] Jacques Maritain, commenting on Aquinas's definition of the beautiful, says: 'The beautiful is that which gives joy, not all joy, but joy in knowledge; not the joy peculiar to the act of knowing, but a joy superabounding and overflowing from such an act because of the object known. If a thing exalts and delights the soul by the very fact of its being given to the intuition of the soul, it is good to apprehend, it is beautiful.'[13]

It is only when one considers the context that Joyce's divergence from Aquinas becomes apparent. Aquinas's definition of beauty appears as a passing reference in a section on 'God, the Divine Unity'. Implied in the above sentences by neo-Thomists is the scholastic understanding of the unity of Being and the presence of God in all beauty. For example, both Joyce and Father Gilby use the word *rest*. What is the orthodox interpretation of *rest*? According to Herbert Ellsworth Cory, Aquinas 'tells us that "it is of the nature of the beautiful that the appetite is allayed by the sight of it." I am sure that he would like us to recall, in this connection, our refrain from St Augustine: "Thou hast made us for Thyself; and our hearts are restless until they find rest in Thee." The aesthetic experience is seldom mystical; but if ever it is *fully* conscious, if its recipient is thoroughly self-disciplined in holiness, and if he is given extraordinary graces by God, it will be mystical.'[14]

Joyce stops short before *what*, according to the Thomists, the aesthetic *stasis* reveals. If the context is denied, the rhythm of art reveals only the mechanical harmony of parts to parts and parts with whole: 'the first formal esthetic relation of part to part in any esthetic whole or of an esthetic whole to its part or parts or of any part to the esthetic whole of which it is a part'. It does not reflect the harmony of God's universe. Seen thus, Joyce is thinking simply of the importance of form, the well-made work of art, and this point of Stephen's theory is closer to Henry James than to Saint Thomas. Joyce's 'rhythm' places no emphasis on the *due* of Aquinas's 'due proportion'. Perhaps this is what Francis

Fergusson had in mind when he wrote that Joyce makes his
Thomism godless.

11 THE BEAUTIFUL, THE GOOD, AND THE TRUE

In *Stephen Hero* the aesthetic theory is presented not as an exposition of abstract principles, but in terms of dramatic conflict. Many
of the points which Stephen explains to Lynch, who offers only
passive resistance and an occasional sarcasm, appear in the earlier
version as part of the paper on 'Art and Life' which Stephen read
before the Literary and Historical Society of University College.
The paper met with a hostile reception, mainly on the charge that
it absolved art and artist from all patriotic and moral obligations.
Previously, Dr Dillon, President of the University, had said to
him : 'This theory you have – if pushed to its logical conclusion –
would emancipate the poet from all moral laws. I notice too that
in your essay you allude satirically to what you call the "antique"
theory – the theory, namely, that the drama should have special
ethical aims, that it should instruct, elevate, and amuse. I suppose
you mean Art for Art's sake.' Stephen replied that he 'only pushed
to its logical conclusion the definition Aquinas has given of the
beautiful' (p. 95). After the reading of his paper, he remained
silent, refusing to debate with his critics. And when, in the process
of revision, the audience of many becomes the single auditor
Lynch, the ethical objections disappear altogether. Thus, the only
defense which Stephen makes at any time to the moralistic criticism
is the testimonial of Saint Thomas – he has simply pushed to its
logical conclusion Aquinas's definition of beauty.

Only by taking the part for the whole is Stephen's summary dis-
missal of the good from any consideration of the beautiful to be
justified in terms of Thomist doctrine. The difference which
Aquinas notes between the aspects of the good and the beautiful
is, in the total theological view, less important than the similarity.

They are 'identical fundamentally', Aquinas said in the passage already quoted, and in another section of the *Summa* :

> The beautiful is the same as the good, and they differ in aspect only. For since good is what all seek, the notion of good is that which calms the desire; while the notion of the beautiful is that which calms the desire, by being seen or known. Consequently those senses chiefly regard the beautiful, which are the most cognitive, viz, sight and hearing, as ministering to reason; for we speak of beautiful sights and beautiful sounds. But in reference to the other objects of the other senses, we do not use the expression *beautiful,* for we do not speak of beautiful tastes, and beautiful odours. Thus it is evident that beauty adds to goodness a relation to the cognitive faculty : so that *good* means that which simply pleases the appetite; while the *beautiful* is something pleasant is apprehend.[15]

It will be noticed that this passage makes beauty and goodness less divergent than does the passage from which Joyce drew his first premise. Aquinas's phrase 'beauty adds to goodness a relation to the cognitive faculty' sanctions the neo-Thomist acceptance of Cajetan's interpretation of this passage : 'Beauty is a certain kind of good.'[16]

Although most neo-Thomists agree with Joyce that art should not be didactic, that the artist's 'only thought for the spectator should be to give him something beautiful, or *well-made*'[17] and that 'the poetic experience in itself teaches nothing, making neither for edification nor appearing to lead onwards to higher truths,'[18] they do feel that art must be subject to moral censorship. This seeming paradox is to be explained by the scholastic distinction between art and artist. Art, says Maritain, is in the realm of Making, which is related solely to the good and perfection of the work produced; it 'remains outside the line of human conduct, with an end, rules, and values, which are not those of the man, but of the work to be produced.'[19] Art is a *habitus* of the practical understanding, and it is always good because it always strives towards perfection. Moral considerations, on the other hand, are in the realm of Doing or Action, the use made of free will. Thus the artist's decisions are ethically vulnerable. Art is infallibly right; when the art-work seems to fail, it is because the artist has failed his art. And since Prudence must rule the affairs of men, the artist must be moral. 'Because art, the virtue of making, is specifically human rather than merely animal or merely mechanical,' Cory explains, 'it can never *persist* in its sanity unless it acts in fellowship with the moral virtues.'[20] Art that is irreverent must be prohibited, for art, says Maritain, 'has no right against God'.[21] The neo-Thomists are not here speaking entirely for themselves; Aquinas himself says, 'In the case of an art that produces things which for the most part some people put to an evil use, although such arts are not unlawful in themselves, nevertheless, according to the teaching of Plato, they should be extirpated from the State by the governing authority.'[22]

The Very Reverend Dr Dillon charged that Stephen's theory would lead him to Art for Art's sake. If this expression means an art which is an escape from life, then the criticism is unjustified, for Joyce had no quarrel with the alliance of art and truth. The Stephen of *Stephen Hero* 'did not attach himself to art in any spirit of youthful dilettantism but strove to pierce to the significant heart of everything' (p. 33), and he told his mother, 'Art is not an escape from life. It's just the very opposite. Art, on the contrary, is the very central expression of life' (p. 86). In the *Portrait,* the theme of the artist's reliance upon life is expressed more symbolically, especially when Stephen, reacting bitterly from his religious crisis, seems to re-affirm the value of life as he watches the young girl wading in the river. In that moment of revulsion from the Church, it is religion – or, at any rate, the religion represented by the Jesuit priests – which seems to stand for the negation of life, and art which affirms the significance of experience. The *Portrait* concludes with the cry, 'Welcome, O life! . . .' Thus, if Stephen is eager to separate beauty from goodness, he is also determined to associate beauty with truth. Joyce's essay on James Clarence Mangan, published in 1902, contains the sentence, 'Beauty, the splendour of truth, is a gracious presence when the imagination contemplates intensely the truth of its own being or the visible world and the spirit which proceeds out of truth and beauty is the holy spirit of joy.'[28] By the time that Joyce wrote the *Portrait,* 'the holy spirit of joy' had become less celestial, but he retained the conviction that beauty is the 'splendour of truth'.

Stephen continues his discourse. He has already cited Aquinas as an authority on the alliance of beauty and truth; he now brings in additional support :

> Plato, I believe, said that beauty is the splendour of truth. I don't think that it has a meaning but the true and the beautiful are akin. Truth is beheld by the intellect which is appeased by the most satisfying relations of the intelligible : beauty is beheld by the imagination which is appeased by the most satisfying relations of the sensible. The first step in the direction of truth is to understand the frame and scope of the intellect itself, to comprehend the act itself of intellection. Aristotle's entire system of philosophy rests upon his book of psychology and that, I think, rests on his statement that the same attribute cannot at the same time and in the same connexion belong to and not belong to the same subject. The first step in the direction of beauty is to understand the frame and scope of the imagination, to comprehend the act itself of esthetic apprehension. (pp. 243–4).

Therefore, the qualities of beauty are akin to the stages of apprehension : 'Though the same object may not seem beautiful to all people, all people who admire a beautiful object find in it certain relations which satisfy and coincide with the stages themselves of all esthetic apprehension. These relations of the sensible, visible to you through one form and to me through another, must be therefore the necessary qualities of beauty' (p. 245).

This part of Stephen's theory clearly agrees with Thomist doctrine. Aquinas wrote that 'since truth is in the intellect in pro-

F

portion to its conformity with the object understood, the idea of
truth must needs flow from the intellect to the object of the intellect, so that the thing understood is said to be true in so far as it
is conformed in relation to the intellect' and that therefore 'truth
is defined by the conformity of intellect and thing.'[24] Cory adds
that 'when we discern the beauty of an object our own spiritual
powers and operations assume themselves a form, a harmony and
equilibrium.'[25] The inter-relationship of subject and object is the
basis of Maritain's definition of poetry : 'that intercommunication
between the inner being of things and the inner being of the human
Self which is a kind of divination'.[26]

What is the significance of this association of beauty with truth,
of the stages of apprehension with the qualities of beauty? For
Joyce, it provided a defense to the charge that his was a dilettante's
art. Art, he insisted, is neither something found, a pretty object
to be copied in a servile manner, nor entirely something invented.
Pure art exists as a delicate balance between the artist-creator and
that which he perceives, between the art-object and the one who
perceives it. Joyce secularizes the Thomist insistence on the moral
obligations of the artist by demanding instead intellectual or
psychological obligations. There are definite standards for art
which are rooted in human psychology. Art is a discipline and the
artist a responsible creature.

III   THE THREE QUALITIES OF BEAUTY

In stating Aquinas's definition of the three qualities of beauty,
Stephen again simplifies and misquotes the original Latin. He tells
Lynch, 'Aquinas says : *Ad pulcritudinem tria requirunter
integritas, consonantia, claritas.* I translate it so : *Three things are
needed for beauty, wholeness, harmony and radiance*' (p. 248).
Actually, Aquinas wrote : '*Nam ad pulchritudinem tria requirun-
tur: primo quidem integritas sive perfectio; quae enim diminuta*

sunt, turpia sunt; et debita proportio sive consonantia; et iterum claritas, unde, quae habent colorem nitidum, pulchra esse dicunter.' This the Dominican Fathers translate: 'For beauty includes three conditions, *integrity* or *perfection,* for those things which are impaired are by the very fact ugly; and then due *proportion* or *harmony* is required; and lastly, *brightness* or *clarity,* whence things are called beautiful which have a bright color.'[27]

We need not linger over the first two of these qualities. *Integritas* Stephen interprets as *wholeness.* In looking at a basket, he tells Lynch, the mind first separates the basket from its surroundings and thus sees it as *one* thing. Joyce's definition is probably even closer to the Latin text than the translation given above, for *integritas* has also the meaning of wholeness or completeness, which fits better the *diminuta.* Father Gilby translates this part of the definition, 'a certain wholeness or perfection, for whatever is incomplete is to that extent ugly'.[28] *Wholeness* obviously has greater application to Joyce's carefully unified art, especially in *Ulysses* and *Finnegans Wake,* than does the more vague *perfection.*

Stephen's interpretation of *consonantia* accords generally with that 'due proportion' Aquinas noted as a characteristic of beauty. Having recognized the basket as *one* thing, Stephen tells Lynch, you now notice 'its formal lines . . . you feel the rhythm of its structure . . . you feel now that it is a *thing*' (p. 249). We have already noted the difference between Aquinas's concept of form and rhythm as a manifestation of Being and Joyce's more mundane, mechanistic interpretation.

With *claritas,* Stephen sharply diverges from the orthodox interpretations of Saint Thomas. On this point we need not assume what would be the attitude of the neo-Thomists towards Joyce's explication. Cory, in his *The Significance of Beauty in Nature and Art,* uses Joyce's explanations of *integritas* and *consonantia* as a rebuttal to an attack on medieval aesthetic theory as sterile and shallow, but he disagrees with Joyce's understanding of *claritas.*

Stephen himself points out the ambiguous nature of the word :
'Aquinas uses a term which seems to be inexact. It baffled me for
a long time. It would lead you to believe that he had in mind
symbolism or idealism, the supreme quality of beauty being a
light from some other world, the idea of which the matter was but
the shadow, the reality of which it was but the symbol. I thought
he might mean that *claritas* was the artistic discovery and representation of the divine purpose in anything or a force of generali-
zation which would make the esthetic image a universal one, make
it outshine its proper conditions' (pp. 249–50). Cory interrupts
his quoting of this passage to remark, 'Precisely so; for Thomists
also like the very powerful word *effulgence*. Joyce, the apostate
here loses his grip.' Stephen continues : 'But that is literary talk.
I understand it so. When you have apprehended that basket as
one thing and have then analysed it according to its form and
apprehended it as a thing you make the only synthesis which is
logically and esthetically permissible. You see that it is that thing
which it is and no other. The radiance of which he speaks is the
scholastic *quidditas*, the *whatness* of a thing' (p. 250). To this,
Cory replies :

> But St Thomas also said elsewhere that one of the three ways in
> which God is present in all things is by His *quidditas*, His
> Essence. Just what *claritas* meant to St Thomas we may gather
> from his account of what the glorified human body will be after
> its resurrection. The glory of the soul, already in heaven, will
> glow through its restored body and make it splendid. For this
> once too often recalcitrant flesh will now be ablaze in its every
> part with the effulgence of the soul which has experienced the
> Beatific Vision. Even so, even on earth, objects inanimate as
> well as animate, though their *claritas* is, of course, immeasurably
> below that of the saints in heaven, yet do, in so far as they are
> beautiful, beacon forth Divine Providence in so far as it is not
> impeded by imperfections which are never created by God. Even
> on earth, then, *claritas*, the crowning attribute of beauty is the
> shining through, to some greater or less degree, of the operative
> and essential presence of God. In his last sentences which I do

not here quote Joyce falteringly reduces this *claritas* to a sort of metaphorical materialistic sentimentality.[29]

Apparently Joyce substituted *quidditas* for *claritas* in order to avoid the spiritual connotation of the latter. He left himself open to the objection of Cory by confusing *quidditas*, which in scholastic philosophy means specific essence (e.g. the manhood of Socrates, the correct answer to What is Socrates?), with the scholastic *haecceitas,* individual thisness.[30] In this instance, as 'the scholastic *quidditas'* seems to imply, Joyce wanted to claim the sanction of Aquinas without accepting the meaning of Aquinas. If the 'bright color' in Aquinas's explanation of *claritas* seems to justify Joyce's mundane interpretation, the context in which it appears does not. The sentence immediately preceding is translated, 'Species or Beauty has a likeness to the property of the Son.' Following the list of the three conditions is Saint Thomas's explanation of how each applies to Christ. *Claritas,* he says, 'agrees with the property of the Son, as the Word, which is the light and splendour of the Intellect.'

To say that beauty is *like* the property of the Son is not, of course, to say that all earthly beauty is but a shadow of divine form. Yet here Aquinas is more conservative than his modern interpreters. Although Maritain, the most authoritative of these commentators, is more cautious than Cory, he says of the third quality of beauty :

A certain splendour is indeed according to all the Ancients the essential character of beauty. . . . *splendor formae,* said St Thomas with the metaphysician's precision of language : for *form,* that is to say the principle determining the peculiar perfection of everything which is, constituting and completing things in their essence and their qualities, the ontological secret, so to speak, of their innermost being, their spiritual essence, their operative mystery, is above all the peculiar principle of intelligibility, the peculiar *clarity* of everything. Every form, moreover, is a remnant or a ray of the creative Mind impressed upon the heart of the being created. All order and proportion, on the other hand, are the work of the mind.[31]

What Joyce called 'epiphany' gives us a clue by which we can trace the gradual development of his alienation from Thomist aesthetic. It is not impossible that Joyce first formulated his theory before his final break with the Church, then altered and modified it to suit his new attitude. We have already noticed that the phrase 'the holy spirit of joy' in his essay on Mangan implies a greater reliance on the spiritual value of art than is apparent in the *Portrait*. In *Stephen Hero* Joyce described *claritas* in terms more congenial to the Thomistic interpretation :

> *Claritas* is *quidditas*. After the analysis which discovers the second quality the mind makes the only logically possible synthesis and discovers the third quality. This is the moment which I call epiphany. First we recognize that the moment is *one* integral thing, then we recognize that it is an organised composite structure, a *thing* in fact : finally, when the relation of the parts is exquisite, when the parts are adjusted to the special point, we recognise that it is *that* thing which it is. Its soul, its whatness, leaps to us from the vestment of its appearance. The soul of the commonest object, the structure of which is so adjusted, seems to us radiant. The object achieves its epiphany. (p. 213)

In this stage, Stephen's interpretation of *claritas* is orthodox.[32] The word *epiphany,* which he defines as 'a sudden spiritual manifestation' (p. 211), has, of course, the religious connotation of Christ's manifestation to the wise men. Stephen speaks of the soul. Maritain says of the third quality of beauty that 'above all it is the profound splendour of the soul shining through'.[33]

In the *Portrait* there is no mention of the epiphany. Here is how Stephen develops his explanation of *claritas* with what Cory calls 'metaphorical materialistic sentimentality' : 'The radiance of which he speaks is the scholastic *quidditas*, that *whatness* of a thing This supreme quality is felt by the artist when the esthetic image is first conceived in his imagination. The mind in that mysterious instant Shelley likened beautifully to a fading coal. The instant wherein that supreme quality of beauty, the clear radiance of the esthetic image, is apprehended luminously by the mind which has been arrested by its wholeness and fascinated by its harmony is the luminous silent stasis of esthetic pleasure' (p. 250). The reference to Shelley is particularly significant because it refers to that passage in *A Defence of Poetry* which describes the creative process as an unfortunate *moving away* from divine inspiration.[34] The man-made nature of art, a condition which Shelley, the translator of Plato's *Ion,* largely regrets, Joyce exalts as the factor which enables the artist to exist as a god in himself.

This explains why the epiphanies, now reduced simply to revelations of whatness rather than of soul, which appear in the *Portrait* and *Ulysses* do not imply the existence of an all-encompassing Unity. In *Ulysses*, for example :

> From the playfield the boys raised a shout. A whirring whistle : goal. . . .
> — The ways of the Creator are not our ways, Mr Deasy said. All history moves towards one great goal, the manifestation of God.
> Stephen jerked his thumb towards the window, saying :
> — That is God.
> Hooray ! Ay ! Whrrwhee !
> — What ? Mr Deasy asked.
> — A shout in the street, Stephen answered, shrugging his shoulders.[35]

Aquinas and Maritain, like Mr Deasy, would undoubtedly agree that God manifests Himself in the shout, but the implication of Stephen's remark is that a shout in the street is all the God there is.

CONCLUSION

We have seen that Joyce consistently secularizes Aquinas. He adheres to the Thomist categories, but interprets them to suit his own purposes. Yet, in doing so, he uses much of Aquinas and does not so much dispute as distort the scholastic argument. At least one important doctrine he accepts completely : the identification of truth as the conformity of mind and object he finds useful because it provides him with a justification of absolute, psychological standards for art and a defense against the charge that his theory is that of a dilettante or an Art-for-Art's-sake advocate. Each of the other principles, however, he interprets – against the spirit, if not the letter, of the *Summa* – in secular, mundane terms that permit him to discard the supernatural implications of Thomist doctrine. Aquinas's 'due proportion' he accepts to the extent that it supports his objective, non-emotional art, but he denies the scholastic interpretation of 'due proportion' as a semblance of Divine Order or Unity. He exalts the art-work as a world in itself, with the appropriate standards of completeness, harmony, and clarity, but he sees it as complete in itself, harmonious in itself, and clear in itself, rather.than as a fragment or a symbol of a broader, more extensive Unity. Thus he makes the artist equal to God and under the guise of traditionalism advances a theory that is revolutionary – or if traditional, closer to the tradition of Gustave Flaubert, Henry James, and Walter Pater than to the tradition of the Thomists.

In the satirical poem 'The Holy Office' (1904), Joyce wrote :

> I turn to view
> The shamblings of that motly crew,
> Those souls that hate the strength that mine has
> Steeled in the school of old Aquinas.
> Where they have crouched and crawled and prayed
> I stand, the self-doomed, unafraid,
> Unfellowed, friendless and alone,
> Indifferent as the herring-bone,
> Firm as the mountain ridges where
> I flash my antlers on the air.[36]

Joyce was steeled in the school of Aquinas to the extent that he could use the scholastic method of logical argument against the vague generalities of the moralists or the dilettantes. But as far as his thought itself was concerned, he stood 'unfellowed, friendless and alone'. *A Portrait of the Artist as a Young Man* tells how Stephen discovered that his weapons were to be 'silence, exile and cunning' (p. 291). The cunning preceded the writing of the novel.

SOURCE: *Philological Quarterly,* XXXVI (January 1957) pp. 20–35.

NOTES

1. *A Portrait of the Artist as a Young Man* (New York, 1916), p. 245. Subsequent references to the *Portrait* appear in the text. Page references otherwise unidentified are to the *Portrait*.

2. *The Road Round Ireland* (New York, 1926), p. 321.

3. 'The Odyssey in Dublin', in *James Joyce: Two Decades of Criticism*, ed. Seon Givens (New York, 1948), p. 222.

4. 'The Critical Theory of James Joyce', *Journal of Aesthetics and Art History*, VIII (1950), 178.

5. *James Joyce* (Norfolk, Conn., 1941), p. 25.

6. *James Joyce, His Way of Interpreting the Modern World* (New York, 1950), p. 20.

7. 'A Reading of *Exiles*', in Joyce's *Exiles* (New York : New Directions, n.d.), p. xvii.

8. Although Joyce's theories of the three forms of art and of the creative process are beyond the province of this study, it may be noted in passing that the parts for which Stephen does not claim Thomist authority appear to be more Thomistic than the parts for which he does claim such authority. See H. M. McLuhan, 'Joyce, Aquinas, and the Poetic Process', *Renascence, IV* (Autumn 1951), pp. 3–11.

9. Herbert Gorman, *James Joyce* (New York, 1948), p. 133; and James Joyce, *Stephen Hero: A Part of the First Draft of A Portrait of the Artist as a Young Man,* ed. Theodore Spencer (Norfolk, 1944), p. 95.

Subsequent page references to *Stephen Hero* appear in the text.

10. *Summa Theologica*, Part I, question 5, article 4. Translations of the *Summa* throughout this essay are taken from *The 'Summa Theologica' of St Thomas Aquinas, Literally Translated by Fathers*

of the English Dominican Province (New York, 1911–12; London, 1913–22), 22 vols.

11. Gorman, p. 97.

12. *Poetic Experience: An Introduction to Thomist Aesthetic* (New York, 1934), pp. 99 and 108.

13. *Art and Scholasticism, with Other Essays*, trs. J. F. Scanlon (London, 1943), p. 23. The most complete statement of the neo-Thomist view of 'due proportion' is Edward I. Watkin, *A Philosophy of Form*, (New York, 1935).

14. *The Significance of Beauty in Nature and Art* (Milwaukee, 1948), p. 67.

15. *Summa Theologica*, Part II, question 27, article 1.

16. *Prima Secundae*, question 27, article 1. Quoted by Maritain, *Art and Scholasticism*, p. 166.

17. Maritain, *Art and Scholasticism*, p. 66.

18. Gilby, *Poetic Experience*, p. 99.

19. Maritain, *Art and Scholasticism*, p. 7.

20. *Significance of Beauty in Nature and Art*, pp. 158–9.

21. Maritain, *Art and Scholasticism*, p. 75.

22. *Summa Theologica*, Part II, question 169, article 2.

23. Quoted by Gorman, p. 80.

24. *Summa Theologica*, Part I, question 16, articles 1 and 2.

25. *Significance of Beauty in Nature and Art*, pp. 66–7.

26. *Creative Intuition in Art and Poetry* (New York, 1953), p. 3.

27. *Summa Theologica*, Part I, question 39, article 8.

28. *Poetic Experience*, p. 89.

29. *Significance of Beauty in Nature and Art*, p. 227.

30. I am indebted to Professor W. K. Wimsatt of Yale University for this information.

31. *Art and Scholasticism*, pp. 24–5.

32. It is perhaps for this reason that Catholic critics of Joyce use the presentation of the theory in *Stephen Hero* as a basis for their argument that the Stephen of the *Portrait* is a satirized, romanticized figure whose statements on art cannot always be taken seriously. See McLuhan, *op cit.* and Hugh Kenner, 'The Portrait in Perspective', in *James Joyce: Two Decades of Criticism*, ed. Givens, p. 154. The assumption that Joyce is speaking for himself in *Stephen Hero*, but not in the *Portrait*, fails to account for the abundant evidence that Joyce shared Stephen's rejection of the Church. See, for example, Mary Colum, *Life and the Dream* (Garden City, 1947), pp. 388–9

and Georges Borach, 'Conversations with James Joyce', trs. Joseph Prescott, *College English*, xv, 326.

33. *Art and Scholasticism*, p. 28.
34. *Works*, ed. Harry Buxton Forman (London, 1880), VIII, 137.
35. *Ulysses* (New York, 1934), p. 35.
36. Quoted by Gorman, p. 140.

Richard Ellmann

THE BACKGROUNDS OF 'THE DEAD' (1959)

> The silent cock shall crow at last. The west shall shake the east awake. Walk while ye have the night for morn, lightbreakfastbringer. . . .
>
> — *Finnegans Wake* (473)

The stay in Rome [from July 1906 until March 1907] had seemed purposeless, but during it Joyce became aware of the change in his attitude toward Ireland and so toward the world. He embodied his new perceptions in 'The Dead'. The story, which was the culmination of a long waiting history, began to take shape in Rome, but was not set down until he left the city. The pressure of hints, sudden insights, and old memories rose in his mind until, like King Midas's barber, he was compelled to speech.

Although the story dealt mainly with three generations of his family in Dublin, it drew also upon an incident in Galway in 1903. There Michael ('Sonny') Bodkin courted Nora Barnacle; but he contracted tuberculosis and had to be confined to bed. Shortly afterwards Nora resolved to go to Dublin, and Bodkin stole out of his sickroom, in spite of the rainy weather, to sing to her under an apple tree and bid her goodbye. In Dublin Nora soon learned that Bodkin was dead, and when she met Joyce she was first attracted to him, as she told a sister, because he resembled Sonny Bodkin.[1]

Joyce's habit of ferreting out details had made him conduct minute interrogations of Nora even before their departure from

Dublin. He was disconcerted by the fact that young men before him had interested her. He did not much like to know that her heart was still moved, even in pity, by the recollection of the boy who had loved her. The notion of being in some sense in rivalry with a dead man buried in the little cemetery at Oughterard was one that came easily, and gallingly, to a man of Joyce's jealous disposition. It was one source of his complaint to his Aunt Josephine Murray that Nora persisted in regarding him as quite similar to other men she had known.[2]

A few months after expressing this annoyance, while Joyce and Nora Barnacle were living in Trieste in 1905, Joyce received another impulsion toward 'The Dead'. In a letter Stanislaus happened to mention attending a concert of Plunket Greene, the Irish baritone, which included one of Thomas Moore's *Irish Melodies* called 'O, Ye Dead!'[3] The song, a dialogue of living and dead, was eerie enough, but what impressed Stanislaus was that Greene rendered the second stanza, in which the dead answer the living, as if they were whimpering for the bodied existence they could no longer enjoy:

> It is true, it is true, we are shadows cold and wan;
> And the fair and the brave whom we loved on earth are gone;
>   But still thus ev'n in death,
>   So sweet the living breath
> Of the fields and the flow'rs in our youth we wandered o'er,
>   That ere, condemn'd, we go
>   To freeze, 'mid Hecla's snow,
> We would taste it awhile, and think we live once more!

James was interested and asked Stanislaus to send the words, which he learned to sing himself. His feelings about his wife's dead lover found a dramatic counterpart in the jealousy of the dead for the living in Moore's song: it would seem that the living and the dead are jealous of each other. Another aspect of the rivalry is suggested in *Ulysses,* where Stephen cries out to his mother's ghost, whose 'glazing eyes, staring out of death, to shake and bend my soul, . . .

to strike me down,' he cannot put out of mind : 'No, mother. Let me be and let me live.'⁴ That the dead do not stay buried is, in fact, a theme of Joyce from the beginning to the end of his work; Finnegan is not the only corpse to be resurrected.

In Rome the obtrusiveness of the dead affected what he thought of Dublin, the equally Catholic city he had abandoned, a city as prehensile of its ruins, visible and invisible. His head was filled with a sense of the too successful encroachment of the dead upon the living city; there was a disrupting parallel in the way that Dublin, buried behind him, was haunting his thoughts. In *Ulysses* the theme was to be reconstituted, in more horrid form, in the mind of Stephen, who sees corpses rising from their graves like vampires to deprive the living of joy. The bridebed, the child-bed, and the bed of death are bound together, and death 'comes, pale vampire, through storm his eyes, his bat sails bloodying the sea, mouth to her mouth's kiss.'⁵ We can be at the same time in death as well as in life.⁶

By February 11, 1907, after six months in Rome, Joyce knew in general what story he must write. Some of his difficulty in beginning it was due, as he said himself,⁷ to the riot in Dublin over *The Playboy of the Western World*. Synge had followed the advice of Yeats that Joyce had rejected, to find his inspiration in the Irish folk, and had gone to the Aran Islands. This old issue finds small echoes in the story. The nationalistic Miss Ivors tries to persuade Gabriel to go to Aran (where Synge's *Riders to the Sea* is set), and when he refuses twits him for his lack of patriotic feeling. Though Gabriel thinks of defending the autonomy of art and its indifference to politics, he knows such a defense would be pretentious, and only musters up the remark that he is sick of his own country. But the issue is far from settled for him.

'The Dead' begins with a party and ends with a corpse, so entwining 'funferal' and 'funeral' as in the wake of Finnegan. That he began with a party was due, at least in part, to Joyce's feeling that the rest of the stories in *Dubliners* had not completed his picture of the city. In a letter of September 25, 1906,[8] he had written his brother from Rome to say that some elements of Dublin had been left out of his stories: 'I have not reproduced its ingenuous insularity and its hospitality, the latter "virtue" so far as I can see does not exist elsewhere in Europe.' He allowed a little of this warmth to enter 'The Dead'. In his speech at the Christmas party Gabriel Conroy explicitly commends Ireland for this very virtue of hospitality, though his expression of the idea is distinctly after-dinner: 'I feel more strongly with every recurring year that our country has no tradition which does it so much honour and which it should guard so jealously as that of its hospitality. It is a tradition that is unique as far as my experience goes (and I have visited not a few places abroad) among the modern nations.' This was Joyce's oblique way, in language that mocked his own, of beginning the task of making amends.

The selection of details for 'The Dead' shows Joyce making those choices which, while masterly, suggest the preoccupations that mastered him. Once he had determined to represent an Irish party, the choice of the Misses Morkans' as its location was easy enough. He had already reserved for *Stephen Hero* a Christmas party at his own house, a party which was also to be clouded by a discussion of a dead man. The other festive occasions of his childhood were associated with his hospitable great-aunts Mrs Callanan and Mrs Lyons, and Mrs Callanan's daughter Mary Ellen, at their house at 15 Usher's Island, which was also known as the 'Misses Flynn school'.[9] There every year the Joyces who were old enough would go, and John Joyce carved the goose and made the speech. Stanislaus Joyce says that the speech of Gabriel Conroy in 'The Dead' is a good imitation of his father's oratorical style.[10]

In Joyce's story Mrs Callanan and Mrs Lyons, the Misses Flynn, become the spinster ladies, the Misses Morkan, and Mary Ellen Callanan becomes Mary Jane. Most of the other party guests were also reconstituted from Joyce's recollections. Mrs Lyons had a son Freddy, who kept a Christmas card shop in Grafton Street.[11] Joyce introduces him as Freddy Malins, and situates his shop in the less fashionable Hénry Street, perhaps to make him need that sovereign Gabriel lent him. Another relative of Joyce's mother, a first cousin, married a Protestant named Mervyn Archdale Browne, who combined the profession of music teacher with that of agent for a burglary insurance company. Joyce keeps him in 'The Dead' under his own name. Bartell d'Arcy, the hoarse singer in the story, was based upon Barton M'Guckin, the leading tenor in the Carl Rosa Opera Company. There were other tenors, such as John McCormack, whom Joyce might have used, but he needed one who was unsuccessful and uneasy about himself; and his father's often-told anecdote about M'Guckin's lack of confidence[12] furnished him with just such a singer as he intended Bartell d'Arcy to be.

The making of his hero, Gabriel Conroy, was more complicated. The root situation, of jealousy for his wife's dead lover, was of course Joyce's. The man who is murdered, D. H. Lawrence has one of his characters say, desires to be murdered;[13] some temperaments demand the feeling that their friends and sweethearts will deceive them. Joyce's conversation often returned to the word 'betrayal',[14] and the entangled innocents whom he uses for his heroes are all aspects of his conception of himself. Though Gabriel is less impressive than Joyce's other heroes, Stephen, Bloom, Richard Rowan, or Earwicker, he belongs to their distinguished, put-upon company.

There are several specific points at which Joyce attributes his own experiences to Gabriel. The letter which Gabriel remembers having written to Gretta Conroy early in their courtship is one of these; from it Gabriel quotes to himself the sentiment, 'Why is it that words like these seem to me so dull and cold? Is it because there is no word tender enough to be your name?' These sentences are taken almost directly from a letter Joyce wrote to Nora in 1904.[15] It was also Joyce, of course, who wrote book reviews, just as Gabriel Conroy does, for the *Daily Express*. Since the *Daily*

Express was pro-English, he had probably been teased for writing for it during his frequent visits to the house of David Sheehy, M.P. One of the Sheehy daughters, Kathleen, may well have been the model for Miss Ivors, for she wore that austere bodice and sported the same patriotic pin.[16] In Gretta's old sweetheart, in Gabriel's letter, in the book reviews and the discussion of them, as well as in the physical image of Gabriel with hair parted in the middle and rimmed glasses, Joyce drew directly upon his own life.

His father was also deeply involved in the story. Stanislaus Joyce recalls that when the Joyce children were too young to bring along to the Misses Flynns' party, their father and mother sometimes left them with a governess and stayed at a Dublin hotel overnight instead of returning to their house in Bray.[17] Gabriel and Gretta do this too. Gabriel's quarrels with his mother also suggest John Joyce's quarrels with his mother, who never accepted his son's marriage to a woman of lower station.[18] But John Joyce's personality was not like Gabriel's; he had no doubts of himself, in the midst of many failures he was full of self-esteem. He had the same unshakable confidence as his son James. For Gabriel's personality there is among Joyce's friends another model.[19] This was Constantine Curran, sometimes nicknamed 'Cautious Con'. He is a more distinguished man than Joyce allows, but Joyce was building upon, and no doubt distorting, his memories of Curran as a very young man. That he has Curran partly in mind is suggested by the fact that he calls Gabriel's brother by Curran's first name Constantine, and makes Gabriel's brother, like Curran's, a priest.[20] Curran has the same high color and nervous, disquieted manner[21] as Gabriel, and like Gabriel he has traveled to the continent and has cultivated cosmopolitan interests. Curran, like Conroy, married a woman who was not a Dubliner, though she came from only as far west as Limerick. In other respects he is quite different. Gabriel was made mostly out of Curran, Joyce's father, and Joyce himself. Probably Joyce knew there was a publican in Howth named Gabriel Conroy; or, as Gerhard Friedrich has proposed,[22] he may have borrowed the name from the title of a Bret Harte novel. But the character, if not the name, was of his own compounding.[23]

Joyce now had his people, his party, and something of its development. In the festive setting, upon which the snow keeps offering a different perspective until, as W. Y. Tindall suggests,[24] the snow itself changes, he develops Gabriel's private tremors, his sense of inadequacy, his uncomfortable insistence on his small pretensions. From the beginning he is vulnerable; his well-meant and even generous overtures are regularly checked. The servant girl punctures his blithe assumption that everyone is happily in love and on the way to the altar. He is not sure enough of himself to put out of his head the slurs he has received long ago; so in spite of his uxorious attitude towards Gretta he is a little ashamed of her having come from the west of Ireland. He cannot bear to think of his dead mother's remark that Gretta was 'country cute', and when Miss Ivors says of Gretta, 'She's from Connacht, isn't she?' Gabriel answers shortly. 'Her people are.' He has rescued her from that bog. Miss Ivors's suggestion, a true Gaelic Leaguer's, that he spend his holiday in the Irish-speaking Aran Islands (in the west) upsets him; it is the element in his wife's past that he wishes to forget. During most of the story, the west of Ireland is connected in Gabriel's mind with a dark and rather painful primitivism, an aspect of his country which he has steadily abjured by going off to the continent. The west is savagery; to the east and south lie people who drink wine and wear galoshes.

Gabriel has been made uneasy about this attitude, but he clings to it defiantly until the ending. Unknown to him, it is being challenged by the song, 'The Lass of Aughrim'. Aughrim is a little village in the west not far from Galway. The song has a special relevance; in it a woman who has been seduced and abandoned by Lord Gregory comes with her baby in the rain to beg for admission to his house. It brings together the peasant mother and the civilized seducer, but Gabriel does not listen to the words; he only watches his wife listening. Joyce had heard this ballad from Nora; perhaps he considered also using Tom Moore's 'O, Ye Dead' in the story, but if so he must have seen that 'The Lass of Aughrim' would connect more subtly with the west and with Michael Furey's visit in the rain to Gretta. But the notion of using a song at all may well have come to him as the result of the excitement generated in him by Moore's song.

And now Gabriel and Gretta go to the Hotel Gresham, Gabriel fired by his living wife and Gretta drained by the memory of her dead lover. He learns for the first time of the young man in Galway, whose name Joyce has deftly altered from Sonny or Michael Bodkin to Michael Furey. The new name suggests, like the contrast of the militant Michael and the amiable Gabriel, that violent passion is in her Galway past, not in her Dublin present. Gabriel tries to cut Michael Furey down. 'What was he?' he asks, confident that his own profession of language teacher (which of course he shared with Joyce) is superior; but she replies, 'He was in the gasworks', as if this profession was as good as any other. Then Gabriel tries again, 'And what did he die of so young, Gretta? Consumption, was it?' He hopes to register the usual expressions of pity, but Gretta silences and terrifies him by her answer, 'I think he died for me.'[25] Since Joyce has already made clear that Michael Furey was tubercular, this answer of Gretta has a fine ambiguity. It asserts the egoism of passion, and unconsciously defies Gabriel's reasonable question.

Now Gabriel begins to succumb to his wife's dead lover, and becomes a pilgrim to emotional intensities outside of his own experience. From a biographical point of view, these final pages compose one of Joyce's several tributes to his wife's artless integrity. Nora Barnacle, in spite of her defects of education, was independent, unself-conscious, instinctively right. Gabriel acknowledges the same coherence in his own wife, and he recognizes in the west of Ireland, in Michael Furey, a passion he has himself always lacked. 'Better pass boldly into that other world, in the full glory of some passion, than fade and wither dismally with age,' Joyce makes Gabriel think. Then comes that strange sentence in the final paragraph : 'The time had come for him to set out on his journey westward.' The cliché runs that journeys westward are towards death, but the west has taken on a special meaning in the story. Gretta Conroy's west is the place where life had been lived simply and passionately. The context and phrasing of the sentence suggest that Gabriel is on the edge of sleep, and half-consciously accepts what he has hitherto scorned, the possibility of an actual trip to Connaught. What the sentence affirms, at last, on the level of feeling, is the west, the primitive, untutored, impulsive country from which Gabriel had felt himself alienated before; in the story, the west is paradoxically linked also with the past and the dead. It is like Aunt Julia Morkan who, though ignorant, old, grey-skinned, and stupefied, seizes in her song at the party 'the excitement of swift and secure flight'.

The tone of the sentence, 'The time had come for him to set out on his journey westward,' is somewhat resigned. It suggests a concession, a relinquishment, and Gabriel is conceding and relinquishing a good deal – his sense of the importance of civilized thinking, of continental tastes, of all those tepid but nice distinctions on which he has prided himself. The bubble of his self-possession is pricked; he no longer possesses himself, and not to possess oneself is in a way a kind of death. It is a self-abandonment not unlike Furey's, and through Gabriel's mind runs the imagery of Calvary. He imagines the snow on the cemetery at Oughterard, lying 'thickly drifted on the crooked crosses and headstones, on the spears of the little gate, on the barren thorns'. He thinks of Michael Furey who, Gretta has said, died for her, and envies him his sacrifice for another kind of love than Christ's. To some extent Gabriel too is dying for her, in giving up what he has most valued in himself, all that holds him apart from the simpler people at the party. He feels close to Gretta through sympathy if not through love; now they are both past youth, beauty, and passion; he feels close also to her dead lover, another lamb burnt on her altar, though she too is burnt now; he feels no resentment, only pity. In his own sacrifice of himself he is conscious of a melancholy unity between the living and the dead.

Gabriel, who has been sick of his own country, finds himself drawn inevitably into a silent tribute to it of much more consequence than his spoken tribute to the party. He has had illusions of the rightness of a way of life that should be outside of Ireland; but through this experience with his wife he grants a kind of bondage, of acceptance, even of admiration to a part of the country and a way of life that are most Irish. Ireland is shown to be stronger, more intense than he. At the end of *A Portrait of the Artist*, too, Stephen Dedalus, who has been so resolutely opposed to nationalism, makes a similar concession when he interprets his departure from Ireland as an attempt to forge a conscience for his race.

Joyce did not invent the incidents that conclude his story, the second honeymoon of Gabriel and Gretta which ends so badly. His method of composition was very like T. S. Eliot's, the imaginative absorption of stray material. The method did not please Joyce very much because he considered it not imaginative enough, but it was the only way he could work. He borrowed the ending for 'The Dead' from another book. In that book a bridal couple receive, on their wedding night, a message that a young woman whom the husband jilted has just committed suicide. The news holds them apart, she asks him not to kiss her, and both are tormented by remorse. The wife, her marriage unconsummated, falls at last to sleep, and her husband goes to the window and looks out at 'the melancholy greyness of the dawn'. For the first time he recognizes, with the force of a revelation, that his life is a failure, and that his wife lacks the passion of the girl who has killed herself. He resolves that, since he is not worthy of any more momentous career, he will try at least to make her happy. Here surely is the situation that Joyce so adroitly recomposed. The dead lover who comes between the lovers, the sense of the husband's failure, the acceptance of mediocrity, the resolve to be at all events sympathetic, all come from the other book. But Joyce transforms them. For example, he allows Gretta to kiss her husband, but without desire, and rarefies the situation by having it arise not from a suicide but from a memory of young love. The book Joyce was borrowing from was one that nobody reads any more, George Moore's *Vain Fortune;* but Joyce read it,[26] and in his youthful essay, 'The Day of the Rabblement', overpraised it as 'fine original work'.[27]

Moore said nothing about snow, however. No one can know how Joyce conceived the joining of Gabriel's final experience with the snow. But his fondness for a background of this kind is also illustrated by his use of the fireplace in 'Ivy Day', of the street-lamps in 'Two Gallants', and of the river in *Finnegans Wake*. It does not seem that the snow can be death, as so many have said, for it falls on living and dead alike, and for death to fall on the dead is a simple redundancy of which Joyce would not have been guilty. For snow to be 'general all over Ireland' is of course unusual in that country. The fine description : 'It was falling on every part of the dark central plain, on the treeless hills, falling softly upon the Bog of Allen and, farther westward, softly falling into the dark mutinous Shannon waves,' is probably borrowed by Joyce from a famous simile in the twelfth book of the Iliad, which Thoreau translates :[28] 'The snowflakes fall thick and fast on a winter's day. The winds are lulled, and the snow falls incessant, covering the tops of the mountains, and the hills, and the plains where the lotus-tree grows, and the cultivated fields, and they are falling by the inlets and shores of the foaming sea, but are silently dissolved by the waves.' But Homer was simply describing the thickness of the arrows in the battle of the Greeks and Trojans; and while Joyce seems to copy his topographical details, he uses the image here chiefly for a similar sense of crowding and quiet pressure. Where Homer speaks of the waves silently dissolving the snow, Joyce adds the final detail of 'the mutinous Shannon waves' which suggests the 'Furey' quality of the west. The snow that falls upon Gabriel, Gretta, and Michael Furey, upon the Misses Morkan, upon the dead singers and the living, is mutuality, a sense of their connection with each other, a sense that none has his being alone. The party-goers prefer dead singers to living ones, the wife prefers a dead lover to a live lover.

The snow does not stand alone in the story. It is part of the complex imagery that includes heat and cold air, fire, and rain, as well as snow. The relations of these are not simple. During the party the living people, their festivities, and all human society seem contrasted with the cold outside, as in the warmth of Gabriel's hand on the cold pane. But this warmth is felt by Gabriel as stuffy and confining, and the cold outside is repeatedly connected with what is fragrant and fresh. The cold, in this sense of piercing intensity, culminates in the picture of Michael Furey in the rain and darkness of the Galway night.

Another warmth is involved in 'The Dead'. In Gabriel's memory of his own love for Gretta, he recalls incidents in his love's history as stars, burning with pure and distant intensity, and recalls moments of his passion for her as having the fire of stars. The irony of this image is that the sharp and beautiful experience was, though he has not known it until this night, incomplete. There is a telling metaphor : he remembers a moment of happiness, standing with Gretta in the cold, looking in through a window at a man making bottles in a roaring furnace, and suddenly calling out to the man, 'Is the fire hot?' The question sums up his naïve deprivation; if the man at the furnace had heard the question, his answer, thinks Gabriel, might have been rude; so the revelation on this night is rude to Gabriel's whole being. On this night he acknowledges that love must be a feeling which he has never fully had.

Gabriel is not utterly deprived. Throughout the story there is affection for this man who, without the sharpest, most passionate perceptions, is yet generous and considerate. The intense and the moderate can meet; intensity bursts out and declines, and the moderated can admire and pity it, and share the fate that moves both types of mankind towards age and death. The furthest point of love of which Gabriel is capable is past. Furey's passion is past because of his sudden death. Gretta is perhaps the most pitiful, in that knowing Furey's passion, and being of his kind, she does not die but lives to wane in Gabriel's way; on this night she too is fatigued, not beautiful, her clothes lie crumpled beside her. The snow seems to share in this decline; viewed from inside at the party, it is desirable, unattainable, just as at his first knowledge of Michael Furey, Gabriel envies him. At the end as the partygoers walk to the cab the snow is slushy and in patches, and then, seen from the window of the hotel room, it belongs to all men, it is general, mutual. Under its canopy, all human beings, whatever their degrees of intensity, fall into union. The mutuality is that all men feel and lose feeling, all interact, all warrant the sympathy that Gabriel now extends to Furey, to Gretta, to himself, even to old Aunt Julia.

In its lyrical, melancholy acceptance of all that life and death offer, 'The Dead' is a linchpin in Joyce's work. There is that basic situation of cuckoldry, real or putative, which is to be found throughout. There is the special Joycean collation of specific detail raised to rhythmical intensity. The final purport of the story, the mutual dependency of living and dead, is something that he meditated a good deal from his early youth. He had expressed it first in his essay on Mangan in 1902, when he spoke already of the union in the great memory of death along with life;[29] even then he had begun to learn like Gabriel that we are all Romes, our new edifices reared beside, and even joined with, ancient monuments. In Dubliners he developed this idea. The interrelationship of dead and living is the theme of the first story in Dubliners as well as of the last; it is also the theme of 'A Painful Case', but an even closer parallel to 'The Dead' is the story, 'Ivy Day in the Committee Room'. This was in one sense an answer to his univer-

sity friends who mocked his remark that death is the most beautiful form of life by saying that absence is the highest form of presence. Joyce did not think either idea absurd. What binds 'Ivy
Day' to 'The Dead' is that in both stories the central agitation
derives from a character who never appears, who is dead, absent.
Joyce wrote Stanislaus that Anatole France had given him the
idea for both stories.[30] There may be other sources in France's
works, but a possible one is 'The Procurator of Judaea'. In it
Pontius Pilate reminisces with a friend about the days he was
procurator in Judaea, and describes the events of his time with
Roman reason, calm, and elegance. Never once does he, or his
friend, mention the person we expect him to discuss, the founder
of Christianity, until at the end the friend asks if Pontius Pilate
happens to remember someone of the name of Jesus, from Nazareth, and the veteran administrator replies, 'Jesus? Jesus of
Nazareth? I cannot call him to mind.' The story is overshadowed
by the person whom Pilate does not recall; without him the story
would not exist. Joyce uses a similar method in 'Ivy Day' with
Parnell and in 'The Dead' with Michael Furey.

In *Ulysses* the climactic episode, *Circe,* whirls to a sepulchral
close in the same juxtaposition of living and dead, the ghost of his
mother confronting Stephen, and the ghost of his son confronting
Bloom. But Joyce's greatest triumph in asserting the intimacy of
living and dead was to be the close of *Finnegans Wake.* Here Anna
Livia Plurabelle, the river of life, flows toward the sea, which is
death; the fresh water passes into the salt, a bitter ending. Yet it is
also a return to her father, the sea, that produces the cloud which
makes the river, and her father is also her husband, to whom she
gives herself as a bride to her groom. Anna Livia is going back to
her father, as Gabriel journeys westward in feeling to the roots
of his fatherland; like him, she is sad and weary. To him the Shannon waves are dark and mutinous, and to her the sea is cold and
mad. In *Finnegans Wake* Anna Livia's union is not only with
love but with death; like Gabriel she seems to swoon away.[31]

That Joyce at the age of twenty-five and -six should have written this story ought not to seem odd. Young writers reach their greatest eloquence in dwelling upon the horrors of middle age and what follows it. But beyond this proclivity which he shared with others, Joyce had a special reason for writing the story of 'The Dead' in 1906 and 1907. In his own mind he had thoroughly justified his flight from Ireland, but he had not decided the question of where he would fly *to*. In Trieste and Rome he had learned what he had unlearned in Dublin, to be a Dubliner. As he had written his brother from Rome with some astonishment, he felt humiliated when anyone attacked his 'impoverished country'.[32] 'The Dead' is his first song of exile.

S O U R C E : *James Joyce* (1959) pp. 252–63.

N O T E S

1. Letter to me from Mrs Kathleen Barnacle Griffin.
2. See Richard Ellmann, *James Joyce* (New York, 1959) p. 222.
3. S. Joyce, 'The Background to "Dubliners" ', *Listener*, LI (25 March 1954) pp. 526-7.
4. *Ulysses* (Random House : 1942; Bodley Head : 1937) p. 12 (8).
5. Ibid. p. 48 (44).
6. The converse of this theme appears in *Ulysses* (p. 113 [107]), when Bloom, walking in Glasnevin, thinks, 'They are not going to get me this innings. Warm beds : warm fullblooded life.'
7. See *James Joyce* p. 248.
8. See ibid. p. 239.
9. Interview with Mrs May Joyce Monaghan, 1953.
10. He excepts the quotation from Browning, but even this was quite within the scope of the man who could quote Vergil when lending money to his son. (See *James Joyce* p. 316.)
11. Interview with Mrs Monaghan.
12. See *James Joyce* p. 14.
13. Birkin in *Women in Love*.
14. Information from Professor Joseph Prescott.
15. At Cornell.

16. Interview with Mrs Mary Sheehy Kettle, 1953.

17. *My Brother's Keeper* (Viking, 1958; Faber, 1958) p. 38 (58).

18. See *James Joyce* p. 17.

19. Interview with S. Joyce, 1953.

20. Suggested to me by Professor Vivian Mercier.

21. See Joyce's letter, *James Joyce* p. 234.

22. Gerhard Friedrich, 'Bret Harte as a Source for James Joyce's "The Dead," ' *Philological Quarterly,* xxxiii (Oct. 1954) pp. 442–4.

23. The name of Conroy's wife Gretta was borrowed from another friend, Gretta (actually Margaret) Cousins, the wife of James H. Cousins. Since Joyce mentioned in a letter at the same time that he was meditating 'The Dead' the danger of becoming 'a patient Cousins' (Letter to S. Joyce, Feb. 1907), this family was evidently on his mind.

24. W. Y. Tindall, *The Literary Symbol* (New York, 1955) p. 227.

25. Adaline Glasheen has discovered here an echo of Yeats's nationalistic play, *Cathleen ni Houlihan* (1902), where the old woman who symbolizes Ireland sings a song of 'yellow-haired Donough that was hanged in Galway'. When she is asked, 'What was it brought him to his death?' she replies, 'He died for love of me; many a man has died for love of me.' (I am indebted to Mrs Glasheen for pointing this out to me.)

26. He evidently refreshed his memory of it when writing 'The Dead', for his copy of *Vain Fortune,* now at Yale, bears the date 'March 1907'.

27. *The Critical Writings of James Joyce,* ed. Ellsworth Mason and Richard Ellmann (Viking: 1959; Faber: 1959) p. 71.

28. Professor Walter B. Rideout kindly called my attention to the similarity of these passages.

29. *Critical Writings* p. 83.

30. Letter to S. Joyce, 11 February 1907.

31. See also *James Joyce* pp. 724–6.

32. Letter to S. Joyce, 25 September 1906.

Wayne C. Booth

THE PROBLEM OF DISTANCE IN
A PORTRAIT OF THE ARTIST (1961)

. . . Jane Austen's implicit apology for Emma said, in effect, 'Emma's vision is your vision; therefore forgive her'. But modern authors have learned how to provide this apology in much more insistent form. The deep plunges of modern inside views, the various streams-of-consciousness that attempt to give the reader an effect of living thought and sensation, are capable of blinding us to the possibility of our making judgments not shared by the narrator or reflector himself.

If a master puzzle maker had set out to give us the greatest possible difficulty, he could not have done more than has been done in some modern works in which this effect of deep involvement is combined with the implicit demand that we maintain our capacity for ironic judgment. The trouble with *Moll Flanders,* such a genius of confusion might be imagined as saying to himself, is that the obvious differences between the female heroine and the author provide too many clues. Let us then write a book that will look like the author's autobiography, using many details from his own life and opinions. But we cannot be satisfied with moral problems, which are after all much less subject to dispute than intellectual and aesthetic matters. Let us then call for the reader's precise judgment on a very elaborate set of opinions and actions in which the hero is sometimes right, sometimes slightly wrong, and sometimes absurdly astray. Just to make sure that things are not too obvious, let us finally bind the reader so tightly to the consciousness of the ambiguously misguided protagonist that nothing will interfere with his delight in inferring the precise though varying degrees of distance that operate from point to point throughout the book. We can be sure that some readers will take the book as strictly autobiographical; others will go sadly astray in overlooking ironies that are intended and in discovering ironies that are not there. But for the rare reader who can make his way through this jungle, the delight will be great indeed.

The giant whom we all must wrestle with in this regard is clearly Joyce. Except for occasional outbursts of bravado nobody has ever really claimed that Joyce is clear. In all the skeleton keys and classroom guides there is open assumption that his later works, *Ulysses* and *Finnegans Wake,* cannot be read; they can only be studied. Joyce himself was always explicating his works, and it is clear that he saw nothing wrong with the fact that they could not be thought of as standing entirely on their own feet. The reader's problems are handled, if they are to be handled at all, by rhetoric provided outside the work.

But the difficulties with distance that are pertinent here cannot be removed by simple study. Obscure allusions can be looked up, patterns of imagery and theme can be traced; gradually over the years a good deal of lore has accumulated, and about some of it by now there is even a certain amount of agreement. But about the more fundamental matters the skeleton keys and guides are of little help, because unfortunately they do not agree, they do not agree at all. It is fine to know that in *Ulysses* Stephen stands in some way for Telemachus and Bloom for his wandering father, Ulysses. But it would also be useful to know whether the work is comic or pathetic or tragic, or, if it is a combination, where the elements fall. Can two readers be said to have read the same book if one thinks it ends affirmatively and the other sees the ending as pessimistic? It is really no explanation to say that Joyce has succeeded in imitating life so well that like life itself his books seem totally ambiguous, totally open to whatever interpretation

the reader wants to place on them. Even William Empson, that
perceptive and somewhat overly ingenious prophet of ambiguity,
finds himself unable to be completely permissive toward conflicting interpretations. In a long, curious essay arguing that the basic
movement of *Ulysses* is toward a favorable ending, with the
Blooms and Stephen united, he admits that there are difficulties,
and that they spring from the kind of book it is: it 'not only
refuses to tell you the end of the story, it also refuses to tell you
what the author thinks would have been a good end to the story.'
And yet almost in the same breath he can write as if he thought
previous critics somehow at fault for not having come to *his*
inferences about the book. 'By the way, I have no patience with
critics who say it is impossible ever to tell whether Joyce means a
literary effect to be ironical or not; if they don't know this part
isn't funny, they ought to.'[1] Well, but why should they know?
Who is to mediate between Empson and those he attacks, or
between Lawrance Thompson, in his interpretation of the book
as comedy, and those critics with whom he is 'decidedly at odds',
Stuart Gilbert, Edmund Wilson, Harry Levin, David Daiches,
and T. S. Eliot, each of whom assumes, he says, that 'Joyce's
artistic mode is essentially a non-comic mode, or that comedy in
Ulysses is an effect rather than a cause'?[2]

Can it possibly make no difference whether we laugh or do not
laugh? Can we defend the book even as a realistic mixture, like
life itself, unless we can state with some precision what the ingre-
dients are that have been mixed together?

Rather than pursue such general questions about Joyce's admit-
tedly difficult later works, it will be more useful to look closely at
that earlier work for which no skeleton key has been thought
necessary, *A Portrait of the Artist as a Young Man* (1916). Everyone seems by now agreed that it is a masterpiece in the modern
mode. Perhaps we can accept it as that – indeed accept it as an
unquestionably great work from any viewpoint – and still feel free
to ask a few irreverent questions.

The structure of this 'authorless' work is based on the growth of a sensitive boy to young manhood. The steps in his growth are obviously constructed with great care. Each of the first four sections ends a period of Stephen's life with what Joyce, in an earlier draft, calls an epiphany : a peculiar revelation of the inner reality of an experience, accompanied with great elation, as in a mystical religious experience. Each is followed by the opening of a new chapter on a very prosaic, even depressed level. Now here is clearly a careful structural preparation – for what? For a transformation, or for a merely cyclical return? Is the final exaltation a release from the depressing features of Irish life which have tainted the earlier experiences? Or is it the fifth turn in an endless cycle? And in either case, is Stephen always to be viewed with the same deadly seriousness with which he views himself? Is it to artistic maturity that he grows? As the young man goes into exile from Ireland, goes 'to encounter for the millionth time the reality of experience and to forge in the smithy' of his soul 'the uncreated conscience' of his race, are we to take this, with Harry Levin, as a fully serious portrait of the artist Dedalus, praying to his name-sake Daedalus, to stand him 'now and ever in good stead'?[3] Or is the inflated style, as Mark Schorer tells us, Joyce's clue that the young Icarus is flying too close to the sun, with the 'excessive lyric relaxation' of Stephen's final style punctuating 'the illusory nature of the whole ambition'?[4] The young man views himself and his flight with unrelieved solemnity. Should we?

To see the difficulties clearly, let us consider three crucial episodes, all from the final section : his rejection of the priesthood, his exposition of what he takes to be Thomistic aesthetics, and his composition of a poem.

Is his rejection of the priesthood a triumph, a tragedy, or merely a comedy of errors? Most readers, even those who follow the new trend of reading Stephen ironically, seem to have read it as a triumph : the artist has rid himself of one of the chains that bound him. To Caroline Gordon, this is a serious misreading. 'I

suspect that Joyce's *Portrait* has been misread by a whole generation.' She sees the rejection as 'the picture of a soul that is being
damned for time and eternity caught in the act of foreseeing and
foreknowing its damnation', and she cites in evidence the fall of
Icarus and Stephen's own statement to Cranly that he is not
afraid to make a mistake, 'even a great mistake, a lifelong mistake
and perhaps for eternity, too'.[5] Well, which *Portrait* do we choose,
that of the artistic soul battling through successfully to his necessary freedom, or that of the child of God, choosing, like Lucifer,
his own damnation? No two books could be further from each
other than the two we envision here. There may be a sufficient
core of what is simply interesting to salvage the book as a great
work of the sensibility, but unless we are willing·to retreat into
babbling and incommunicable relativism, we cannot believe that
it is *both* a portrait of the prisoner freed *and* a portrait of the
soul placing itself in chains.

Critics have had even more difficulty with Stephen's aesthetic
theory, ostensibly developed from Aquinas. Is the book itself, as
Grant Redford tells us,[6] an 'objectification of an artistic proposi-
tion and a method announced by the central character', achieving
for Joyce the 'wholeness, harmony, and radiance' that Stephen
celebrates in his theory? Or is it, as Father Noon says, an ironic
portrait of Stephen's immature aesthetics? Joyce wanted to qualify
Stephen's utterances, Father Noon tells us, 'by inviting attention
to his own more sophisticated literary concerns', and he stands
apart from the Thomist aesthetics, watching Stephen miss the
clue in his drive for an impersonal, dramatic narration. 'The
comparison of the artist with the God of the creation', taken
'straight' by many critics, is for Father Noon 'the climax of Joyce's
ironic development of the Dedalus aesthetic'.[7]

Finally, what of the precious villanelle? Does Joyce intend it to
be taken as a serious sign of Stephen's artistry, as a sign of his
genuine but amusingly pretentious precocity, or as something else
entirely?

> Are you not weary of ardent ways,
> Lure of the fallen seraphim?
> Tell no more of enchanted days.
>
> Your eyes have set man's heart ablaze
> And you have had your will of him.
> Are you not weary of ardent ways? . . .

Hardly anyone has committed himself in public about the quality of this poem. Are we to smile at Stephen or pity him in his tortured longing? Are we to marvel at his artistry, or scoff at his conceit? Or are we merely to say, 'How remarkable an insight into the kind of poem that would be written by an adolescent in love, if he were artistically inclined'? The poem, we are told, 'enfolded him like a shining cloud, enfolded him like water with a liquid life : and like a cloud of vapour or like waters circumfluent in space the liquid letters of speech, symbols of the element of mystery, flowed forth over his brain.' As we recall Jean Paul's formula for 'romantic irony', 'hot baths of sentiment followed by cold showers of irony', we can only ask here which tap has been turned on. Are we to swoon – or laugh?

Some critics will no doubt answer that all these questions are irrelevant. The villanelle is not to be judged but simply experienced; the aesthetic theory is, within the art work, neither true nor false but simply 'true' to the art work – that is, true to Stephen's character at this point. To read modern literature properly we must refuse to ask irrelevant questions about it; we must accept the 'portrait' and no more ask whether the character portrayed is good or bad, right or wrong than we ask whether a woman painted by Picasso is moral or immoral. 'All facts of any kind', as Gilbert puts it, 'mental or material, sublime or ludicrous, have an equivalence of value for the artist.'[8]

This answer, which can be liberating at one stage of our development in appreciating not only modern but all art, becomes less and less satisfactory the longer we look at it. It certainly does not

G

seem to have been Joyce's basic attitude, though he was often
misleading about it.[9] The creation and the enjoyment of art can
never be a completely neutral activity. Though different works
of art require different kinds of judgment for their enjoyment, the
position taken . . . [elsewhere in *The Rhetoric of Fiction*] must
stand : no work, not even the shortest lyric, can be written in
complete moral, intellectual and aesthetic neutrality. We may
judge falsely, we may judge unconsciously, but we cannot even
bring the book to mind without judging its elements, seeing them
as shaped into a given kind of thing. Even if we denied that the
sequence of events has meaning in the sense of being truly sequen-
tial, that denial would itself be a judgment on the rightness of
Stephen's actions and opinions at each stage : to decide that he is
not growing is as much a judgment on his actions as to decide that
he is becoming more and more mature. Actually everyone reads the
book as some kind of progressive sequence, and to do so we judge
succeeding actions and opinions to be more or less moral, sensitive,
intellectually mature, than those they follow.[10] If we felt that the
question of Joyce's precise attitude toward Stephen's vocation, his
aesthetics, and his villanelle were irrelevant, we would hardly
dispute with each other about them. Yet I count in a recent check
list at least fifteen articles and one full book disputing Joyce's
attitude about the aesthetics alone.[11]

Like most modern critics, I would prefer to settle such disputes
by using internal rather than external evidence. But the experts
themselves give me little hope of finding answers to my three
problems by re-reading *Portrait* one more time. They all clutch
happily at any wisp of comment or fragmentary document that
might illuminate Joyce's intentions.[12] And who can blame them?

The truth seems to be that Joyce was always a bit uncertain
about his attitude toward Stephen. Anyone who reads Ellmann's
masterful biography with this problem in mind cannot help being
struck by the many shifts and turns Joyce took as he worked
through the various versions. There is nothing especially strange

in that, of course. Most 'autobiographical' novelists probably encounter difficulty in trying to decide just how heroic their heroes are to be. But Joyce's explorations came just at a time when the traditional devices for control of distance were being repudiated, when doctrines of objectivity were in the air, and when people were taking seriously the idea that to evoke 'reality' was a sufficient aim in art; the artist need not concern himself with judging or with specifying whether the reader should approve or disapprove, laugh or cry.

Now the traditional forms *had* specified in their very conceptions a certain degree of clarity about distance. If an author chose to write comedy, for example, he knew that his characters must at least to some degree be 'placed' at a distance from the spectator's norms. This predetermination did not, of course, settle all of his problems. To balance sympathy and antipathy, admiration and contempt, was still a fundamental challenge, but it was a challenge for which there was considerable guidance in the practice of previous writers of comedy. If, on the other hand, he chose to write tragedy, or satire, or elegy, or celebration odes, or whatever, he could rely to some extent on conventions to guide him and his audience to a common attitude toward his characters.

The young Joyce had none of this to rely on, but he seems never to have sensed the full danger of his position. When, in his earliest years, he recorded his brief epiphanies – those bits of dialogue or description that were supposed to reveal the inner reality of things – there was always an implied identification of the recorder's norms and the reader's; both were spectators at the revealing moment, both shared in the vision of one moment of truth. Though some of the epiphanies are funny, some sad, and some mixed, the basic effect is always the same : an overwhelming sense – when they succeed – of what Joyce liked to call the 'incarnation' : Artistic Meaning has come to live in the world's body. The Poet has done his work.

Even in these early epiphanies there is difficulty with distance;

the author inevitably expects the reader to share in his own pre-
conceptions and interests sufficiently to catch, from each word or
gesture, the precise mood or tone that they evoke for the author
himself. But since complete identification with the author is a
silent precondition for the success of such moments, the basic
problem of distance is never a serious one. Even if the author and
reader should differ in interpretation, they can share the sense
of evoked reality.

It is only when Joyce places at the center of a long work a
figure who experiences epiphanies, an epiphany-producing device,
as it were, who is himself used by the real author as an object
ambiguously distant from the norms of the work, that the com-
plications of distance become incalculable. If he treats the author-
figure satirically, as he does in much of *Stephen Hero,* that earlier,
windier version of *Portrait,*[13] then what happens to the quality of
the epiphanies that *he* describes? Are they still genuine epiphanies
or only what the misguided, callow youth *thinks* are epiphanies?
If, as Joyce's brother Stanislaus has revealed, the word 'hero' is
satiric, can we take seriously that anti-hero's vision? Yet if the
satirical mode is dropped, if the hero is made into a real hero,
and if the reader is made to see things entirely as he sees them,
what then happens to objectivity? The portrait is no longer an
objective rendering of reality, looked at from a respectable aesthetic
distance, but rather a mere subjective indulgence.

Joyce can be seen, in Ellmann's account, struggling with this
problem throughout the revisions. Unlike writers before Flaubert,
he had no guidance from convention or tradition or fellow artists.
Neither Flaubert nor James had established any sure ground to
stand on. Both of them had, in fact, stumbled on the same hurdles,
and though each had on occasion surmounted the difficulties,
Joyce was in no frame of mind to look behind their claims as
realists to the actual problems and lessons that lay beneath their
evocative surfaces. A supreme egoist struggling to deal artistically
with his own ego, a humorist who could not escape the comic

consequences of his portrait of that inflated ego, he faced, in the completed *Stephen Hero,* what he had to recognize as a hodge-podge of irreconcilables. Is Stephen a pompous ass or not? Is his name deliberately ridiculous, as Stanislaus, who invented it, says? Or is it a serious act of symbolism? The way out seems inevitable, but it seems a retreat nonetheless : simply present the 'reality' and let the reader judge. Cut all of the author's judgments, cut all of the adjectives, produce one long, ambiguous epiphany.[14]

Purged of the author's explicit judgment, the resulting work was so brilliant and compelling, its hero's vision so scintillating, that almost all readers overlooked the satiric and ironic content – except, of course, as the satire operated against *other* characters. So far as I know no one said anything about irony against Stephen until after *Ulysses* was published in 1922, with its opening in which Icarus–Stephen is shown with his wings clipped. Ironic readings did not become popular, in fact, until after the fragment of *Stephen Hero* was published in 1944. Readers of that work found, it is true, many authoritative confirmations of their exaltation of Stephen – for the most part in a form that might confirm any-one's prejudice against commentary. '. . . When he [Stephen] wrote it was always a mature and reasoned emotion which urged him' (p. 155). 'This mood of indignation which was not guiltless of a certain superficiality was undoubtedly due to the excitement of release. . . . He acknowledged to himself in honest egoism that he could not take to heart the distress of a nation, the soul of which was antipathetic to his own, so bitterly as the indignity of a bad line of verse : but at the same time he was nothing in the world so little as an amateur artist' (p. 130). 'Stephen did not attach himself to art in any spirit of youthful dilettantism but strove to pierce to the significant heart of everything' (p. 25). But readers were also faced with a good many denigrations of the hero. We can agree that *Portrait* is a better work because the immature author has been effaced; Joyce may indeed have found

that effacing the commentary was the only way he could obtain
an air of maturity. But the fact remains that it is primarily to
this immature commentary that we must go for evidence in de-
ciphering the ironies of the later, purer work.

What we find in *Stephen Hero* is not a simple confirmation of
any reading that we might have achieved on the basis of *Portrait*
alone. Rather we find an extremely complicated view, combining
irony and admiration in unpredictable mixtures. Thus the Thomist
aesthetics 'was in the main applied Aquinas and he set it forth
plainly with a naif air of discovering novelties. This he did partly
to satisfy his own taste for enigmatic roles and partly from a
genuine predisposition in favour of all but the premisses of scholasticism' (p. 64). No one ever inferred, before this passage was
available, anything like this precise and complex judgment on
Stephen. The combination of blame and approval, we may be
sure, is different in the finished *Portrait;* the implied author no
doubt often repudiates the explicit judgments of the younger
narrator who intrudes into *Stephen Hero.* But we can also be sure
that his judgment has not become less complex. Where do we
find, in any criticism of *Portrait* based entirely on internal evidence, the following kind of juxtaposition of Stephen's views with
the author's superior insight? 'Having by this *simple process*
established the literary form of art as the most excellent he *proceeded to examine it in favour of his theory,* or, *as he rendered
it,* to establish the relations which must subsist between the literary
image, the work of art itself, and that energy which had imagined
and fashioned it, the center of conscious, re-acting, particular
life, the artist' (p. 65; italics mine). Can we infer, from *Portrait,*
that Joyce sees Stephen as simply rationalizing in favor of his
theory? Did we guess that Joyce could refer to him mockingly
as a 'fiery-hearted revolutionary' and a 'heaven-ascending
essayist'?[15]

In *Stephen Hero,* the author's final evaluation of the aesthetics
is favorable but qualified : 'Except for the eloquent and arrogant

peroration Stephen's essay was a careful exposition of a carefully meditated theory of esthetic' (p. 68). Though it might be argued that in the finished book he has cut out some of the negative elements, such as the 'eloquent and arrogant peroration', and has presented the pure theory in conversational form, it is clear that Joyce himself judged his hero's theory in greater detail than we could possibly infer from the final version alone.

Similar clarifications can be found in *Stephen Hero* of our other two crucial problems, his rejection of the priesthood and his poetic ability. For example, 'He had swept the moment into his memory . . . and . . . had brought forth some pages of sorry verse' (p. 57). Can the hero of *Portrait* be thought of as writing 'sorry verse'? One would not think so, to read much of the commentary by Joyce's critics.

But who is to blame them? Whatever intelligence Joyce postulates in his reader – let us assume the unlikely case of its being comparable to his own – will not be sufficient for precise inference of a pattern of judgments which is, after all, private to Joyce. And this will be true regardless of how much distance from his own hero we believe him to have achieved by the time he concluded his final version. We simply cannot avoid the conclusion that to some extent the book itself is at fault, regardless of its great virtues. Unless we make the absurd assumption that Joyce had in reality purged himself of all judgment by the time he completed his final draft, unless we see him as having really come to look upon all of Stephen's actions as equally wise or equally foolish, equally sensitive or equally meaningless, we must conclude that many of the refinements he intended in his finished *Portrait* are, for most of us, permanently lost. Even if we were now to do our homework like dutiful students, even if we were to study all of Joyce's work, even if we were to spend the lifetime that Joyce playfully said his novels demand, presumably we should never come to as rich, as refined, and as varied a conception of the quality of Stephen's last days in Ireland as Joyce had in mind. For some of us the air of detachment and objectivity may still be worth the price, but we must never pretend that a price was not paid.

SOURCE: *The Rhetoric of Fiction* (1961) pp. 324–36.

NOTES

1. 'The Theme of *Ulysses*', *Kenyon Review*, xviii (Winter, 1956) pp. 36, 31.

2. *A Comic Principle in Sterne – Meredith – Joyce* (Oslo, 1954) p. 22.

3. *James Joyce* (Norfolk, Va., 1941) pp. 58–62.

4. 'Technique as Discovery', *Hudson Review*, i (Spring, 1948) pp. 79–80.

5. *How To Read a Novel* (New York, 1957) p. 213.

6. 'The Role of Structure in Joyce's "Portrait" ', *Modern Fiction Studies*, iv (Spring 1958) p. 30. See also Herbert Gorman, *James Joyce* (London, 1941) p. 96, and Stuart Gilbert, *James Joyce's Ulysses* (London, 1930) pp. 20–2.

7. William T. Noon, S.J., *Joyce and Aquinas* (New Haven, Conn., 1957) pp. 34, 35, 66, 67. See also Hugh Kenner, 'The *Portrait* in Perspective', *Kenyon Review*, x (Summer, 1948) pp. 361–81.

8. *James Joyce's Ulysses*, p. 22.

9. Richard Ellmann concludes that whether we know it or not, 'Joyce's court is, like Dante's or Tolstoy's, always in session' (*James Joyce* [New York, 1959] p. 3).

10. Norman Friedman considers it a 'tribute to Joyce's dramatic genius that a Catholic can sympathize with the portrayal of Catholic values in the novel which the hero rejects' ('Point of View in Fiction', *PMLA*, lxx [December, 1955] pp. 11–84). But this is not to say that the Catholic readers are right, or that we need not make up our minds about the question.

11. *Modern Fiction Studies*, iv (Spring, 1958) pp. 72–99.

12. See, for example, J. Mitchell Morse's defense of a fairly 'straight' reading of *Ulysses*, based largely on Gorman's reading of Joyce's *Notebooks* ('Augustine, *Ayenbite*, and *Ulysses*', *PMLA*, lxx [December, 1955] p. 1147, n. 12).

13. Ed. Theodore Spencer, 1944. Only part of the MS. survives.

14. See Denis Donoghue's 'Joyce and the Finite Order', *Sewanee*

Review, LXVIII (Spring, 1960) pp. 256–73. 'The objects [in *Portrait*] exist to provide a suitably piteous setting for Stephen as Sensitive Plant; they are meant to mark a sequence of experiences in the mode of *pathos*. . . . The lyric situation is insulated from probes, and there is far too much of this cosseting in the *Portrait*. . . . Drama or rhetoric should have warned Joyce that Stephen the aesthetic *alazon* needed nothing so urgently as a correspondingly deft *eiron;* lacking this, the book is blind in one eye' (p. 258). Joyce would no doubt reply – I think unfairly – that he intended Stephen as both *alazon* and *eiron*.

15. One reviewer of *Stephen Hero* was puzzled to notice in it that the omniscient author, not yet purged in accordance with Joyce's theories of dramatic narration, frequently expresses biting criticism of the young Stephen. The earlier work thus seemed to him 'much more cynical', and 'much, much farther from the principles of detached classicism that had been formulated before either book was written'. How could the man who wrote *Stephen Hero* go on and write, 'in a mood of enraptured fervour' a work like *Portrait?* (*T.L.S.*, 1 February 1957, p. 64).

It is true that, once we have been alerted, signs of ironic intention come rushing to our view. Those of us who now believe that Joyce is not entirely serious in the passages on aesthetics must wonder, for example, how we ever read them 'straight'. What did we make out of passages like the following, in those old, benighted days before we saw what was going on? 'The lore which he was believed to pass his days brooding upon so that it had rapt him from the companion-ship of youth was only a garner of slender sentences from Aristotle's Poetics and Psychology and a *Synopsis Philosophiæ Scholasticæ ad mentem divi Thomæ*. His thinking was a dusk of doubt and selfmis-trust, lit up at moments by the lightnings of intuition. . . .' 'In those moments the world perished about his feet as if it had been [with] fire consumed : and thereafter his tongue grew heavy and he met the eyes of others with unanswering eyes for he felt that the spirit of beauty had folded him round like a mantle and that in reverie at least he had been acquainted with nobility. But, when this brief pride of silence upheld him no longer, he was glad to find himself still in the midst of common lives, passing on his way amid the squalor and noise and sloth of the city fearlessly and with a light heart' (opening pp. of chap. v). If this is not mockery, however tender, it is fustian.

J. I. M. Stewart

DUBLINERS (1963)

Joyce early found himself in difficulties with doubting publishers
and timid printers. *Dubliners,* when it appeared in 1914, contained
fifteen sketches or short stories which, nine years before, he had
endeavoured to recommend in the following terms :

> My intention was to write a chapter of the moral history of
> my country and I chose Dublin for the scene because the city
> seemed to me the centre of paralysis. . . . I have written it for
> the most part in a style of scrupulous meanness and with the
> conviction that he is a very bold man who dares to alter in the
> presentment, still more to deform, whatever he has seen and
> heard.

This is a little manifesto of naturalism; but its most significant
phrase is 'moral history'. Stephen Dedalus, paraphrasing Flaubert,
was to describe the writer as one who 'remains within or behind
or beyond or above his handiwork, invisible, refined out of existence, indifferent, paring his fingernails' and was to sketch an
aesthetic in consonance with this. Yet when writing to his brother
about *Dubliners* Joyce condemns Maupassant's moral sense as
'rather obtuse'. And it is apparent in the stories that he does not
differ from other young writers in having as his chief impulsion
a set of powerful emotional responses before the spectacle of fallen
humanity – here mostly represented, it seems, by his own relations
and their circle. It is urged upon us that almost every aspect of
Dublin life is horrifying or pitiful or degraded; that everything is
nasty and that nothing nice gets a square deal; and that to the

effective asserting of this the artist must bend all his cunning.
Joyce will allow no half-measures. His book is about paralysis –
both the word and the thing fascinate a small boy on the first
page – and paralysis is uncompromisingly asserted as something to
make the flesh creep. Each one of the stories cries out against the
frustration and squalor of the priest-ridden, pub-besotted, cultur-
ally decomposing urban lower-middle-class living it depicts, and
aims at exhaling – so Joyce declared – 'the odour of ashpits and
old weeds and offal'. An elderly priest dies in a state of mental
and perhaps moral degeneration, and a small boy to whom he
has given some instruction learns from whispering women that
the trouble began when he dropped and broke a chalice. Two
boys play truant and have a casual encounter with an ineffective
pervert. A coarse amorist, to the admiration of a less accomplished
friend, gets money out of a servant girl. A drunken clerk is scolded
by a bullying employer and humiliated in a public house; he goes
home and flogs a small boy. In another public house a traveller
in tea falls down the steps of a lavatory and injures himself. While
convalescent he is visited by friends, who talk tediously and ignor-
antly about ecclesiastical matters, and then endeavour to reform
him by taking him to hear a sermon for business men. It is recorded
by Joyce's brother that lavatory, bedside, and church in this story
are designed in a ludicrous correspondence to Dante's Inferno,
Purgatorio, and Paradiso. Such 'correspondences' were to exercise
an increasing fascination over Joyce later on.

We may well agree that the style in which incidents like these
are recounted should be 'scrupulously mean'. A great part of their
effect lies in Joyce's virtuosity here, and particularly in his em-
ployment of a mimetic or semi-ventriloquial technique. Thus in
a story about a very simple girl we read : 'One time there used
to be a field there in which they used to play every evening with
other people's children. Then a man from Belfast bought the field
and built houses in it.' And similarly with the adults. The quality
of their living is defined by the language :

One said that he had seen Mac an hour before in Westmoreland Street. At this Lenehan said that he had been with Mac
the night before in Egan's. The young man who had seen Mac
in Westmoreland Street asked was it true that Mac had won a
bit over a billiard match. Lenehan did not know : he said that
Holohan had stood them drinks in Egan's.

Even an exclamation mark may be made to do this sort of work :
'Just as they were naming their poisons who should come in but
Higgens!' Higgens, thus acclaimed, is a cipher; he has not appeared before and will not appear again. Such effects would be
oppressive if unrelieved, and so the texture of the prose is bound
to show inconsistency. The first story, that of the priest who broke
the chalice, begins in a child's words of one syllable, but presently
the priest has a handkerchief which is 'inefficacious', and he lies
'solemn and copious' in his coffin. And everywhere the description
and evocation have a precision and economy and sensitiveness
which constitute the substance of the book's style just as the
'scrupulous meanness' constitutes its ironic surface. For the
method is essentially ironic. The meanness of language has an
air of accepting and taking for granted the meanness of what is
described. It is contrived to expose what it affects to endorse.

A special use of this technique occurs at the end of 'Ivy Day
in the Committee Room'. We are introduced to a group of can-
vassers in a Dublin municipal election. They are working only
for the money they hope to get from their candidate, whom they
despise and distrust and would be quite ready to desert. This,
and much more of the degradation of civic and national life they
represent, emerges in their talk. Because Ivy Day commemorates
the anniversary of Parnell's death one of those present is persuaded
to recite an appropriate poem of his own composition. It begins :

> He is dead. Our Uncrowned King is dead.
>   O, Erin, mourn with grief and woe
> For he lies dead whom the fell gang
>   Of modern hypocrites laid low.

The verses, which continue in a vein of facile patriotic sentiment and factitious indignation, read as if they might have been picked out of a forgotten nationalist newspaper, but are a clever fabrication by Joyce himself. The effect achieved is subtle. The poem is fustian. Its massed clichés and threadbare poeticisms declare it to belong to the same world of impoverished feeling conveyed in the preceding conversations. But this is not quite all. There is a ghost in the poem – the ghost of generous enthusiasms and of strong and sincere attachment to large impersonal purposes. We respond both ways, as we are later to do to analogous outcrops of romantic clichés in the reveries of Dedalus.

It is in the last and longest story in *Dubliners,* 'The Dead', that Joyce's stature as a writer first declares itself unmistakably. Two old ladies and their niece, all obscure figures in the musical life of Dublin, are giving their annual party, and to this their nephew Gabriel Conroy, a schoolmaster with literary tastes, brings his wife Gretta. The party, which is an undistinguished, rather vulgar, but entirely human affair, is described in great detail. Gabriel takes prescriptively a leading part, although his superior education and his sensitiveness prevent his doing it easily, and he makes a speech which we are given in full. This speech, like the poem in 'Ivy Day in the Committee Room', is an example of Joyce's deftest double-talk. It is full of trite and exaggerated sentiment, dwelling on spacious days gone beyond recall, absent faces, memories the world will not willingly let die, and so forth. Gabriel is himself aware of its insincerity as he speaks. But we ourselves are contrastingly aware that it represents a sincere attempt to perform a duty and give innocent pleasure. Our attitude to Gabriel remains sympathetic even while we are being afforded a searching view of him. After the party he and his wife drive through snow to the hotel where they are to spend the night. He is full of desire for her, but she does not respond. Presently he learns that a song heard at the party has reminded her of a boy, Michael Furey, of whom he has never heard, and who died long ago as the result of a

passionate vigil he had kept for Gretta when he was already very
ill. Gabriel's realization that he has been a stranger to what is thus
revealed as the deepest experience of his wife's life now becomes
the deepest experience of his :

> While he had been full of memories of their secret life to-
> gether, full of tenderness and joy and desire, she had been
> comparing him in her mind with another. A shameful conscious-
> ness of his own person assailed him. He saw himself as a ludi-
> crous figure, acting as a pennyboy for his aunts, a nervous, well-
> meaning sentimentalist, orating to vulgarians and idealizing
> his own clownish lusts, the pitiable fatuous fellow he had caught
> a glimpse of in the mirror. . . .
> Generous tears filled Gabriel's eyes. He had never felt like
> that himself towards any woman, but he knew that such a feel-
> ing must be love. The tears gathered more thickly in his eyes
> and in the partial darkness he imagined he saw the form of a
> young man standing under a dripping tree. Other forms were
> near. His soul had approached that region where dwell the vast
> hosts of the dead. He was conscious of, but could not apprehend,
> their wayward and flickering existence. His own identity was
> fading out into a grey impalpable world : the solid world itself,
> which these dead had one time reared and lived in, was dis-
> solving and dwindling.
> A few light taps upon the pane made him turn to the window.
> It had begun to snow again. He watched sleepily the flakes, silver
> and dark, falling obliquely against the lamplight. The time had
> come for him to set out on his journey westward. Yes, the
> newspapers were right : snow was general all over Ireland. It
> was falling on every part of the dark central plain, on the tree-
> less hills, falling softly upon the Bog of Allen and, farther west-
> ward, softly falling into the dark mutinous Shannon waves. It
> was falling, too, upon every part of the lonely churchyard on the
> hill where Michael Furey lay buried. It lay thickly drifted on
> the crooked crosses and headstones, on the spears of the little
> gate, on the barren thorns. His soul swooned slowly as he heard
> the snow falling faintly through the universe and faintly falling,
> like the descent of their last end, upon all the living and the
> dead.

It appears that this great story, while owing something to George Moore's *Vain Fortune,* is implicated not only with three generations of Joyce's family but also with Nora Barnacle, who had been wooed in Galway by a youth called Sonny Bodkin when he was in an advanced stage of consumption. A sister of Nora's – a woman seemingly altogether too simple to elaborate a myth – has recorded the circumstances as being in detail those of Joyce's fiction. That Sonny Bodkin should become Michael Furey may stand as an epitome of the transmuting power evinced in 'The Dead'. The story mingles naturalism and symbolism with a new confidence and richness. Tragic ironies play across it subtly and economically. Its parts are proportioned to each other strangely but with a brilliant effectiveness. And if its artistry looks forward to a great deal in Joyce's subsequent writing, its charity and compassion are qualities to which he was never to allow so free a play again.

Source: *Eight Modern Writers* (1963) pp. 431-5.

Morris Beja

THE WOODEN SWORD: THREATENER AND THREATENED IN THE WORLD OF JAMES JOYCE (1964)

– Do you think you impress me, Stephen asked, when
you flourish your wooden sword?[1]

Despite Stephen's bravado, he and indeed all Joyce's fictional
heroes are keenly receptive to the impressions created by the men
of this world who carry wooden swords, the men who flourish
them literally as well as figuratively and symbolically. It has
become a commonplace to recognize the close kinship among protagonists like Stephen Dedalus, the narrator or narrators of the
first three stories in *Dubliners,* Richard Rowan, Shem, H.C.E.
and Bloom. But little has been done to show that there are many
basic and revealing affinities between the antagonists who menace
them – and, as I hope to show, between the protagonists and
antagonists as well.

As a start, a reminder of the presentation of one of the menacing
figures may be helpful. Among the earliest and most haunting is
the stranger whom the narrator and his friend Mahony meet in
'An Encounter'. In our very first glimpse of him, before we hear
of his 'bottle-green' eyes, we are told that in one hand 'he held a
stick with which he tapped the turf lightly', and again that he is
'always tapping the ground with his stick'.[2] He asks the two boys
how many sweethearts they have; when the narrator replies that he

has none, the stranger does not believe him. He demands the boy admit the truth; after all, 'there was nothing' that even the stranger 'liked, he said, so much as looking at a nice young girl' (p. 26). As the boy continues through his silence to refuse to confess, the stranger forgets his 'liberalism' and remarks that there is 'nothing in this world he would like so well' as whipping a boy who 'had a girl for a sweetheart and told lies about it' : 'He described . . . how he would whip such a boy as if he were unfolding some elaborate mystery. He would love that, he said, better than anything in this world' (p. 27). Frightened, the boy escapes as soon as he feels he safely can.

There are in Joyce's fiction numerous figures whose roles very much resemble – both in detail and in broad significance – that of the stranger in this story. Of course, there are still others whose mere features or characteristics may remind us of him, but who do not serve the same functions; I am not concerned with them. Or, characters may share with him functions other than the particular ones I am examining : Marvin Magalaner, for example, uses a number of interesting associations between this stranger and 'the captain' in *A Portrait of the Artist* to illustrate Joyce's 'stock characterization of the abnormal male personality'.[3] My concern, however, is with an even more pervasive 'stock characterization' exemplified by the stranger, that of the man who threatens someone with violent punishment – a man who, it turns out, is all too normal.

The presentation of this figure is strikingly consistent throughout Joyce's career. Even those whom the figure threatens tend to fall into a pattern : there is often a boy, more often two, who are perhaps poor and 'ragged'. Frequently, the threats to these boys are much cruder than those uttered by the mild-mannered stranger to Mahony and the narrator in *Dubliners*. But as in that case, the threats ordinarily arise out of a demand for some kind of acknowledgment of guilt : a demand that the threatened confess to some sin, admit some frailty, apologize for some transgression. In this confrontation, someone's eyes are almost always stressed – usually those of the threatener, from the stranger in 'An Encounter' with his 'bottle-green eyes' to the 'greeneyed mister' of *Finnegans Wake*.[4] Occasionally, the focus is on the eyes of the prey, or on *both* his and his attacker's.

Above all, the threatening figure can almost always back up his menacing gestures with a 'wooden sword' : a stick, perhaps, or a cane, or a pandybat. The stick has generally been felt to be, in Joyce's work, something beneficial, a symbol of the tree of life, a phallic image of creative power. Of course it is at times all these things. For example, when, as cane, it serves as the blind man's substitute for eyes, it suggests a positive force, a guide through darkness. But a stick may also be a power to be feared – and surely the symbolic reference to masculine virility is no less pertinent here, though with typical dexterity Joyce also takes advantage of the connotations in the fact that a stick is in a sense a dead tree rather than a tree of life – a 'deathbone' (*Wake,* p. 193). In this role, again as cane, it is sometimes associated with lameness, a symbolic castration which in Joyce frequently has sinister overtones. (The demons of hell, of course, have cloven feet. In the *Wake,* the personification of evil, Ahriman – Mr R. E. Meehan – is depicted as having foot trouble, 'in misery with his billyboots', while we are also told that 'there's not so much green in his Ireland's eye' – p. 466.) On the other hand the cane may be simply a 'walking-stick', such as the one with which Farrington – who is continually described as having 'heavy dirty eyes' – beats his small boy at the end of 'Counterparts', 'striking at him viciously with the stick' (*Dubliners,* pp. 86, 94, 98).

An ominous figure who *is* lame is the sour, violent, one-legged sailor who fascinates 'two barefoot urchins' in the Wandering Rocks episode of *Ulysses,*[5] a character strongly reminiscent of one who appears in a newly discovered passage of the manuscript of *Stephen Hero.* There, a 'ragged boy' and 'an equally ragged friend' are confronted by another 'lame beggar', who 'gripping his stick' demands that the two boys confess it was they who called out names after him the day before. When the boys deny their guilt, the beggar thrusts 'his malign face down at their faces . . . moving his stick up and down' : 'D'ye see that stick?' he asks. 'Well, if ye call out after me the next time I'll cut [yous] yez open with that stick.' With a relish for detail worthy of the stranger in 'An Encounter', he proceeds to explain himself to the frightened children : 'I'll cut yez open with that stick,' he repeats; 'I'll cut the livers and the lights out of ye.'[6] Joyce had himself witnessed just such a scene, and he recorded it in an 'epiphany' which is extremely close to the version eventually written into *Stephen Hero*.

> [In Mullingar : an evening
> in autumn]
> The Lame Beggar – (*gripping his stick*) . . . . It was
> you called out after me yesterday.
> The Two Children – (*gazing at him*) . . . No, sir.
> The Lame Beggar – O, yes it was, though. . . . (*moving
> his stick up and down*) . . . . But
> mind what I'm telling you. . . .
> D'ye see that stick?
> The Two Children – Yes, sir.
> The Lame Beggar – Well, if ye call out after me
> any more I'll cut ye open with
> that stick. I'll cut the livers
> out o' ye. . . . (*explains himself*)
> . . . D'ye hear me? I'll cut ye
> open. I'll cut the livers and
> the lights out o' ye.[7]

That this scene powerfully impressed Joyce is no surprise considering the significance of the exact nature of the lame beggar's threats, and considering the threats made against Joyce's eyes by Mr Vance which I shall come to shortly. Marvin Magalaner points out that 'though Joyce must have known that "lights" commonly

signified "lungs", figurative use of the word to connote "eyes" was
an easy and logical artistic step.' This is certainly true, but perhaps
unnecessary. Partridge says that 'lights' meant 'eyes' in standard
English until the early nineteenth century, and that from then on
it continued to carry that sense in boxing.[8]

Clearly, this incident was somehow revelatory to the young
author who recorded it as an epiphany. Just as clearly, it is profoundly revealing to Stephen, who witnessing it feels that he has
'never before seen such evil expressed in a face. He had sometimes
watched the faces of prefects as they "pandied" boys with a broad
leather bat but those faces had seemed to him less malicious than
stupid, dutifully inflamed faces. The recollection of the beggar's
sharp eyes struck a fine chord of terror in the youth' (*Stephen
Hero*, p. 245). Although Stephen recalls the priests as a contrast,
their very association with the lame beggar inevitably suggests a
comparison. And in the *Portrait*, during a conversation with the
dean of studies, Stephen sees 'the silent soul of a jesuit look out
at him from the pale loveless eyes. Like Ignatius he was lame but
in his eyes burned no spark of Ignatius' enthusiasm' (*Portrait*,
p. 186).

But of course the person in the *Portrait* most evocative of
'prefects' who ' "pandied" boys with a broad leather bat' is the
prefect of studies, Father Dolan, with his 'nocoloured eyes' (p. 50).
In the account of him as still another tormentor of two little boys a
new element is brought in. The entire incident is prefaced by a
conversation Stephen and his classmates have about some boys who
are going to be punished. Hearing cricket bats in the distance,
Stephen thinks of the sounds a pandybat makes as it strikes.
'The fellows said it was made of whalebone and leather with lead
inside : and he wondered what was the pain like' : unmistakably
mingled with his fear is a distinct fascination with the punishment,
looking forward to the more emphatic masochism evident in
Bloom's relationships with those who torment him. 'A long thin
cane', Stephen reflects, 'would have a high whistling sound and

he wondered what was that pain like'. In class, Stephen is excused
from schoolwork by his teacher because he has broken his glasses.
But such an excuse does not suit the sadistic Father Dolan, who
first uses his stick on Fleming ('an idler of course. I can see it in
your eye'), a rough boy rather like Mahony of 'An Encounter'.
Then he approaches Stephen, accuses him of guilt, and demands
that he hold out his hand. The astonished boy does so and is struck
by a 'blow like the loud crack of a broken stick . . . and at the sound
and the pain scalding tears were driven into his eyes.' Stephen
feels within him 'a prayer to be let off', but he does not plead for
mercy, he does not submit – even 'though the tears scalded his
eyes'. Stephen never forgets this incident; it reveals to him a totally
new aspect of the Church, which, he realizes for the first time, can
be oppressive and unjust : 'The prefect of studies was a priest but
that was cruel and unfair' (*Portrait*, pp. 45–52). The importance of
such a revelation in Stephen's development is obvious and indeed
can hardly be exaggerated.

   Moreover, in his presentation of other oppressive figures in the
Portrait, Joyce strengthens the association between the Church
and the attempt to make Stephen submit. The very first pages of
the book, for example, include the scene in which Dante (associated, in the entry in *Scribbledehobble* for the first chapter of
A Portrait of the Artist, with 'all the bespectable people'[9]) threatens
Stephen with the loss of his eyes if he does not apologize for some
vague sin. In the original 'epiphany' upon which that passage is
based, the antagonist is not Dante but Mr Vance, who *'comes in
with a stick'* :

> [Bray : in the parlour of the house
> in Martello Terrace]
> Mr Vance – (*comes in with a stick*) . . . O, you know,
>   he'll have to apologise, Mrs Joyce.
> Mrs Joyce – O yes . . . Do you hear that, Jim?
> Mr Vance – Or else – if he doesn't – the eagles'll
>   come and pull out his eyes.

Mrs Joyce – O, but I'm sure he will apologise.
Joyce – (*under the table, to himself*)
    – Pull out his eyes,
    Apologise,
    Apologise,
    Pull out his eyes.

    Apologise,
    Pull out his eyes,
    Pull out his eyes,
    Apologise.   (*Workshop of Daedalus*, p. 11)

Naturally it was no mere whim that led Joyce, in his novel, to take the main inquisitional role from Mr Vance and give it to Dante. She has just been connected with Irish nationalism through her two brushes, one for Michael Davitt and one for Parnell. Soon, however, she turns against this cause in the primary vehemence of her defense of the Church – the central reason for taking the role from Mr Vance, who is a Protestant.

Later, after his English master has accused him of having heresy against the Church in an essay, some of Stephen's classmates bully him. He recalls that event years later while talking to Heron, the leader of those boys. Heron, who likes 'to poke the ground with his cane', is now teasing Stephen by trying to make him 'admit' his relationship with Emma – striking him 'lightly across the calf of the leg with his cane'. 'Admit!' Heron repeats, 'striking him again with his cane', a blow that is 'not so lightly given as the first one had been'. Going along with the jest, if not with its spirit, Stephen begins to recite the *Confiteor*. Meanwhile, 'the familiar stroke of the cane' and 'the familiar word of admonition' cause him to recapture 'as if by magic' a past moment. Years before, after the English master's accusation, the younger Heron – who even then used to cleave 'the air before him with a thin cane' – had led the other boys in the attempt to 'catch hold of this heretic' and force him to conform, by 'cutting at Stephen's legs with his cane'. 'Admit that Byron was no good,' they had demanded as they struck him, 'Admit.' But Stephen had resisted, finally succeeding in driving his tormentors off – though not until his eyes were 'half blinded with tears' (*Portrait,* pp. 75, 77–8, 80–2).

Stephen Dedalus, to be sure, is not the only hero in Joyce's fiction – which is to say, he is not the only victim. There is also, for one, Leopold Bloom, all of whose tormentors appear during one or another of his visions in the Circe episode. Some are relatively minor, such as the First Watch who 'draws his truncheon' to threaten him, or the volunteer-hangman H. Rumbold, who displays both 'a life preserver and a nail-studded bludgeon' as he answers a call for someone to execute Bloom (*Ulysses,* pp. 471–2). More important is the Citizen with his prototypical Irish weapon, the 'shillelagh' (p. 593). The major encounter with him, of course, is given full treatment in an earlier episode, where he is epically portrayed as possessing 'a mighty cudgel rudely fashioned out of paleolithic stone' (p. 297). We are nevertheless given a comically ironic account of his own horror at the survival of flogging in the British navy; he pitifully describes 'a young lad brought out, howling for his ma', while 'the master at arms comes along with a long cane and he draws out and he flogs the bloody backside off of the poor lad till he yells meila murder.' Despite his own obviously graphic interest in such goings on, the Citizen attacks all those who 'believe in rod, the scourger almighty' (p. 329). But soon the brutality of his own nature gets the upper hand, and he threatens Bloom with violence. Luckily, he is too drunk to be effective : 'the sun was in his eyes or he'd have left him for dead' (p. 343). Surely, some sort of triumph for Bloom inheres in the fact that it is not his but the Citizen's eyes that are – at least figuratively – blinded. Ulysses-Bloom no more yields to the violent threats of the Cyclops-Citizen than does Stephen to Dante's, or Father Dolan's, or Heron's. For in Joyce's world there is an ultimate futility in the threatening figures, a futility which I hope is becoming clearer now. Even Bella Cohen, the most formidable of Bloom's oppressors, is triumphant only briefly : as we shall see, it is Bloom rather than Bella who effectively wields the wooden sword.

This is an important point, and I shall return to it, but first we must look at the figure of the man with the stick in Joyce's final work, where once again – as the ballad about Tim Finnegan's wake puts it – 'shillelagh law' is 'all the rage'. The key incident in which such a figure appears is also the key incident in the book, the encounter in Phoenix Park. Like most of the other scenes it appears in various guises and versions, but its general presentation parallels in curious ways the experience related in 'An Encounter'. This association is reinforced by *Scribbledehobble*, Joyce's so-called 'Ur-Workbook' for *Finnegans Wake*. In an entry among the pages on 'An Encounter', Joyce writes of 'self & onanism : . . . Oscar=beggar' (p. 37). 'Oscar' presumably refers to Oscar Wilde, who through his role as representative of homosexuality recalls (although with crude injustice) the ominous stranger of the story. The 'beggar' refers to the assailant-beggar who confronts H.C.E. in the park, and probably back to the lame beggar of Joyce's earlier work as well. (Elsewhere in *Scribbledehobble*, p. 125, the 'unknown beggar' is associated with the 'Murray vultures . . . on the prowl' – Mr Vance's eagles, perhaps? Or those of Joyce's mother, Mary Jane Murray?) In one scene of the *Wake* the beggar is 'the attackler' who 'catching holst of an oblong bar he had and with which he usually broke furnitures . . . rose the stick at' his victim. There is an odd mixing of roles in this version, though odd only in relation to what the previous works might have led us to expect, for this time it is the victim who is apparently lame, having 'more in his eye than was less to his leg' (p. 81; earlier, we have been told how H.C.E. was 'torn . . . limb from lamb' by a mob waving 'green boughs o'er him', p. 58). Such mixing of roles is to be expected in *Finnegans Wake*, and indeed as often as not the hitherto customary roles are almost completely reversed. For example, in the initial presentation of the encounter in the park, between H.C.E. and the cad with a pipe, it is the frightened figure

who is to be suspected of 'perversion', not the menacing one. And
H.C.E. is frightened despite the fact that it is he who has a stick
with which he timidly shows himself ready to fight, trying to make
it seem more formidable by bending deeply 'to give more pondus
to the copperstick he presented' (p. 35).

Although taking all his guises together the 'greeneyed mister'
encountered 'on the fair green' (pp. 87–8) is the most complete
presentation in *Finnegans Wake* of the man with a stick, a more
prominent figure who occasionally takes on this role is Shaun.
Ironically, as Jaun he presents in his sermon advice on how to 'put
your swell foot foremost', preaching that although 'whalebones
and buskbutts may hurt you (thwackaway thwuck!)', you must
'never lay bare your breast secret' (p. 434). More obviously in
character, as Kevin he boasts, 'I . . . curry nothung up my sleeve'
(p. 295) – 'nothung' being Siegfried's sword and, in *Ulysses*,
Stephen's ashplant. At the climax of the Shem the Penman
episode, Shaun 'points the deathbone and the quick are still.' Yet
the final triumph is far from being clearly his, and the culminating
act is certainly not : that is reserved for Shem, who immediately
afterward 'lifts the lifewand and the dumb speak' (pp. 193, 195;
cf. *Isaiah,* 35 :6 : 'Then shall the lame man leap as an hart, and
the tongue of the dumb sing'). It is helpful to remember that in
Finnegans Wake all contests may be regarded as contests between
brothers, and therefore ('therefore', anyway, in Joyce's world)
between two aspects of one personality. Hindsight shows us many
forecasts of the battle between Shaun and Shem in Joyce's earlier
fiction too. Among the chief models for Shaun was Joyce's own
brother Stanislaus, just as he himself was one of the chief models
for Shem; another important fictional depiction of Stanislaus is
Mr Duffy of 'A Painful Case', who 'never gave alms to beggars
and walked firmly, carrying a stout hazel' (*Dubliners,* p. 108). Yet
in *My Brother's Keeper* (p. 126) Stanislaus says that it is he who is
represented by the 'arctic beast' in the 'obscure pool' of an early
epiphany, in which Joyce writes : 'I thrust in my stick and as he

rises out of the water I see that his back slopes towards the croup and that he is very sluggish. I am not afraid but, thrusting at him often with my stick drive him before me.'[10] Once again it is the Shem who wields the stick – just as, in *Ulysses,* Stephen reflects that the Shaun-figure Buck Mulligan 'fears the lancet of my art as I fear that of his'.[11] As I have already indicated, in fact, the retaliation by the victim against his attacker – with the attacker's own weapons – is an important element in Joyce's fiction. If in the hand of a threatener a stick can be a 'deathbone', in the hand of the threatened it may be a 'lifewand' – the 'curved stick of an augur' of which Stephen's ashplant reminds him in the *Portrait* (p. 225), or the 'augur's rod of ash' it is called in *Ulysses* (pp. 48, 574).

When one of Joyce's major victims uses a stick menacingly, he invariably does so in self-defence against threats, not for any purposes of aggression of his own. He will not serve, but neither will he impose his rule upon others. Stephen, frightened by a dog, thinks, 'Lord, is he going to attack me? Respect his liberty. You will not be master of others or their slave. I have my stick' (*Ulysses,* p. 45). And although at one point Stephen thinks of his stick as his 'sword', whenever he actually '*flourishes his ashplant*' he does so not out of aggressive intent, but with the purpose – if possible – of '*shattering light over the world*' (pp. 210, 432). No scene in *Ulysses* is more climactic in regard to Stephen than the one in which, after '*a green crab with malignant red eyes sticks deep its grinning claws in Stephen's heart*', he frees himself with his ashplant as he shouts his Satanic cry of rebellion : '*Non serviam!*'

> Break my spirit all of you if you can ! . . .
> *Nothung!*
>> (*He lifts his ashplant high with both hands and smashes the chandelier. Time's livid final flame leaps and, in the following darkness, ruin of all space, shattered glass and toppling masonry.*) (Pp. 582–3)

Stephen's accomplishment here is apparently real enough for him to be able to abandon his stick for a time, so that someone else may assert himself with it.

For it is with Stephen's ashplant that Bloom is at last victorious over the terrifying figure of Bella Cohen. Claiming that the ten shillings she demands are too much for the damage Stephen has done, Bloom – who has picked up the young man's abandoned cane – angers Bella by mildly pointing out that only the chimney of the lamp is broken. As he tries to show what he means, '*he raises the ashplant*'. With fine parody of the parallel scene in the *Odyssey*, Bella misinterprets his action, '*shrinks back and screams*' and eventually yields. Moreover, Bloom's triumph is one that unites him with his spiritual son through the weapon he uses – and with his dead son too, through a subsequent vision : for as he stands over the prostrate Stephen after the encounter with Private Carr, and as he nervously '*tightens and loosens his grip on the ashplant*' (Stephen's ashplant), he envisions his son Rudy – who '*holds a slim ivory cane*' (pp. 584, 609).

Thus, in Joyce's work we see not merely that a bond connects all the threateners with one another, or all the threatened with one another, but that threatener and threatened become inextricably associated as well. Instead of a confrontation in which one side is completely controlled by hatred or anger or self-righteousness, and the other side by fear or rebelliousness or doubt, we have a complex pattern in which each side displays many or all of these emotions and others too. But above all both share the same sense of guilt.

Joyce's characters are often hounded by feelings of guilt – and he indicates in many ways that they must be, ought to be so hounded, because such feelings are valid. It is a gross misreading of Joyce's fiction to allow our sympathy for the victims' plight to delude us into assuming that they are innocent. The punishment they undergo may often seem arbitrary, yet in some subtle way it is always a true retribution. As Heron reminds Stephen while he strikes him with the cane, 'You can't play the saint on me any more' (*Portrait*, p. 77). Joyce's depiction of crime and punishment no more indicates that he views the world as *essentially* unjust or 'absurd' than does Dostoevsky's, or Kafka's. To Joyce as to them, certain clichés of contemporary criticism notwithstanding, the world is not absurd but profoundly meaningful – mysterious, but meaningful. Even the classic case of injustice in Joyce, Stephen's pandying by Father Dolan – ignoring in fact the additional implications in the possibility we have seen that Stephen unconsciously almost invites the punishment – is significantly illuminated by a comment in the *Portrait* which has been ignored by too many readers for too long : 'During all the years . . . in Clongowes and in Belvedere he had received only two pandies and, though these had been dealt him in the wrong, he knew that he had often escaped punishment' (p. 156). Of course, punishment does often come to Stephen in other ways, but though the process of retribution may be incomprehensible to us, as it is when it strikes down Kafka's victims, the guilt and sin are no less pervasive here than they are in Kafka. And they are no less so in, say, the fate of the 'unjustly' convicted Dmitri at the end of *The Brothers Karamazov* than in the fate of the 'justly' convicted Raskolnikov at the end of *Crime and Punishment* – or no less so in the fate of Darl Bundren or Joe Christmas than in that of Popeye in Faulkner. Or perhaps I can express my sense of Joyce's world by quoting Kafka, in a paradox which Joyce's Jesuit training would have made quite comprehensible to him : 'The state in which we are is sinful, irrespective of guilt.'[12] But to claim some sort of *refuge* through such a notion of universal or original sin, to claim that it takes away each man's final responsibility, would be no less self-deceptive than to claim innocence. As the priest in Kafka's *The Trial* puts it (when K. asks, 'how can any man be called guilty? We are all simply men here, one as much as the other') : 'That is true . . . but that's how all guilty men talk.'[13] Joyce, nevertheless, did not talk that way. In a notebook, under the entry 'Nora', he wrote,

'She speaks as often of her innocence as I do of my guilt' (*Workshop of Daedalus,* p. 103).

All these stresses are evident throughout Joyce's work; they become more or less explicit when martyr and criminal and jailor and judge and executioner all tend to merge into one another in the Circe episode of *Ulysses,* equally innocent and equally guilty. They are most manifest in *Finnegans Wake;* nevertheless, in that book, where almost everybody is almost everybody else sooner or later anyway, these facts are easily lost sight of. They are, however, still especially distinct in the story with which I began my essay.

The stranger in 'An Encounter' meets not one but two boys, who have been playing truant together. In addition to the narrator there is Mahony, a rougher boy. Early in the day, before meeting the stranger, Mahony chases 'a crowd of ragged girls', threatening them with his catapult; we are specifically told that he brandishes an 'unloaded catapult', so it would seem that he threatens them by using it as a club or stick. The girls are defended, 'out of chivalry', by two boys smaller than Mahony – 'two ragged boys'. Mahony proposes that they charge the rescuers, but the narrator objects that 'the boys were too small' (*Dubliners,* p. 22) – a point no one raises to the lame beggar when *he* encounters two ragged boys, or to Father Dolan, or to Mr Vance, or to Farrington. In one sense, Mahony is the counterpart of all these figures – and, more relevantly, of the stranger who confronts him in turn shortly later.

While he is talking to the two boys, the stranger at one point interrupts his monologue to excuse himself. After he has been gone for a few minutes, Mahony exclaims, 'I say! Look what he's doing!' But the narrator declines to do so: 'I neither answered nor raised my eyes.' Refusing to have anything to do with whatever strange act the 'queer old josser' may be committing, he says instead, 'In case he asks us for our names . . . let you be Murphy and I'll be Smith' (p. 26). Such a combination of a retreat from awareness and a recourse to deception does not bode well for a favorable reaction to the man's silent but unmistakable plea that the narrator 'should understand him' (p. 27); and in fact the narrator clearly fears to do so, as if he might experience an unsettling awareness of self. Left alone with the stranger when Mahony has run off to chase a cat, he is uncomfortable and afraid; he feels he must escape from the stranger, abandon him. With forced bravery, he shouts 'Murphy!' – but, interestingly, is immediately 'ashamed' of his 'paltry stratagem'. Then he follows with a similar reaction to Mahony, for as his friend comes running across the field as if to bring him aid he is again shamed. 'And I was penitent; for in my heart I had always despised him a little' (p. 28). However falteringly and hesitantly, he is on his way to accepting the need for human sympathy, and his own responsibility for the plea of the strange man with the stick that someone 'should understand him'.

S o u r c e : *James Joyce Quarterly*, 2 (Fall 1964) pp. 33–41 [revised].

NOTES

1. *A Portrait of the Artist as a Young Man*, ed. Chester G. Anderson and Richard Ellmann (Viking, 1964) p. 197.
2. *Dubliners*, ed. Robert Scholes and Richard Ellmann (Viking, 1967) p. 24.
3. *Time of Apprenticeship: The Fiction of Young James Joyce* (Abelard-Schuman, 1959) p. 106. If Mr Magalaner's comparison needs further corroboration, one may point out that according to the account in *My Brother's Keeper* of the true incident behind the short story, Stanislaus Joyce gave the stranger he and his brother met the nickname of 'the captain of fifty' (Viking, 1958) p. 62.
4. *Dubliners*, p. 27; *Finnegans Wake* (Viking, 1947) p. 88.
5. (Random House, 1961) p. 225.
6. *Stephen Hero*, ed. Theodore Spencer, Rev. John J. Slocum and Herbert Cahoon (New Directions, 1963) p. 244.
7. *The Workshop of Daedalus: James Joyce and the Raw Materials for A Portrait of the Artist as a Young Man*, ed. Robert Scholes and Richard M. Kain (Northwestern University, 1965) p. 25.

8. Magalaner, *Time of Apprenticeship,* p. 30; Eric Partridge, *A Dictionary of Slang and Unconventional English* (Macmillan [New York], 1961) p. 482.

9. *Scribbledehobble: The Ur-Workbook for Finnegans Wake,* ed. Thomas E. Connolly (Northwestern University, 1961) p. 70.

10. *Workshop of Daedalus,* p. 26. Cf. Stephen, in *Ulysses:* 'Bath a most private thing. I wouldn't let my brother, not even my own brother, most lascivious thing. Green eyes, I see you' (p. 43). -

11. P.7. Cf. an entry in Joyce's 'Trieste Notebook' under '*Gogarty* (Oliver Saint John)' : 'He fears the lancet of my art as I fear that of his.' The next note reads : 'He addresses lifeless objects and hits them smartly with his cane : the naturalism of the Celtic mind' (*Workshop of Daedalus,* p. 97).

In the same notebook, incidentally, the sole entry under '*Skeffington* (Francis Joseph Christopher)' is, 'He wields a wooden sword' (p. 105).

12. 'Reflections on Sin, Suffering, Hope, and the True Way', in *Dearest Father,* trans. Ernst Kaiser and Eithne Wilkins (Schocken, 1954) p. 43.

Readers of Samuel Beckett's *Molloy, Malone Dies,* and *The Unnamable* may already have recalled, as this essay has proceeded, the many similar associations within Beckett's trilogy among various characters, often lame, who carry sticks or are threatened or beaten by figures who do; in the present context, a passage early in *Molloy* is perhaps especially interesting : 'It was a stout stick, he used it to thrust himself onward, or as a defence, when the time came, against dogs and marauders. Yes, night was gathering, but the man was innocent, greatly innocent, he had nothing to fear, though he went in fear, he had nothing to fear, there was nothing they could do to him, or very little. . . . Yes, he saw himself threatened, his body threatened, his reason threatened, and perhaps he was, perhaps they were, in spite of his innocence. What business has innocence here?' (Calder & Boyars, 1959) p. 10.

13. Trs. Willa and Edwin Muir, with additional materials trs. E. M. Butler (Random House, 1956) p. 264.

Anthony Burgess

A PARALYSED CITY (1965)

Joyce's first piece of published juvenilia was a verse encomium on dead Parnell and an attack on Parnell's chief enemy. It was called *Et Tu, Healy* and it was written when he was nine. Here ends the bibliography of Joyce the committed or *engagé*. His student writings praised Ibsen and poured scorn on the Irish Literary Theatre ('The Day of the Rabblement'). Before leaving Ireland, almost for ever, he wrote a Swiftian – or Hudibrastic – poem called *The Holy Office,* in which the parochial poetlings of the Celtic Twilight have a few drops of acid thrown at them :

> So distantly I turn to view
> The shamblings of that motley crew,
> Those souls that hate the strength that mine has
> Steeled in the school of old Aquinas.
> Where they have crouched and crawled and prayed
> I stand, the self-doomed, unafraid,
> Unfellowed, friendless and alone,
> Indifferent as the herring-bone,
> Firm as the mountain-ridges where
> I flash my antlers on the air.

Bold words, and a bold manifesto :

> But all these men of whom I speak
> Make me the sewer of their clique.
> That they may dream their dreamy dreams
> I carry off their filthy streams
> For I can do those things for them
> Through which I lost my diadem,

Those things for which Grandmother Church
Left me severely in the lurch.
Thus I relieve their timid arses,
Perform my office of Katharsis.

Joyce, at twenty-two, had no doubt of his artistic function, nor of its importance. The office of purgation, of making art a kind of sewer for the draining-off of man's baser elements, was not what the Church would call holy; still, Aristotle – who gave him the word *katharsis* – was sponsored by St Thomas Aquinas, and St Thomas Aquinas was not of the same world as the Christian Brothers and the Maynooth priests. Joyce has the image of a great traditional intellectual aristocracy, to which he himself belongs. Prettiness, fancy, devotionalism have no place in the austerity and self-dedication of its creed. It is demanding, and one must be prepared to be damned for it (Joyce sees himself in a sort of hell of artists, 'self-doomed, unafraid, unfellowed, friendless and alone'). And so the deliberate cutting-off, the exile.

The first big fruit of Joyce's exile was the volume of short stories, *Dubliners*. It seems a very mild purge to us now, chiefly because it is the first in a whole pharmocopoeia of cathartics to which we have developed a tolerance. To its eponyms it seemed strong enough; printers and publishers would not at first administer it; its little saga of rejections, bowdlerisations, burnings looks forward to the epic struggle of *Ulysses* (itself originally conceived as a story for *Dubliners*) to get itself first into print and then past the customs-houses. The book was mainly written in Trieste in 1905, worked up from notes Joyce had made while still in Dublin. Grant Richards, to whom it was first sent, would and would not publish it. In 1909, Joyce gave it to Maunsel and Co. in Dublin. In 1910, Maunsel and Co. grew frightened of it and postponed publication. In 1912, the type was broken up by the printer and Joyce, in a broadside called 'Gas from a Burner', made the printer say :

H

. . . I draw the line at that bloody fellow
That was over here dressed in Austrian yellow,
Spouting Italian by the hour
To O'Leary Curtis and John Wyse Power
And writing of Dublin, dirty and dear,
In a manner no blackamoor printer could bear.
Shite and onions! Do you think I'll print
The name of the Wellington Monument,
Sydney Parade and Sandymount tram,
Downes's cakeshop and Williams's jam?
. . . Who was it said: Resist not evil?
I'll burn that book, so help me devil.
I'll sing a psalm as I watch it burn
And the ashes I'll keep in a one-handled urn.
I'll penance do with farts and groans
Kneeling upon my marrowbones.
This very next lent I will unbare
My penitent buttocks to the air
And sobbing beside my printing press
My awful sin I will confess.
My Irish foreman-from Bannockburn
Shall dip his right hand in the urn
And sign crisscross with reverent thumb
Memento homo upon my bum.

But printing the name of the Wellington Monument and Downes's cakeshop was, after all, the thin end of the wedge. Admit the naturalism of a picture postcard and you must soon admit also *graffiti* on lavatory walls, the blaspheming of jarveys, and what goes on in the back bedrooms of Finn's Hotel. *Dubliners* was totally naturalistic, and no kind of truth is harmless; as Eliot says, mankind cannot bear very much reality.

And yet, first as last, Joyce did not want merely to record the current of ordinary life. There was this business of epiphanies, defined in *Stephen Hero* (the first draft of *A Portrait*):

By an epiphany he meant a sudden spiritual manifestation, whether in the vulgarity of speech or of gesture or in a memorable phase of the mind itself. He believed that it was for the man of letters to record these epiphanies with extreme care, seeing that they themselves are the most delicate and evanescent of moments.

Stephen Dedalus tells his friend Cranly (as, in *A Portrait,* he is to tell Lynch – more eloquently and at much greater length) that Aquinas's three prerequisites for beauty are integrity, symmetry and radiance. First the apprehending mind separates the object – 'hypothetically beautiful' – from the rest of the universe and perceives that 'it is one integral thing'; it recognises its integrity or wholeness. Next, 'the mind considers the object in whole and in part, in relation to itself and to other objects, examines the balance of its parts, contemplates the form of the object, traverses every cranny of the structure'. As for the third stage – 'radiance' – that is Stephen's translation of Aquinas's *claritas* – it is a sort of *quidditas* or whatness shining out of the object :

> . . . finally, when the relation of the parts is exquisite, when the parts are adjusted to the special point, we recognise that it is *that* thing which it is. Its soul, its whatness, leaps to us from the vestment of its appearance. The soul of the commonest object, the structure of which is so adjusted, seems to us radiant. The object achieves its epiphany –

The term seems ironic when applied to the 'showings forth' of *Dubliners,* but, after all, the original Epiphany was ironic enough to the Magi – a child in a dirty stable.

The glory and mystery of art can lie in the tension between the appearance and the reality, or, rather, between the subject-matter and what is made out of it. The view that subject-matter should be in itself enlightening still persists, chiefly because a moral stock-response comes more easily to most people than a genuine aesthetic transport. When Grant Richards eventually got round to publishing *Dubliners* – as he did on 15 June 1914 : very nearly the tenth

anniversary of the Bloomsday that had not yet happened – few
people were ready for it : the taste was for the didacticism, the
pedestrian moral lessons of a less naturalistic fiction. In *Dubliners*
the reader was not told what to think about the characters and
their actions, or rather inactions. There were no great sins, nor any
performance of great good. Out of drab ordinariness a purely
aesthetic *quidditas* leaps out.

All the stories in *Dubliners* are studies in paralysis or frustration,
and the total epiphany is of the nature of modern city life – the
submission to routines and the fear of breaking them; the emancipation that is sought, but not sought hard enough; the big noble
attitudes that are punctured by the weakness of the flesh. The first
story, 'The Sisters', presents the key-word in its very first paragraph :

> Every night as I gazed up at the window I said softly to myself
> the word paralysis. It had always sounded strangely in my ears,
> like the word gnomon in the Euclid and the word simony in the
> Catechism. But now it sounded to me like the name of some
> maleficent and sinful being. It filled me with fear, and yet I
> longed to be nearer to it and to look upon its deadly work.

The narrator is a young boy. Behind the window Father Flynn
lies dead. The boy, like Joyce himself, is drawn not only to the
mystery of words but to the terrifying complexities of the rites
that the priest has administered. As for the priest himself – old and
retired and dying – the boy's feelings have been a mixture of awed
fascination and repugnance. Father Flynn looks forward to the
unpleasant priests of Graham Greene and the dramatic possibilities
of the contrast between their function and their nature. He has
been a messy snuff-taker. 'When he smiled he used to uncover his
big discoloured teeth and let his tongue lie upon his lower lip.' But
now he is dead, and the boy goes with his aunt to see the body in
the house of the Misses Flynn, the sisters of the priest. He learns,
over a glass of defunctive sherry, that Father Flynn's illness began

with the breaking of a chalice, that this affected his mind : '. . . And what do you think but there he was,' says Eliza Flynn, 'sitting up by himself in the dark in his confession-box, wide-awake and laughing-like softly to himself?' Meanwhile, the dead priest is 'lying still in his coffin as we had seen him, solemn and truculent in death, an idle chalice on his breast'.

That is the whole story, and it is more an attempt at establishing a symbol than manufacturing a plot : a broken chalice, an idle chalice. The shameful discoveries about the adult world continue in the next story, 'An Encounter', in which the boy-narrator and his friend Mahony play truant from school for a day. Their heads full of *The Union Jack, Pluck,* and *The Halfpenny Marvel,* they meet adventure, but not in the form of the innocent violence of their little Wild West mythologies. A shabby man accosts them, full of perverse fantasies. Mahony runs away, but the narrator has to listen to the man's monologue about whipping boys who have sweethearts. 'He described to me how he would whip such a boy, as if he were unfolding some elaborate mystery. He would love that, he said, better than anything in this world; and his voice, as he led me monotonously through the mystery, grew almost affectionate and seemed to plead with me that I should understand him.' The narrator gets away from the demented babbling, calling Mahony. 'How my heart beat as he came running across the field to me ! He ran as if to bring me aid. And I was penitent; for in my heart I had always despised him a little.'

'Araby' is the last of this opening trilogy of stories in which the world is seen from a child's-eye view. Here, though, the passionate frustration belongs to the boy himself. He is past the stage of encountering external mysteries – ritual and dementia – and is now learning about love's bitter mystery through pubescent experience. Here comes the eucharist symbol : 'I imagined that I bore my chalice safely through a throng of foes. Her name sprang to my lips at moments in strange prayers and praises which I myself did not understand.' We are to meet this symbolism again, in the

'Villanelle of the Temptress' – named in *Stephen Hero,* presented
in *A Portrait.* In 'Araby', though, the loved one is no temptress but
a girl at a convent-school. She wants to go to the bazaar called
Araby (this, like all the public events in Joyce, is historical : it was
held in Dublin – from May 14th to 19th 1894, in aid of Jervis
Street Hospital); unfortunately there is a retreat at the convent
and she has to be disappointed. The boy promises to go instead
and bring her back a present. It is the last night of Araby, he must
get some money from his uncle, and his uncle comes home late and
fuddled. When he arrives at the bazaar it is closing down; the
lights are going out.

> Gazing up into the darkness I saw myself as a creature driven
> and derided by vanity; and my eyes burned with anguish and
> anger.

The seeming triviality of the frustration and the violence of the
language which expresses it are, as it were, reconciled by the
aesthetic force of the epiphany : here, drawn from commonplace
experience, is a symbol for the frustration of adolescence and, by
extension, of maturity too.

The rest of the frustrations and cases of paralysis belong to the
adult secular world. The heroine of 'Eveline' longs to escape from
her drab Dublin life and she has her chance. But, on the very point
of embarking for Buenos Aires with the man who loves her, 'all the
seas of the world tumbled about her heart. He was drawing her
into them : he would drown her.' Her heart says no; she sets 'her
white face to him, passive, like a helpless animal. Her eyes gave
him no sign of love or farewell or recognition.' Little Chandler, in
'A Little Cloud', re-meets the great Ignatius Gallaher, who has
made good in London journalism (in *Ulysses* he has already
become a Dublin newspaper-man's myth : he telegraphed details
of the Phoenix Park murders to the *New York World,* using a code
based on a *Freeman* advertisement. This was a memorable scoop).

Little Chandler makes the inevitable comparison between the richness of Gallaher's life, all whiskey and advances from moneyed
Jewesses, and his own – the mean job, the insipid wife, the bawl-
ing child. If only he could make his name with a little book of
Celtic Twilight poems, go to London, escape ghastly provincial
Dublin. But it is too late. The epiphany flowers in the rebukes of
his wife for making the brat scream, while his cheeks are 'suffused
with shame' and 'tears of remorse' start to his eyes. The cage is
tight-shut.

One need not be a negative and timid character, like Eveline
or Little Chandler, to exhibit the syndrome of soul-rot. Farrington,
in 'Counterparts', is burly, red-faced, perpetually thirsty, and he
fancies himself as a pub strong man. But he has the shiftlessness of
all virile Dubliners, and even the job of copy-clerk in a solicitor's
office is too much for him. The little heaven of release from
actuality is always the 'hot reeking public-house', the tailor of malt,
the dream of high-class women, but the money always runs out, the
sponging cronies fade away, and heaven is thoroughly dissolved
by the time he has reached the tram-stop on O'Connell Bridge.
'He cursed everything', waiting for the Sandymount tram. 'He
had done for himself in the office, pawned his watch, spent all his
money; and he had not even got drunk.' All that is left is to go
home and beat his son Tom for letting the fire go out. Tom cries :
'I'll say a *Hail Mary* for you, pa, if you don't beat me . . . I'll say
a *Hail Mary*. . . .' But a *Hail Mary* won't do for any of these
Dubliners.

Nothing will really do. Lenehan, in 'Two Gallants' as in *Ulysses,*
carries his seedy scraps of culture round ('That takes the solitary,
unique, and, if I may so call it, *recherché* biscuit !') in the service of
a sports paper and the office of jester to whoever – even a boor
like Corley – has, or is able to get, a little bit of spending money.
But even where there *is* money, and education, and a fair cultivated and cosmopolitan acquaintance, there is something missing.
In 'After the Race' the city wears 'the mask of capital' for Jimmy

and his European friends, who have come 'scudding in towards Dublin, running evenly like pellets in the groove of the Naas Road' in their racing cars.

> At the crest of the hill at Inchicore sightseers had gathered in clumps to watch the cars careering homeward, and through this channel of poverty and inaction the Continent had sped its wealth and industry. Now and again the clumps of people raised the cheer of the gratefully oppressed. . . .

There are drinking and gambling and song on board the American's yacht in Kingstown Harbour, but Jimmy is fuddled and is one of the heaviest losers. 'They were devils of fellows, but he wished they would stop : it was getting late.' It is all folly, and he will regret it all in the morning. At the end of the story – Joyce's only incursion into the world of the moneyed – morning has come. 'Daybreak, gentlemen!'

High ideals are betrayed – not with renegade force but through submission to compromise, the slow silting away of conviction that, it seems, only the Irish fanatic can hold. Mr Henchy, in 'Ivy Day in the Committee Room', says :

> 'Parnell is dead. Now, here's the way I look at it. Here's this chap come to the throne after his old mother keeping him out of it till the man was grey. He's a man of the world, and he means well by us. He's a jolly decent fellow, if you ask me, and no damn nonsense about him. He just says to himself : "The old one never went to see these wild Irish. By Christ, I'll go myself and see what they're like." And are we going to insult the man when he comes over here on a friendly visit?'

It is Parnell's anniversary, and the corks pop round the fire in the committee room. The impending visit of Edward VII is folded into the warmth of convivial tolerance ('The King's coming here will mean an influx of money into this country'). Joe Hynes recites a poem called 'The Death of Parnell', in which the lost leader is presented as a betrayed Christ. There is applause, another cork pops, and Mr Crofton says that it is 'a very fine piece of writing'. Parnell has joined a harmless pantheon, no legitimate Jesus but an ikon. This is one of the stories that held back publication of the whole book. A libel on the Irish spirit, a too free bandying of the name of a living monarch, an intolerable deal of demotic speech : naturalism had gone too far altogether.

With 'Grace', the penultimate story, the heady wine of religious faith is decently watered for the children of this world, who – as the text of Father Purdon's sermon reminds us – are wiser in their generation than the children of light. The story begins with the fall of man :

> Two gentlemen who were in the lavatory at the time tried to lift him up : but he was quite helpless. He lay curled up at the foot of the stairs down which he had fallen. They succeeded in turning him over. His hat had rolled a few yards away and his clothes were smeared with the filth and ooze of the floor on which he had lain, face downwards. His eyes were closed and he breathed with a grunting noise. A thin stream of blood trickled from the corner of his mouth.

This is Mr Kernan, 'a commercial traveller of the old school which believed in the dignity of its calling'. He is one of a group of small tradesmen, clerks, employees of the Royal Irish Constabulary, workers in the office of the Sub-Sheriff or the City Coroner – good bibulous men who are to be the backbone of *Ulysses*. Mr Power promises Mrs Kernan that he and his friends will make a new man of her husband : no more drunken fallings, regeneration with God's grace. And so, without solemnity and even with a few harmless Catholic jokes, we move towards a businessmen's retreat, a renewal of baptismal vows, and a sermon from Father Purdon. It is a manly, no-nonsense sermon, in which Jesus Christ is presented as a very understanding master, asking little, forgiving much.

> We might have had, we all had from time to time, our tempta-
> tions : we might have, we all had, our failings. But one thing
> only, he said, he would ask of his hearers. And that was : to be
> straight and manly with God. If their accounts tallied in every
> point to say :
> 'Well, I have verified my accounts. I find all well.'
> But if, as might happen, there were some discrepancies, to
> admit the truth, to be frank and say like a man :
> 'Well, I have looked into my account. I find this wrong and
> this wrong. But, with God's grace, I will rectify this and this. I
> will set right my accounts.'

Thus this rather mean city is spread before us, its timidity and
the hollowness of its gestures recorded with economy and a kind of
muffled poetry, its bouncing cheques of the spirit endorsed with
humour but with neither compassion nor censoriousness, for the
author must be totally withdrawn from his creation. The book
begins, in 'The Sisters', with the image of a paralysed priest and a
broken chalice; it might have ended, in 'Grace', with the sacrament of provincial mock-piety and a blessing for small and dirty
minds. But it does not end there. The longest and best story which
concludes the book is an afterthought. Dublin may be an impotent
city, but Ireland is more than Dublin. Life may seem to lie in
exile, 'out in Europe', but it is really waiting coiled up in Ireland,
ready to lunge from a wilder west than is known to the reading
boys of 'An Encounter'. This story about life is called 'The
Dead'.

Everything in Joyce's writing is an enhanced record of the
author's own experience, but perhaps 'The Dead' is the most personal item in the long chronicle of Dublin which was his life's
work. Gabriel Conroy is a sort of James Joyce – a literary man,
college teacher, contributor of a literary column to the Dublin
Daily Express, Europeanised, out of sympathy with Ireland's

nationalistic aspirations, aware that his own culture is of a different, superior, order to that which surrounds him in provincial Dublin. He has married a girl of inferior education ('country cute' is what his own mother once called her), but he does not despise her : Gretta Conroy has the Galway firmness of character of her prototype, Nora Joyce; she is beautiful; Gabriel is a possessive husband. On New Year's Eve they go to the annual party given by Gabriel's aunts – Miss Kate and Miss Julia – and, as the house is some way out of Dublin, they have booked a hotel room for the night. It is a good convivial evening, full of piano solos, song, quadrilles, food. As Gabriel and Gretta go to their hotel room in the early hours, a wave of desire comes over him : the possessive wants to possess. But Gretta is distracted. At the end of the party the tenor Bartell D'Arcy sang a song called *The Lass of Aughrim,* and she is thinking about the song. A young boy she once knew in Galway used to sing it. His name was Michael Furey and he was 'in the gasworks'. He died young. Gabriel asks whether he died of consumption, and Gretta replies : 'I think he died for me.'

The complex of emotions which takes possession of Gabriel's soul on this disclosure and on Gretta's transport of re-lived grief needs something more than a naturalistic technique for its expression. We see, the emergence of a new Joyce, the deployment of the cunning of the author of *Ulysses,* and experience a visitation of terrible magic. As Gabriel analyses his tepid soul we see that his name and that of his dead rival have taken on a strange significance – Gabriel the mild angel, Michael the passionate one; and that dead boy, possessed of an insupportable love, was rightly called Furey.

> The air of the room chilled his shoulders. He stretched himself cautiously along under the sheets and lay down beside his wife. One by one, they were all becoming shades. Better pass boldly into that other world, in the full glory of some passion, than fade and wither dismally with age.

Gabriel becomes aware of the world of the dead, into which the living pass. That world goes on with his own life, and its purpose is to qualify, literally to haunt, the world of those not yet gone. The living and the dead coexist; they have strange traffic with each other. And there is a sense in which that dead Michael Furey is more alive, through the passion which killed him, than the living Gabriel Conroy with his bits of European culture and his intellectual superiority. Meanwhile, in the all too tangible world of Dublin, the snow is coming down, general all over Ireland. 'The time had come for him to set out on his journey westwards.' The west is where passion takes place and boys die for love : the graveyard where Michael Furey lies buried is, in a sense, a place of life. As for the snow, it unites the living and the dead and, by virtue of this supernatural function, it ceases to be the sublunary snow that drops on a winter city. Gabriel's soul swoons slowly as he hears 'the snow falling faintly through the universe and faintly falling, like the descent of their last end, upon all the living and the dead'. We have broken, with him, through the time-space veil; we are in the presence of a terrible ultimate truth.

Ellmann's biography of Joyce tells us, in detail, about the real-life materials which went to the making of 'The Dead'. Gabriel's revelation of the community of dead and living was also his creator's, derived from a similar jealousy of his wife's dead lover, a jealousy which had to yield to acquiescence and a sort of surrender. By extension, jealousy of a living rival becomes equally futile : it is best to accept philosophically, even gladly; we can even end by deliberately willing the cuckold's role. When, towards the end of *Ulysses*, Bloom reflects on his wife's adultery (multiple – the names of her fellow-sinners are fully listed), he considers the responses of 'envy, jealousy, abnegation, equanimity' and justifies the last of these with thoughts about the 'futility of triumph or protest or vindication; the inanity of extolled virtue; the lethargy of nescient matter; the apathy of the stars'. But, earlier, in the brothel scene, his imagination has called up the enactment of adultery between his wife and Blazes Boylan and he himself, in imagination, has urged it on :

> B L O O M : (*His eyes wildly dilated, clasps himself*) Show ! Hide ! Show ! Plough her ! More ! Shoot !

Similarly, Richard in the play *Exiles* has a shameful desire to give his wife to his friend Robert : '. . . In the very core of my ignoble heart I longed to be betrayed by you and her – in the dark, in the night – secretly, meanly, craftily. By you, my best friend, and by her. I longed for that passionately and ignobly, to be dishonoured for ever in love and in lust, to be . . .' This yielding urge, shared by three of Joyce's characters, and even given mythical status (it is imposed on Shakespeare, for instance) in *Ulysses,* is an aspect of the 'womanly' in the Joyce man, the *yin* that qualifies the *yang.* Bloom undergoes many metamorphoses in Mabbot Street, and perhaps the least spectacular of these is his change of sex.

As for the bigger, and more creative, theme of the one world of living and dead, this may be thought of as having its roots in Joyce's Catholicism : the striving living are militant and the beatified dead triumphant, but they are members of one Church. Dead and alive meet naturally in the phantasmagoria of the brothel scene; in the deeper dream of *Finnegans Wake* the unity of human history depends on the simultaneous existence of all its periods. But, in the interests of economy, one man and one woman must play many parts. The table called, Joyceanly, 'Who is Who When Everybody is Somebody Else' in Adaline Glashcen's *A Census of Finnegans Wake,* makes Earwicker play God the Father, Adam the sinner, Adam the father, Abraham, Isaac, Noah, Buddha, Mohammed, Finn MacCool, Tim Finnegan, King Leary and some twenty-odd other roles, and Earwicker's family is quick to find appropriate supporting parts. This is the Occam's Razor of the mature artist. At the close of 'The Dead' Gabriel feels his own identity fading out and his soul swooning as the solid world dissolves : it is dissolving, proleptically, into the huge empyrean of *Finnegans Wake*; the seeds are being sown.

The importance of *Dubliners* in the entire Joyce canon cannot be exaggerated. There may seem to be little remarkable in the technique nowadays, but this is because Joyce himself, through his followers as well as in the book, has habituated us to it : we take for granted the bareness of the prose, the fact that originality may well consist in taking away as much as in adding. Joyce's later work is, in fact, an art of adding, of building on to a simple enough structure incrustations of deeper and deeper richness : *Finnegans Wake* represents the possible limit of loading statements with layers of significance. In *Dubliners* his task was different. He had to deromanticise fictional prose, stripping off the coloured veneers that had passed for poetic brilliance in the heyday of the late Victorian novel. To write like Meredith or Hardy or Moore (or anybody else, for that matter) was not difficult for the author who was to create the 'Oxen of the Sun' episode in *Ulysses*. He naturally tended to richness, but richness was not wanted in this study of a drab modern city which should flash out its epiphanies from the commonplace. Where cliché occurs, cliché is intended, for most of the inhabitants of the city live in clichés. Where a stale bit of romanticism is used – as in 'Two Gallants' : 'His harp, too, heedless that her coverings had fallen about her knees, seemed weary alike of the eyes of strangers and of her master's hands, – that also is in keeping, underlining the poverty of the Irish dream of the past. As for the management of humour, as in 'Grace' and 'Clay', this is as deadpan as anything in the contemporary American tradition and a world away from the whimsy and heavy-footed japing of what passed for comedy in Joyce's youth. But the miraculous ear for verbal nuance is seen best in the dialogue.

Joyce's books are about human society, and most social speech is 'phatic', to use Malinowski's useful term. It concerns itself less with conveying information, intention or need than with establishing or maintaining contact – mere comfortable noise in the dark.

Irish town speech is the most phatic of the entire English-speaking world : it is all colour, rhythm and gesture. It is the very voice of charming apathy and shiftlessness, a deadly Siren trap for the author who is concerned with strong plot and dramatic action, for the creation of Irish characters within the structure of a plot must either lead to the destruction of the plot or the falsifying of those who must enact it. When we see *Juno and the Paycock* we feel somehow let down when action occurs : the play stands or falls on what the characters say, and what they say does not take us towards a final curtain. Joxer and the Paycock, like *Finnegans Wake* itself, are destined to go round and round in a circle, lamenting the 'chassis' of the world but never doing anything about it, asking 'What is the stars?' but never troubling to find out. And so with Joyce's Dubliners, whose totem is Johnny the horse in Gabriel Conroy's story :

> 'And everything went on beautifully until Johnny came in sight of King Billy's statue : and whether he fell in love with the horse King Billy sits on or whether he thought he was back again in the mill, anyhow he began to walk round the statue. Round and round he went. . . .'

The exactly caught speech of these harnessed citizens is the true voice of paralysis. Realising how essential its tones are to Joyce's art, we begin to understand his need for finding action outside, for his garrulous pub-crawlers will not generate it. Action has to come from an exterior myth, like that of the Odyssey, or a circular theory of history which suggests, even if it does not fulfil, an image of purposive movement.

Finally, *Dubliners* is important because it provides *Ulysses* with a ready-made cast of extras. We shall meet them all again or, if they are dead, hear about them – Bartell D'Arcy, Mr Power, Martin Cunningham, Hynes, Mrs Sinico and the rest. If we have not yet met Mr Bloom, it is because, though he was intended for this gallery, he had to be lifted out to be groomed for greater things. And if we have not yet met Stephen Dedalus and his university cronies, it is because they had already been set down in a novel of their own, along with a roaring father and a sweet doomed mother.

SOURCE: *Here Comes Everybody: An Introduction to James Joyce for the Ordinary Reader* (1965) pp. 35–47.

John Gross

THE VOYAGE OUT (1970)

... In a sense, Joyce was running ahead of himself when he wrote
'The Dead'. Younger and fiercer than Gabriel Conroy, he was not
yet ready to renounce the proud intransigence that had inspired
the other stories in *Dubliners* – not, at least, until he had created
as definitive a version of the romantic rebel as he had of the society
against which he was in revolt. The problem as it now presented
itself was how best to extract a valid work of art from the crude
ore of *Stephen Hero,* and the apparently paradoxical solution that
Joyce hit on was to intensify rather than tone down the egoism of
the earlier work. In the *Portrait of the Artist,* hero and novel are
coextensive. Everything that happens to Stephen is registered in
terms of his sensibility at that particular stage, while events are
important purely insofar as they help to shape his inner development : the other characters only exist, as it were, when Stephen's
around in the quad. Moreover, his superiority is now assumed
rather than argued as it was in *Stephen Hero.* He is quite simply
made of finer clay than his fellows, and the implications of his
being called Dedalus in a world of Dolans and Lynches are reinforced by an elaborate system of imagery involving birds, water,
and the Icarus legend generally. Yet the more arrogant of the two
books is also artistically the more detached. In the psuedo-objec-
tive *Stephen Hero* Joyce is constantly pleading Stephen's case or
nudging us into applauding his virtues; in the *Portrait,* on the
other hand, he confines himself to hammering out an image and
offering it for our inspection. We may approve or disapprove,
but there at any rate it stands, plain for all to see.

To describe the book in these terms is not necessarily to endorse the famous distinction that Stephen draws in the last chapter between 'static' and 'kinetic' art, between art that 'arrests the mind' (as he thinks it should) and the inferior variety that plays directly on our emotions and moves us to 'desire or loathing'. If stasis simply means that the artist has remained in control of his materials and avoided inflicting his designs upon us too palpably, well and good. But if the assumption is that ideally a work of literature ought to elicit as purely aesthetic a response as, say, a still life or a Persian carpet, then Stephen is involved in a major contradiction, since the whole tenor of the *Portrait* itself runs counter to any such theory. In the finest scenes of the novel – the Christmas dinner with its bitter quarrel over Parnell, the unjust pandybatting, the visit to Cork, Father Arnall's fearful sermons – we tremble with Stephen as we might with a child in Dickens, and enter his feelings as deeply (or as kinetically) as those of a Dostoevskian raw youth. The intricacies of the symbolism and the closely calculated narrative shifts do nothing to diminish the emotional impact, any more than, say, the Arnall sermons are a mere clever pastiche because it turns out that, far from being written at white heat, they were to a considerable extent carefully adapted from a tract by a little-known seventeenth-cenury Italian Jesuit, Pinamonti's *Hell Opened to Christians.* We react to the preacher wholly in the context of Stephen's adolescent sexual guilt, and our reaction in turn helps to bring home the nature of Stephen's anguish – including its melodramatic aspects – as no amount of direct description could.

Few readers of the *Portrait,* once they have got the hang of Joyce's stylistic innovations, can have found much to quarrel with in the first two-thirds or so of the book. As a bewildered child or as a schoolboy buffeted by the storms of puberty, Stephen is a victim who automatically enlists our support; it is only when he begins to assert himself and to proclaim his artistic creed that we start having doubts. If we are adolescents ourselves when we first come across the *Portrait,* we may possibly take him at his own valuation, but after that it is hard not to be repelled, or on occasion amused, by his posturing and his moist romanticism. He is utterly self-absorbed; his reveries are rendered in the over-exquisite accents of the House Beautiful; the one specimen of his poetry we are shown might almost have been written by Enoch Soames. And yet at the same time he is the undisputed hero of the piece, striding radiantly forward to embrace his destiny as the curtain falls.

How exactly are we to take all this? If we assume that Joyce completely identifies himself with Stephen, the final section of the book becomes an exercise in naïve self-glorification, chiefly interesting for what it unconsciously reveals about the author's blind spots and immature yearnings. Anxious to acquit Joyce of having perpetrated anything so disagreeable, a number of critics have gone to the opposite extreme in their interpretation, treating the *Portrait* as the deliberate and systematic exposé of a radically false attitude to life. Stephen's style betrays him because it is meant to; his absurdities and inadequacies supply the dry light of irony by which his grandiose gestures are to be judged. Depending on whether we prefer the satirical or the naturalistic variant of this approach, he is either a monster of conceit or the hapless product of a blighting environment, but in either case he is essentially sterile, and the principal characteristic that he shares with his exemplar Icarus is that he is heading for a fall. The portrait of the artist turns out to be the dissection of a second-rate aesthete.

A plausible case has more than once been constructed along these lines, and undoubtedly the idea of everything that Stephen says or does being held up for our unqualified approval is not one that will bear much inspection. There can be no mistaking the calculated manner in which his rhapsodizings are periodically set off against his unheroic behavior or punctured by the irruption of crude Dublin reality. Yet despite this, the tone and overall momentum of the book, in my experience at least, are not primarily those of a cautionary tale. If they were, and if Stephen's condition was really hopeless, Joyce could legitimately be taxed with a certain gratuitous cruelty : why dispatch so small a victim at such length, in such intimate detail, when he might have been decently disposed of in a short story? As it is, however, the *Portrait* is surely meant to leave us with equivocal feelings about its hero's potentialities. For much of the time Stephen embodies an aspect of Joyce's nature that he repeatedly punished in his books but that he could never finally quell : the egoarch, the poseur with a smack of Hamlet, the narcissist who dedicated his first extended work (a play written at the age of eighteen and subsequently lost) 'to My own Soul'. But he also represents Joyce by virtue of his unaccommodating ideals and his restless imagination : even the purple patches hold out the promise of a more authentic, more distinctive lyricism. And he has the courage of his immaturity, which means having the capacity to grow and change, of not being afraid of a plunge into the unknown. Whether he will ultimately justify his presumptuousness and succeed in writing his masterpiece is an open question as the book ends, but given his youth and his vulnerability it is a question that would scarcely arise at all if he had not armored himself against the claims of conventional society with a defiantly romantic and Promethean conception of the artist's calling. . . .

SOURCE : *James Joyce* (1970) pp. 37–41.

SELECT BIBLIOGRAPHY

See, also, the various books and essays discussed in the Introduction. Given the thousands of essays and books devoted in whole or in part to Joyce, any 'select bibliography' must omit many items of genuine value and interest. For more complete bibliographies, see, below, the checklist by Beebe, Herring and Litz, and the full bibliography by Deming.

Chester G. Anderson (ed.), *James Joyce's A Portrait of the Artist as a Young Man: Text, Criticism, and Notes* (Viking, 1968).
A handy volume, containing the novel itself, 'Related Texts by Joyce', critical studies, and 'Explanatory Notes'. Cf. the Scholes and Litz volume for *Dubliners*.

James R. Baker and Thomas F. Staley (eds.), *James Joyce's Dubliners: A Critical Handbook* (Wadsworth, 1969).
A collection of previously published essays, most of them devoted to studies of individual stories.

Maurice Beebe, Phillip F. Herring, and Walton Litz, 'Criticism of James Joyce : A Selected Checklist', in *Modern Fiction Studies*, xv (Spring 1969) 105–82.
A carefully compiled list, with useful categories, including one for each story in *Dubliners*.

Morris Beja, *Epiphany in the Modern Novel* (London : Peter Owen; Seattle : University of Washington, 1971).
On Joyce, see pp. 13–23, 71–111.

Edward Brandabur, *A Scrupulous Meanness: A Study of Joyce's Early Work* (University of Illinois, 1971).
A psychoanalytic study of *Dubliners* and *Exiles*, with a brief look at *Portrait* and *Ulysses*.

Anthony Burgess, *Here Comes Everybody: An Introduction to James Joyce for the Ordinary Reader* (Faber, 1965).
Published in the U.S. as *Re Joyce* (Norton, 1965).

Thomas E. Connolly (ed.), *Joyce's Portrait: Criticisms and Critiques* (London : Peter Owen, 1964; New York : Appleton–Century–Crofts, 1962).

> Over 100 pages of this collection are devoted to essays on 'The Aesthetic Theory'.

Robert H. Deming, *A Bibliography of James Joyce Studies* (University of Kansas Libraries, 1964).

> Has useful divisions, with sections on each major work and various aspects of it, and on each story in *Dubliners*.

———— (ed.), *James Joyce: The Critical Heritage,* two volumes (Routledge & Kegan Paul, 1970).

> Reprints or excerpts reviews and criticisms, 1902–41.

Richard Ellmann, *James Joyce* (Oxford, 1959).

> The authoritative biography, and a monumental one.

Edmund L. Epstein, *The Ordeal of Stephen Dedalus: The Conflict of the Generations in James Joyce's A Portrait of the Artist as a Young Man* (London : Feffer and Simons; Carbondale : Southern Illinois University, 1971).

> A broader study than its title suggests, since it also examines both *Ulysses* and *Finnegans Wake*. Not introductory.

Don Gifford, with Robert J. Seidman, *Notes for Joyce: Dubliners and A Portrait of the Artist as a Young Man* (Dutton, 1967).

> Annotations, keyed to the pagination of various American editions.

Seon Givens (ed.), *James Joyce: Two Decades of Criticism* (Vanguard, 1963).

> Originally published in 1948, contains a number of important studies.

Arnold Goldman, *James Joyce* (Routledge & Kegan Paul, 1968).

> A volume in the Profiles in Literature series; an introduction to Joyce by the author of *The Joyce Paradox* (Northwestern, 1966).

John Gross, *Joyce* (Collins, 1971).

> Published in the U.S. as *James Joyce* (Viking, 1970). Pays special attention to the figure of the father in Joyce's fiction.

Leslie Hancock, *Word Index to James Joyce's Portrait of the Artist* (Southern Illinois University, 1967).

> A computerised concordance.

Clive Hart (ed). *James Joyce's Dubliners* (London : Faber; New York : Viking, 1969).
New essays by a number of critics, one on each of the stories.

Stanislaus Joyce, *My Brother's Keeper: James Joyce's Early Years,* ed. Richard Ellmann (London : Faber; New York : Viking, 1958).
A fascinating memoir.

Harry Levin, *James Joyce: A Critical Introduction* (New Directions, 1941, rev. edn. 1960).
Perhaps still the best introductory study.

A. Walton Litz, *James Joyce* (Twayne, 1966).
A concise general introduction, with a chapter on each of the major prose works.

Marvin Magalaner, *Time of Apprenticeship: The Fiction of Young James'Joyce* (Abelard–Schuman, 1959).
Especially valuable for its examinations of early versions of both *Dubliners* and *Portrait.*

————— and Richard M. Kain, *Joyce: The Man, the Work, the Reputation* (New York University, 1956).

William E. Morris and Clifford A. Nault, Jr (eds.), *Portraits of an Artist: A Casebook on James Joyce's A Portrait of the Artist as a Young Man* (Odyssey, 1962).

J. Mitchell Morse, *The Sympathetic Alien: James Joyce and Catholicism* (New York University, 1959).

John Ryan (ed.), *A Bash in the Tunnel: James Joyce by the Irish* (Clifton, 1970).
In addition to some already well known pieces, this collection publishes some new essays. John Jordan's 'Joyce Without Fears : A Personal Journey' is an interesting record of the effect of Joyce's books on a young Dubliner of a later generation.

Robert Scholes and A. Walton Litz (eds.), *James Joyce's Dubliners: Text, Criticism, and Notes* (Viking, 1969).
Contains the stories, a section on 'Background', critical essays, and 'Notes to the Stories'; cf. Anderson's volume for *Portrait.*

————— and Richard M. Kain (eds.), *The Workshop of Daedalus: James Joyce and the Raw Materials for A Portrait of the Artist as a Young Man* (Northwestern, 1965).
For a brief description of this important collection, see the Introduction to the present volume.

W. M. Schutte (ed.), *Twentieth Century Interpretations of A Portrait of the Artist as a Young Man* (Prentice-Hall, 1968).

Thomas F. Staley (ed.), *James Joyce Today: Essays on the Major Works* (Indiana University, 1966).

A collection of new essays presenting an overview of the critical situation in the mid-1960s for each of the major works. See, e.g. J. S. Atherton, 'The Joyce of *Dubliners*', and W. T. Noon, S.J., '*A Portrait of the Artist as a Young Man:* After Fifty Years'.

Kevin Sullivan, *Joyce Among the Jesuits* (Columbia, 1958).

A 'factual and biographical rather than critical or theoretical' study of Joyce's relationship with the Jesuits.

William York Tindall, *A Reader's Guide to James Joyce* (Noonday, 1959).

Emphasises Joyce's symbolism; often ingenious, but to be used with caution.

ADDENDA 1978

Homer Obed Brown, *James Joyce's Early Fiction: The Biography of a Form* (Case Western Reserve University, 1972).

Thomas F. Staley and Bernard Benstock (eds), *Approaches to Joyce's Portrait: Ten Essays* (University of Pittsburgh, 1977).

NOTES ON CONTRIBUTORS

MAURICE BEEBE. Teaches at Temple University. Editor of the *Journal of Modern Literature*, and former editor of *Modern Fiction Studies*. Author of *Ivory Towers and Sacred Founts: The Artist as Hero in Fiction from Goethe to Joyce* (1964).

MORRIS BEJA. Teaches at Ohio State University. While editing this book, was visiting professor at University College, Dublin, during which time he was also the recipient of Fulbright and Guggenheim Fellowships. Author of *Epiphany in the Modern Novel* (1971); editor of *Psychological Fiction* (1971), and of *Virginia Woolf: 'To the Lighthouse'* (1970) in the same series as the present volume.

WAYNE C. BOOTH. George M. Pullman Professor of English at the University of Chicago. Author of *The Rhetoric of Fiction* (1961) and *A Rhetoric of Irony* (1974).

ANTHONY BURGESS. Active as both a critic and a novelist. Among his novels are *A Clockwork Orange* (1962), *The Wanting Seed* (1962), *Honey for the Bears* (1963), *Nothing Like the Sun* (1964), *Inside Mr. Enderby* (1966), and *Abba Abba* (1977).

RICHARD ELLMANN. Goldsmith Professor of Literature, Oxford, since 1970. His *James Joyce* (1959) won the National Book Award for non-fiction. Editor of several volumes of Joyce material and author of *Ulysses on the Liffey* (1972) and *The Consciousness of Joyce* (1977), he has also published studies on Yeats and other modern writers.

EDWARD GARNETT (1868-1937). Editor, critic, poet, aand novelist. The literary supporter of (and correspondent with) a number of important novelists of the early twentieth century, notably Conrad, Galsworthy and Lawrence. His books include *Tolstoy: His Life and Writings* (1914), *Turgenev: A Study* (1917), *Friday Nights: Literary Criticism and Appreciations* (1922), as well as *Light and Shadow: A Novel* (1889).

BREWSTER GHISELIN. Professor Emeritus of English at the University of Utah. Editor of *The Creative Process* (1963).

GERALD GOULD (1885–1936). Critic and poet, author of many books, including *The English Novel of To-Day* (1924) and *All About Women: Essays and Parodies* (1931). His *Collected Poems* appeared in 1929.

JOHN GROSS. Editor of *TLS* (1974–81), his publications include *The Rise and Fall of the Man of Letters* (1969).

JOHN STANISLAUS JOYCE (1849–1931). James Joyce's father.

STANISLAUS JOYCE (1884–1955). James Joyce's younger brother, and the counterpart to 'Maurice' in *Stephen Hero*. Author of the autobiographical *My Brother's Keeper* (1958).

HUGH KENNER. Professor of English at Johns Hopkins University. Author of many books on modern literature, including *The Invisible Poet: T. S. Eliot* (1959), *Samuel Beckett: A Critical Study* (1961), *Flaubert, Joyce and Beckett: The Stoic Comedians* (1962), and *The Pound Era* (1972).

HARRY LEVIN. Irving Babbit Professor of Comparative Literature at Harvard University. Editor of *The Portable James Joyce* (1947; in England, *The Essential James Joyce* [1948]), and the author of *The Power of Blackness* (1958), *The Gates of Horn: A Study of Five French Realists* (1963), and numerous other critical studies.

FRANK O'CONNOR (1903–66); born Michael O'Donovan. The author of numerous collections of short stories, for which he is best known. Also the author of *The Big Fellow: A Life of Michael Collins* (1937, rev. edn 1965; in the U.S., *Death in Dublin: Michael Collins and the Irish Revolution* [1937, 1966]), and of *The Backward Look: A Survey of Irish Literature* (1967; in the U.S., *A Short History of Irish Literature: A Backward Look*).

J. I. M. STEWART. Formerly Reader in English Literature, Oxford. His many critical books include studies of Conrad (1968) and Hardy (1971). Among his novels are *Mungo's Dream* and volumes in the 'Patullo' sequence; his crime fiction is published under the pen-name of Michael Innes.

INDEX

Page numbers in bold type denote essays or extracts in this Case-book; entries in small capitals denote characters in Joyce's works.